What people are saying about

The Fresh Life Series

"I'm touched and blessed by Lenya and Penny's heart for His kingdom."

—KAY ARTHUR, BIBLE TEACHER AND
AUTHOR OF MANY BEST-SELLING BIBLE STUDIES

"What a great way for women to learn to study the Bible: interesting stories, thought-provoking questions, and a life-changing approach to applying Scripture. Lenya and Penny provide a great method so women can succeed and grow spiritually in a short period of time. Kudos!"

—FRANKLIN GRAHAM, PRESIDENT AND CEO OF
BILLY GRAHAM EVANGELISTIC ASSOCIATION AND SAMARITAN'S PURSE

"Skip and Lenya Heitzig have been friends of my wife, Cathe, and I for more than twenty years. Lenya loves to study God's Word and teach it to women in a way that is both exciting and accessible. I trust her latest book will be a blessing to you."

—GREG LAURIE, PASTOR AND EVANGELIST OF HARVEST MINISTRIES

"Lenya and Penny's love for the Lord and knowledge of His Word uniquely equips them to help other women discover the pathway to God through these in-depth Bible studies."

—KAY SMITH, WIFE OF CHUCK SMITH (CALVARY CHAPEL)

"The Fresh Life Series is an insightful and in-depth look at God's Word. Through these Bible studies Lenya Heitzig and Penny Rose lead women to deeper intimacy with God."

—K. P. YOHANNAN, PRESIDENT OF GOSPEL FOR ASIA

"Lenya and Penny have created another wonderful Bible study series that invites participants to spend time in God's Word and then see the Word come to fruition in their lives. What a blessing! These studies are perfect for small groups or personal daily devotions."

—ROBIN LEE HATCHER, WOMEN'S EVENT SPEAKER
AND AWARD-WINNING AUTHOR

Live Intimately

Fresh Life
Bible Study Series

A 20-MINUTES-A-DAY STUDY

Live Intimately

Lessons from the Upper Room

Lenya Heitzig & Penny Rose

David C Cook®

transforming lives together

LIVE INTIMATELY
Published by David C. Cook
4050 Lee Vance View
Colorado Springs, CO 80918 U.S.A.

David C. Cook Distribution Canada
55 Woodslee Avenue, Paris, Ontario, Canada N3L 3E5

David C. Cook U.K., Kingsway Communications
Eastbourne, East Sussex BN23 6NT, England

The Web site addresses recommended throughout this book are offered
as a resource to you. These Web sites are not intended in any way to be or imply
an endorsement on the part of David C. Cook, nor do we vouch for their content.

Additional material provided by Maria Guy, Misty Foster, and Judy Sutton.

ISBN 978-1-4347-6790-5

The Team: Terry Behimer, Karen Lee Thorpe, Amy Kiechlin, and Jaci Schneider
Cover/Interior Design: ThinkPen Design, Greg Jackson

Printed in the United States of America
First Edition 2008

1 2 3 4 5 6 7 8 9 10

033108

With Gratitude

Special thanks to Pastor Skip Heitzig for your spiritual influence; Pastor Chip Lusko for your media expertise; Pastor Kerry Rose for your steadfast guidance; and Pastor Levi Lusko for your fresh vision.

Contents

Lesson Nine

Lesson Ten

Introduction

LIVE INTIMATELY

If you knew it was your last evening on earth, what would you do? Most of us wouldn't go to our jobs. We wouldn't watch television. We wouldn't do dishes or clean the house. We would gather together the people we love and spend quality time with them. We would shower them with affection. We would impart any words of wisdom we could possibly share. And we would warn them to watch out for any dangers that might be lurking. We would want to spend an intimate time with those we hold near and dear.

Jesus was no different. The time had come for Him to depart this world. So He did what any loving human being would do—He gathered His loved ones for a final meal and taught them the secret of how to live intimately.

WHO WAS INVITED?

Those invited to the upper room were a small group of people. Previously Jesus had been ministering to the multitudes in Jerusalem and Galilee. Members of His audience had included Romans, religious leaders, tainted women, tax collectors—a menagerie of men, women, and children from all walks of life. Sadly, the "world at large" did not receive Jesus as the Messiah. With His departure imminent, Jesus focused His special attention on His twelve apostles, drawing them deeper into His inner circle. He would lavish them with love and impart some heavenly secrets.

WHAT WAS DISCUSSED?

In essence, Jesus had invited His twelve friends to a going-away party. The Upper Room Discourse was Jesus' farewell speech. It started with love in action as Jesus modeled the role of servant leadership by washing His disciples' feet. He next warned the disciples about deniers, quitters, and betrayers. He offered insight and instruction about spreading

Author: John

Audience: The Twelve and all Christ's followers

Theme: So people will believe that Jesus is the Christ, the Son of God, and that by believing, they will have life in His name.

Date: Probably AD 85–90, before the exile to Patmos.

Setting: An upper room, Jerusalem

Scripture: "I am the way, the truth, and the life. No one comes to the Father except through Me" (John 14:6).

the gospel message after He departed. He taught His friends key lessons about abiding in the Father and about the divine nature of the triune God. He ended with what is in reality the Lord's Prayer, as He interceded for His people both present and in the future. It was a personal conversation that would change the world.

WHEN DID THIS HAPPEN?

Our text begins by setting the time as "before the Feast of the Passover, when Jesus knew that His hour had come that He should depart from this world to the Father" (John 13:1). From this verse, we are given two timetables. In the earthly realm, this was the season for the Jewish Passover meal. In the eternal realm, the time had drawn nigh for Jesus to return to the Father. Earlier in His ministry, Jesus predicted, "My hour has not yet come" (John 2:4). Now this meal signaled that what had once been spoken of in the future tense was near—the final hour was upon Him.

WHERE WERE THEY GATHERED?

While no one knows the exact location of the upper room, scholars tell us that the room was located in Jerusalem. Upper rooms were usually large, spacious rooms used for feasts and entertaining. As the master of the feast, Jesus chose the upper room and had everything ready for the Twelve. Mark gives the following account.

Now on the first day of Unleavened Bread, when they killed the Passover lamb, His disciples said to Him, "Where do You want us to go and prepare, that You may eat the Passover?" And He sent out two of His disciples and said to them, "Go into the city, and a man will meet you carrying a pitcher of water; follow him. Wherever he goes in, say to the master of the house, 'The Teacher says, "Where is the guest room in which I may eat the Passover *with My disciples?"' Then he will show you a large upper room, furnished and prepared; there make ready for us." So His disciples went out, and came into the city, and found it just as He had said to them; and they prepared the Passover.* Mark 14:12–16

May you live intimately,
Lenya Heitzig and Penny Rose

How to Get the Most Out of This Study

Are you living a life that leads you into a deeper relationship with God? The secret to spiritual intimacy is found in God's Word. We know that God reveals Himself through His Word. That's why doing a Bible study like this is so vital—because God's Word has the power to do His work in our lives. It is the catalyst that refreshes your heart, renews your mind, and restores your soul—it makes life worth living!

This study focuses on the last evening of Jesus' life when He spent some precious time with His close friends. They were engaged in a conversation that is commonly called the Upper Room Discourse. During this time, Jesus wanted to prepare His disciples for His departure. He expressed His deep love not only for His disciples, but also for all of His people throughout the ages. He urged us to love one another in the power of His Holy Spirit. Jesus shared some great secrets with His followers and drew them into an even closer relationship with their Lord and Savior. We pray that as you participate in this study, you, too, will learn to live a life that is even more deeply connected to Him. We trust that each week you will learn to *Live Intimately* with Jesus!

Each week of the study is divided into five days for your personal time with God. Each day's lesson contains five elements. They are designed to help you fully "live" as you apply the truths you learn to your life:

1. Lift up … Here we ask you to "Lift up" prayers to God, asking Him to give you spiritual insight for the day.

2. Look at … This portion of the study asks you to "Look at" the Scripture text, using inductive questions. These questions help you to discover *What are the facts?* You'll learn the basic who-what-when-where-how aspects of the passage as well as some of the important background material.

3. Learn about … The "Learn about" sidebars correlate to specific questions in order to help you understand *What does this text mean?* These sidebar elements

offer cultural insight, linguistic definitions, and biblical commentary.

4. Live out … These questions and exercises are designed to help you investigate How should this change my life? Here you are challenged to personally apply the lessons you have learned as you "Live out" God's principles in a practical way. We encourage you to write out all of the answers to the questions in this study. You may want to write the answers to the personal application questions in a journal to ensure privacy. By writing your insights from God day by day, you'll have a record of your relationship with Him that you can look back on when you need a faith boost.

5. Listen to … We finish with inspiring quotes from authors, speakers, and writers. You'll be able to "Listen to" the wisdom they've gleaned in their lives and relate it to your own.

Live Intimately is ideal for discussion in a small-group setting as well as for individual study. The following suggestions will help you and your group get the most out of your study time:

PERSONAL CHECKLIST

- Be determined. Examine your daily schedule, then set aside a consistent time for this study.

- Be prepared. Gather the materials you'll need: a Bible, this workbook, a journal in which to write your thoughts, and a pen.

- Be inspired. Begin each day with prayer, asking the Holy Spirit to be your teacher and to illuminate your mind.

- Be complete. Read the suggested Bible passage and finish the homework each day.

- Be persistent. Answer each question as fully as possible. If you're unable to answer a question, move forward to the next question or read the explanation in the "Learn about …" section, which may offer further insight.

- Be consistent. Don't get discouraged. If you miss a day, use the weekend to catch up.

- Be honest. When answering the "Live out …" questions, allow the Lord to search your heart and transform your life. Take time to reflect honestly about your feelings, experiences, sins, goals, and responses to God.

- Be blessed. Enjoy your daily study time as God speaks to you through His Word.

SMALL-GROUP CHECKLIST

- Be prayerful. Pray before you begin your time together.

- Be biblical. Keep all answers in line with God's Word; avoid personal opinion.

- Be confidential. Keep all sharing within your small group confidential.

- Be respectful. Listen without interrupting. Keep comments on track and to the point so that all can share.

- Be discreet. In some cases, you need not share more than absolutely necessary. Some things are between you and the Lord.

- Be kind. Reply to the comments of others lovingly and courteously.

- Be mindful. Remember your group members in prayer throughout the week.

SMALL-GROUP LEADER CHECKLIST

- Be prayerful. Pray that the Holy Spirit will "guide you into truth" so that your leadership will guide others.

- Be faithful. Prepare by reading the Bible passage and studying the lesson ahead of time, highlighting truths and applying them personally.

- Be prompt. Begin and end the study on time.

- Be thorough. For optimum benefit, allot one hour for small-group discussion. This should allow plenty of time to cover all of the questions and exercises for each lesson.

- Be selective. If you have less than an hour, you should carefully choose which questions you will address and summarize the edited information for your group. In this way, you can focus on the more thought-provoking questions. Be sure to grant enough time to address pertinent "Live out ..." exercises, as this is where you and the women will clearly see God at work in your lives.

- Be sensitive. Some of the "Live out ..." exercises are very personal and may not be appropriate to discuss in a small group. If you sense that this is the case, feel free to move to another question.

- Be flexible. If the questions in the study seem unclear, reword them for your group. Feel free to add your own questions to bring out the meaning of a verse.

- Be inclusive. Encourage each member to participate in the discussion. You may have to draw some out or tone some down so that all have the opportunity to participate.

- Be honest. Don't be afraid to admit that you don't have all the answers! When in doubt encourage ladies to take difficult questions to their church leadership for clarification.

- Be focused. Keep the discussion on tempo and on target. Learn to pace your small group so that you complete a lesson on time. When participants get sidetracked, redirect the discussion to the passage at hand.

- Be patient. Realize that not all people are at the same place spiritually or socially. Wait for the members of your group to answer the questions rather than jumping in and answering them yourself.

The Prince and the Pauper
John 13:1–17

Mark Twain's *The Prince and the Pauper* tells the tale of two boys born into opposite social circles in Tudor England. After a chance encounter, the look-alike boys decide to exchange clothes to discover how the "other half" lives. Prince Edward adapts to life as a beggarly child born to an abusive father, and the pauper, Tom Canty, adjusts to life full of palace protocol and intrigue.

After a series of adventures, in which the prince (Tom in disguise) is declared insane and the pauper (Edward) endures a stint in prison, the boys switch back just in time for Edward to celebrate his coronation after the death of his father, King Henry VIII. But Tom and Edward meet resistance when the nobles refuse to believe that the beggarly child is the rightful king. Things are set straight when the real Edward produces the Great Seal he's hidden before leaving the palace. To show his gratitude for supporting Edward's claim to the throne, Tom is named "The King's Ward," a lifelong privileged position.

The incarnation of Jesus truly portrays the Prince of Peace becoming a pauper among humankind. In John 13—17, known as the Upper Room Discourse, we see the King of Kings condescend to become a servant as He washes His followers' feet. Although He is the rightful heir to the throne, His temporary role reversal will lead Him to endure a humiliating arrest, torture, and execution, which will begin just after he celebrates this Passover Feast with the twelve men He loves so dearly. John 13—17 contains our Lord's beautiful farewell speech in which He imparts His most deeply held values and advice.

Because Jesus became a pauper, we have been made princes and princesses of the kingdom of heaven for all eternity. What an undeserved reversal of roles we have inherited!

Day 1: John 13:1–4   **CHANGING CLOTHES**

Day 2: John 13:5–8   **CHANGING ROLES**

Day 3: John 13:9–10   **CHANGING MINDS**

Day 4: John 13:11–13   **CHANGING HEARTS**

Day 5: John 13:14–17   **CHANGING EXPECTATIONS**

DAY I

Changing Clothes

LIFT UP ...

Jesus, how unfathomable it is that You would leave the glory of heaven to live in this world in order to exchange places with me. I can't wait for the day when I cast down every crown at Your feet and declare, "Worthy, worthy, worthy, is the Lord God Almighty." Amen.

LOOK AT ...

We jump into our study in the midst of what must have been a long week for the Savior. On Sunday Jesus made His triumphal entry into Jerusalem. On Monday He cleansed the temple of money changers. On Tuesday He confronted the religious leaders who sought to have Him arrested (see Matthew 21—25). While Jesus spent Wednesday with His good friends in Bethany, Judas conspired with the chief priests (see Matthew 26). That brings us to Thursday, the first day of the Feast of Unleavened Bread. Jesus and His disciples have gone to an upper room in the home of an unnamed friend to celebrate the feast.

In the Upper Room Discourse, we discover that what Jesus *knew* compelled Him to follow through with what He had to *do*—sacrifice His life for the sins of the world. He modeled the principle that information should lead to transformation. As you'll see, one of the key words in today's study is "knew." We'll come to understand that Jesus *knew* where He came from and where He was going. He *knew* that "His hour had come" to leave this world and depart to the next. Therefore He would not only tell His disciples that He loved them, He would show them the extent of His love through His actions. He would stoop to wash their feet in humility. That way, they would begin to know how to become servant leaders. As you study this passage, may you begin to know Jesus as the greatest servant leader of all. And may you know that the way to lead is by serving others.

LEARN ABOUT ...

2 His Hour

"His hour had come" speaks of the divinely appointed time when Jesus would be glorified through His death and resurrection. Previously in John's gospel, this phrase had referred to a time yet to come. Now it had arrived. His departure from earth and homecoming in heaven was imminent.

3 His Love

The phrase "loved them to the end" in some translations is "to the uttermost" or "to the full extent." It can be interpreted three different ways: 1) loving to the end of Jesus' life; 2) loving to the end of the disciples' lives; 3) loving to the very end or without end, meaning forever.

7 His Humility

Surely servants could have performed this menial task. Therefore Jesus' actions must have surprised the disciples, because previously "on the road they had disputed among themselves who would be the greatest" (Mark 9:34). Jesus had told them that the greatest must be the servant of all. Now He showed them this through His humble actions.

READ JOHN 13:1–4.

Now before the Feast of the Passover, when Jesus knew that His hour had come that He should depart from this world to the Father, having loved His own who were in the world, He loved them to the end.

And supper being ended, the devil having already put it into the heart of Judas Iscariot, Simon's son, to betray Him, Jesus, knowing that the Father had given all things into His hands, and that He had come from God and was going to God, rose from supper and laid aside His garments, took a towel and girded Himself. John 13:1–4

1. What holiday did these events precede? What, if anything, do you know about that holiday?

2. Explain what Jesus knew about His destiny.

3. Who had Jesus loved and for how long?

4. Describe what you learn about Judas Iscariot in the passage.

5. What three things do you learn about Jesus' knowledge of Himself and the Father toward the end of this passage?

6. List the four verbs that describe the actions Jesus took after supper.

7. How would what Jesus knew and the way He behaved seem to be a contradiction?

LIVE OUT...

8. In the following chart, recount the circumstances in which Jesus alluded to the "hour" of His death to reveal God's heavenly

timetable. (Look at the context of each verse to see what was going on.)

Scripture	Heavenly Timetable
John 2:4	
John 7:30	
John 8:20	
John 12:23	
John 17:1	

LEARN ABOUT ...

8 Your Hour

The Lord knows the beginning and end of your life. "Lord, make me to know my end, And what is the measure of my days, That I may know how frail I am" (Ps. 39:4). Isn't it comforting to know that until our hour comes, we are invincible? Like Jesus, this should embolden us.

10 Your Service

A servant is under another's authority. Servants are not free to do as they please. Jesus declared that the greatest people are those who serve: "If anyone desires to be first, he shall be last of all and servant of all" (Mark 9:35).

9. a. Either here or in your journal, fill in a personal timeline noting some of the high and low points of your life, from the past leading to the present.

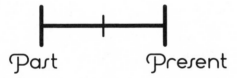

Past   Present

b. How does it make you feel to know that the Lord will love you to the very end?

10. a Read Philippians 2:3–11. Today we learned that Christ's knowledge led Him to take humble actions. If we have Christ's mind, list how we should and should not behave (see vv. 3–5).

b. How does acting in this manner model Christlike behavior (see vv. 6–8)?

c. In what three ways is Christ glorified based upon His obedience (see vv. 9–11)?

d. In what ways have you been a servant this week? How do you think your heavenly Father feels about your actions?

○ ○ ● ○ ○

Do clothes really make the man? Many actors reveal that the secret to capturing a character's personality lies in the wardrobe. They believe the costume helps dictate their demeanor, stance, and gestures. Think about it, Scarlett O'Hara just couldn't be the genteel and prissy spoiled socialite without her corset, petticoats, and fancy fan. Vivien Leigh in full costume seemed to float across the silver screen as the perfect Southern belle, even though she was really an English actress.

Geoffrey Rush explained that the key to unlocking the sinister persona of Captain Barbossa in Disney's hit trilogy *Pirates of the Caribbean* was a hat. Not just any hat, but one with an exaggerated brim, large plumage, and at a cocked position on his head. This helped the actor embody the larger-than-life braggadocio and deceptive outlaw.

When Jesus wanted to relate to humanity, He divested Himself of His glory and took the form of a man. Mary wrapped Him in swaddling cloths at His humble birth. Throughout His life He chose the simple garments of a carpenter. In the upper room, He showed His disciples how to dress by taking off His simple tunic and girding Himself with a servant's towel. On earth, the only time our Savior wore the purple robes of royalty was when He was being mocked and beaten.

If you're having a difficult time taking on the role of a servant, perhaps you need to follow Christ's example and "be clothed with humility, for 'God resists the proud, But gives grace to the humble'" (1 Peter 5:5). When you dress down, you'll be dressed for success.

LISTEN TO ...

He clothed himself with our lowliness in order to invest us with his grandeur.

—*Richardson Wright*

DAY 2

Changing Roles

Role playing is very enlightening. Counselors call this exercise "role reversal." It's a technique where one person is asked to exchange roles with another person. Each assumes as many of the character traits of the other as possible. In that way one is able not only to experience a different perspective in a situation (to walk in another's shoes), but also to examine one's own behavior from the other's point of view. As a result, role reversals bring significant insight and transformation.

For instance, before disciplining a child, a parent might swap roles and ask, "If you were mommy and your little boy used bad words, what would you do?" Often the erring child suggests more severe discipline than the parent would offer on her own.

Or imagine your workplace. What if next Friday were declared role reversal day? The executives would become administrators and vice versa. Morale would skyrocket as participants became more empathetic to the duties and responsibilities of everyone in the company.

Jesus understood the power of changing roles. Though He could have demanded that the disciples serve Him, He chose instead to wait on them. And He decided to perform the lowest task of all—washing dirty feet. It must have been mind blowing for these twelve men to watch the Savior wrap Himself with a towel, fill a basin with water, and stoop at their feet. What lessons do you think they might have learned? Would they be more willing to serve one another or those less fortunate than themselves? How would you feel if the Creator of the universe dressed as a servant, knelt down, and offered to wash your feet?

LIFT UP ...

Jesus, Your condescension is humbling. I am ashamed of the times that I demand my rights when You willingly laid Your majesty aside to serve others. Help me to follow Your example. Amen.

LOOK AT ...

Yesterday we joined the disciples and our Lord in the upper room. We discovered what was on the Savior's mind and how His actions seemed counterintuitive. We also witnessed Judas lose the battle between the flesh and the spirit as he succumbed to satanic influence. The stage was set for Judas to make his ultimate betrayal.

Today we find that the reason Jesus changed His clothes was to change roles and wash His disciples' feet. While it must have perplexed all of the men, Peter was overwhelmed. Throughout Scripture we discover that Peter was an outspoken, often presumptuous individual. Jesus had to correct Him on more than one occasion. Remember the time Peter resisted the idea of Jesus' death? "He rebuked Peter, saying, 'Get behind Me, Satan! For you are not mindful of the things of God, but the things of men'" (Mark 8:33).

Have you ever misinterpreted something the Lord has done in your life? Perhaps you have been presumptuous like Peter, assuming God was being capricious when, in fact, He meant it for your good. Learn from Peter's poor example by surrendering your will to God's.

READ JOHN 13:5–8.

After that, He poured water into a basin and began to wash the disciples' feet, and to wipe them with the towel with which He was girded. Then He came to Simon Peter. And Peter said to Him, "Lord, are You washing my feet?"

Jesus answered and said to him, "What I am doing you do not understand now, but you will know after this."

Peter said to Him, "You shall never wash my feet!"

Jesus answered him, "If I do not wash you, you have no part with Me." John 13:5–8

1. "After that" is a transitional phrase. Recount what happened in the preceding verses to bring us to this point.

2. Now describe in detail what Jesus did "after that."

3. a. In your own words, recount Peter's initial question when Jesus approached him.

b. Why do you think he questioned Christ's actions?

4. a. How did Jesus answer Peter?

   b. Put yourself in Peter's place: Do you think you would have felt comfortable with the answer, or would you have still been confused?

5. Recount the exclamatory statement Peter made to Jesus. Knowing what you know about Peter, why do you think he said this?

6. Why would Peter have "no part with" Jesus if Jesus didn't wash him?

LIVE OUT...

7. a. Foot washing was performed as a hospitable service as well as for sacramental reasons. However, there is a third aspect of this lovely ceremony: worship. Read John 12:1–8. When and where did these events occur, and what previously took place there (see v. 1)?

   b. Describe how Mary attended the Lord's feet (see v. 3).

   c. Explain how Judas responded to this action (see vv. 4–6).

   d. How did the Lord respond, and how would this have made the others feel (see vv. 7–8)?

8. Today we see that Peter misunderstood the Lord's intent. But Peter is not the only biblical person to question God.

   a. Use a Bible concordance to search for various forms of the

LEARN ABOUT ...

2 Foot Washing

Washing feet was an expression of hospitality extended to guests in Bible times. People traveling dusty roads in Palestine needed to wash their feet for comfort and cleanliness. The lowliest servant in the household generally performed this task. Guests could also be offered water and vessels for washing their own feet.[1]

5 Foot Cleansing

This foot washing can also be seen as a ritual known as ablution, meaning to cleanse ceremonially as a rite of purification. It served a fourfold purpose: 1) to initiate into a higher condition; 2) to prepare for a special act of religious service; 3) to purify from defilement; 4) to declare freedom from guilt.

6 Foot Soldier

The word *part* in the original language means division, share, or portion. It carries the idea of "participation" as in having a share in someone or something. Jesus was warning Peter that if he did not receive this ceremonial ablution, he would not become "part and parcel" with the Lord.

LEARN ABOUT ...

7 Foot Balm

Spikenard was one of the most valued aromatics known to the ancients, with the exception perhaps of saffron. It was very costly since it was obtained by foreign commerce from distant countries such as Persia, Africa, and India. Often it was shipped in expensive alabaster containers.[2]

---

8 Foot in Mouth

Peter often put his foot in his mouth by speaking before thinking. Beware! If you don't control your tongue, it can burn others and backfire to burn you: "The tongue is a fire, a world of iniquity.... It defiles the whole body, and sets on fire the course of nature; and it is set on fire by hell" (James 3:6).

words "question," "doubt," or "ask" and describe another person from Scripture who doubted the Lord. Include the biblical reference.

b. Now describe a time when you did the very same thing. What were the circumstances? How did the Lord correct you?

9. Jesus warned Peter that to abstain from this ceremonial foot washing was to reject communion with Him. Which of the following spiritual disciplines are you neglecting? Next to the box, describe how you will reengage with the Lord.

- ❏ Baptism
- ❏ Communion
- ❏ Fellowship
- ❏ Intercession
- ❏ Repentance
- ❏ Worship
- ❏ Prayer
- ❏ Bible study

10. Journal a prayer asking God to forgive you for your carelessness. Then reaffirm your allegiance to Him.

° ° ● ° °

Did you know that there are laws both past and present concerning your bathing habits? In 1842, the first bathtub was denounced publicly as a "luxurious and democratic vanity." The city of Boston made it unlawful to bathe except by doctor's prescription. In 1843, Philadelphia made bathing illegal between November 1 and March 15. In Kansas, it was once illegal to swim with a polka-dotted bathing suit before noon. To this day unusual bathing laws are on the books in many U.S. cities. For instance, in Albuquerque, New Mexico, you can bathe publicly, but in Asheville, North Carolina, you cannot. If you move to Kentucky, the law mandates that people must bathe at least once per year. If you've ever raised a preadolescent boy, you can understand why mandated bathing is important.

Would it surprise you to know that the Bible had bathing laws too? Apparently it was legal to bathe publicly in Egypt, as the pharaoh's daughter did when she discovered baby Moses. Bathing was required by God's law for purification from uncleanness of any kind, such as leprosy (see Lev. 15) or betrothal (see Ruth 3:3). The high priest underwent ritual cleansing on the Day of Atonement before dressing in his holy garments.

In the next few verses, Jesus will reveal the full symbolism behind washing the disciples' feet. However, the interesting fact is that Jesus knew His disciples needed cleansing. He didn't mandate it with a law but enforced it by warning them that to avoid this bath was tantamount to rejecting the Lord. It's astounding that Jesus washed Judas's feet, though his heart was tainted and may never be cleansed. Sadly, taking a bath cannot cleanse a heart.

LISTEN TO ...

A closed mouth gathers no foot.

—*Unknown*

DAY 3

Changing Minds

How often do you change your mind? Howard Gardner explains in his book *Changing Minds: The Art and Science of Changing Our Own and Other People's Minds* that "people underestimate how difficult it is to change minds. When you're little, your mind changes pretty readily, even if nobody pushes it. We are natural mind-changing entities until we are ten or so. But as we get older and have acquired more formal and informal knowledge, then it's very, very hard to change our minds."[3]

Minor issues are not where folks become close-minded, like whether dinner is served at six or seven. But try to get people to alter their thoughts on major issues, such as their worldviews, life's goals, or belief systems, and their brains cling tenaciously to the status quo. By the time we're adults, our way of thinking works for us largely because the neural pathways in our brains become set.

Perhaps this phenomenon explains why the odds of a person becoming a Christian as they age decrease precipitously. In fact, a senior citizen who converts to Christianity is a statistical miracle! Throughout His ministry, Jesus' mission was to change minds and hearts. The religious leaders whose neural pathways were set in stone proved to be His greatest challenge. Although His disciples had mind-changing experiences, they still possessed vestiges of stinking thinking. During the Upper Room Discourse, Jesus sought to revolutionize their concepts of love, unity, and His deity. Peter, specifically, would have to surrender his misconceptions of an austere, aloof God for one who was humble and meek. He would have to learn that Jesus was fully God and fully man willing to wash His disciples' feet.

LIFT UP ...

I confess that my thoughts are not Your thoughts. I'm certain there are many areas where I could use a change of mind. Lord, I surrender my thoughts to You. Please transform me and renew my mind. Amen.

Look at ...

Peter had misunderstood the Lord's intent in washing his feet. True to form, Peter thought he knew best and spoke out of turn. The Lord challenged him to decide whether Jesus was Lord of all. Today we'll see Peter go from one extreme to the other in his words and deeds.

We can all sympathize with Peter's need to please and perhaps his desire to impress others. There's no doubt that Peter loved Jesus passionately. Unfortunately, his passion could lead him in the wrong direction. No doubt the Lord preferred Peter's extreme enthusiasm over apathy. In the book of Revelation, Jesus warned the Laodiceans that He just couldn't tolerate people with tepid temperatures. He said, "So then, because you are lukewarm, and neither cold nor hot, I will vomit you out of My mouth" (Rev. 3:16). If the Lord asks you to jump, do you ask, "How high?" or do you immediately obey? Better to be jumpy than to sit idly by.

Learn about ...

3 Shower
The Greeks had two different words for bath/wash. Verses 4, 6, 8, 12, and 14 use *nipto*, meaning "to wash a part of the body." In verse 10, *louo* is employed, which means "to bathe all over." Repentance leading to regeneration cleanses sinners "all over." Henceforth, our "sins and lawless deeds [are] remember[ed] no more" (Heb. 10:17).

Read John 13:9–10.

Simon Peter said to Him, "Lord, not my feet only, but also my hands and my head!"

Jesus said to him, "He who is bathed needs only to wash his feet, but is completely clean; and you are clean, but not all of you." John 13:9–10

1. Recount the conversation Simon Peter and Jesus had in yesterday's lesson. What ultimatum did Jesus give Peter?

2. In your own words, describe what parts of his body Peter offered for Jesus to wash also. What do you think he was trying to convey to Jesus?

LEARN ABOUT …

4 Sinless

Salvation wipes away all sin, but afterward we may become defiled again. When we fall into sin, we don't need to be saved again but simply to have the defilement washed away. "If we confess our sins, He is faithful and just to forgive us our sins and to cleanse us from all unrighteousness" (1 John 1:9).

---

6 Stained

Scripture differentiates between Judas and Peter and the status of their hearts. Both received a foot washing. The implication is that Peter was cleansed "all over," but Judas was *not*. Some commentators believe Judas was saved but backslid. Here, Jesus implies that Judas was never a true believer.

---

7 Scriptural Shower

Salvation brings complete cleansing from original sin and past personal sins. But for a Christian there is no such thing as sinless perfection. Instead we're to sin less and less. If you need a bath, the Bible says you can be cleansed by "the washing of water by the word" (Eph. 5:26).

3. Jesus' answer to Peter was profound. Let's break it down so we can discover the meaning behind each phrase. According to Jesus, what was the only thing one who had bathed needed to wash?

4. What did He reveal about the state of the rest of that person's body?

5. Jesus' point was really about spiritual cleanliness. How would you explain what He was trying to tell Peter?

6. What did He reveal about one of the disciples? Who do you think He was talking about?

LIVE OUT…

7. We, too, have been "bathed all over." But like the disciples, sometimes we need cleansing in a particular area of our lives. Fill in the chart to discover what might need cleansing and why.

SCRIPTURE	WHAT NEEDS CLEANSING AND WHY
Psalm 51:2	
Psalm 119:37	
Matthew 18:8–9	
James 4:8	

8. In the following illustration, circle or draw an arrow to the body part that you personally need cleansed. Journal a description of how you became defiled, and write a prayer of repentance, asking God to wash you as white as snow.

9. In John 13:10, Jesus speaks of Judas as an unbeliever. This is a startling reality, because Judas was close to Jesus for years, heard His teaching, and saw His miracles. Read John 6:64–71.

   a. What knowledge did Jesus possess (see v. 64)?

   b. Who grants access to Jesus (see v. 65)? Why does this matter to us?

   c. Some of Jesus' disciples stopped following Him because of His shocking teaching (see v. 66). Why didn't Peter and the other apostles depart too (see vv. 67–69)?

   d. What do you make of the fact that Jesus knew Judas was "a devil" (see vv. 70–71) yet allowed Judas to be one of His closest companions?

° ° ● ° °

Chen-Bo Zhong and Katie Liljenquist, two research workers at the University of Toronto, have recently been preoccupied with hand washing. They say that compulsive germophobics, who obsessively wash or disinfect their hands, suffer from "the Macbeth hand-washing syndrome."

They recount that:

Lady Macbeth, long after she had washed her hands dripping with Duncan's blood, continued to be preoccupied by hand washing. So great was her sense of guilt that no amount of water and the ritual incantation of "Out, damned spot! out, I say" could restore her peace of mind or ability to sleep.

Compulsive hand washing in those who are either guilt-ridden or suffer from obsessive compulsive disorder has intrigued generations of psychiatrists. Obsessions are persistent anxieties, impulses, and ideas, including feelings of guilt, that are as intrusive as they are senseless. Compulsions refer to ritualistic, repetitive behavioral patterns that obsessed people adopt. Hand washing, a vain attempt at ridding body and mind of the evidence of some real or imagined guilt, is a common example of compulsive behavior.[4]

Peter went from refusing a foot bath to requesting a thorough dunking from head to toe. Jesus affirmed that believers don't become unregenerate, just defiled in spots as they walk through this world. When this happens, they need cleansing only from specific sins. Sadly, there are some believers who incessantly fear that they're not *really* saved. They seem stuck on some past sin that Jesus has already cleansed. When He forgives, He forgets. He "will cast all our sins Into the depths of the sea (Mic. 7:19). Don't live like Lady Macbeth, wringing your hands furtively over a past sin. Allow Jesus to do a little spot cleaning.

LISTEN TO ...

They tell me a revival is only temporary; so is a bath, but it does you good.

—*Billy Sunday*

DAY 4

Changing Hearts

Criminals rarely have a change of heart while committing a crime, but that's exactly what happened to an armed robber who crashed a dinner party in Washington, D.C. *The Washington Post* reports:[5]

[A] grand feast of marinated steaks and jumbo shrimp was winding down, and a group of friends was sitting on the back patio of a Capitol Hill home, sipping red wine. Suddenly, a hooded man slid in through an open gate and put the barrel of a handgun to the head of a 14-year-old guest.

"Give me your money, or I'll start shooting," he demanded.

The five other guests froze—and then one spoke. "We were just finishing dinner," Cristina Rowan blurted out. "Why don't you have a glass of wine with us?"

The intruder took a sip of their Chateau Malescot St-Exupéry and said, "!@#, that's good wine."

The girl's father, Michael Rabdau, 51, suggested that he take the whole glass. Then Rowan offered him the bottle. The would-be robber, his hood now down, took another sip and had a bite of Camembert cheese. Astonishingly, he then tucked the gun into the pocket of his sweatpants and said, "I think I may have come to the wrong house. I'm sorry,"

Then he asked the group, "Can I get a hug?"

Rowan, who works part time at her children's school, stood up and wrapped her arms around him. Then it was Rabdau's turn. Then his wife's. The other two guests complied. With that, the man walked out with a crystal wine glass in hand. No one was hurt, and nothing was stolen.

Apparently, acts of love and compassion can change the hearts of some hardened criminals. Sadly, they cannot change the hearts of everyone.

LIFT UP ...

Jesus, thank You for being the embodiment of love and for changing my heart. I beg You to change the hearts of my friends and family who have not yet accepted You as Lord and Savior. Please show them Your love and mercy. Amen.

LOOK AT ...

We've seen that Peter zealously offered his whole body for Jesus to wash. Jesus replied that Peter only needed for his feet to be cleaned. Warren Wiersbe wrote: "Peter had a difficult time accepting Christ's ministry to him because Peter was not yet ready to minister to the other disciples. It takes humility and grace to serve others, but it also takes humility and grace to allow others to serve us. The beautiful thing about a beautiful spirit is that it can both give and receive to the glory of God."[6]

In theological terms Jesus was showing Peter the difference between being justified and sanctified. When you're saved/justified by the blood of the Lamb, you can say it's "just as if I'd" never sinned. After that, the Holy Spirit's process of sanctifying you from glory to glory lets you know you can be a "saint if I'd" obey the Lord. Justification happens once; sanctification is a lifelong process. Today we'll see whether the disciples were gaining insight into Jesus' loving actions.

READ JOHN 13:11–13.

For He knew who would betray Him; therefore He said, "You are not all clean."
So when He had washed their feet, taken His garments, and sat down again, He said to them, "Do you know what I have done to you? You call Me Teacher and Lord, and you say well, for so I am." John 13:11–13

1. We've learned that one of the key words in this week's study is the word "knew."

What did Jesus know according to today's text?

2. Notice what Jesus said because of what He knew. How would you restate this in your own words?

3. "So" is another transitional word. "So," according to our text, what had ended?

4. Describe what two actions Jesus took after washing the disciples' feet.

5. What question did He ask them? Restate it in your own words.

6. The text implies that the disciples answered in some manner. How do you think they answered? How might you have answered if you were with them that night?

7. Based on the text, what two titles did the disciples probably call Jesus? What did these titles signify about their relationship to Him?

Live out...

8. a. Only three times in the New Testament does a reference to betrayal focus on the betrayal of someone other than Christ. Fill in the following chart to discover who was betrayed by whom.

Scripture	Who Betrayed Whom
Matthew 24:10	
Mark 13:12	
Luke 21:16	

Learn about ...

1 Brotherly Betrayal

To betray means to give a person over to prison or judgment through treachery. In order to betray a person, one has to be intimate. In the New Testament, the word is used thirty-nine times. Thirty-six of these refer to Judas' betrayal of Christ.

4 Lordly Level

The NIV translates this verse "returned to his place" rather than "sat down again." Though He had condescended to act like a servant, He again took His rightful place as the Master of the feast. Today He is exalted even higher: "When He had by Himself purged our sins, [He] sat down at the right hand of the Majesty on high" (Heb. 1:3).

7 Proper Label

Teacher literally means doctor, master, or instructor. This indicates that in the disciples' eyes Jesus was highly qualified to instruct them in spiritual matters. The term "Lord" or "Master" was one of the disciples' favorite titles for Jesus. They often used it in times of confusion or trouble, such as when the windstorm overtook them: "Master, Master, we are perishing!" (Luke 8:24).

8 Love Unconditional

Jesus washing His disciples' feet is indeed beautiful. But the poignancy is magnified by the fact that He also washed His betrayer Judas' feet. Scripture tells us, "God demonstrates His own love toward us, in that while we were still sinners, Christ died for us" (Rom. 5:8).

---

10 Eternal Title

The disciples called Jesus "Teacher" and "Lord." But Jesus gave them further insight into His divine nature by saying, "And so *I am*" (emphasis added). I AM is one of the most important names for God in the Old Testament. The four-letter Hebrew word YHWH was how God revealed Himself to Moses at the burning bush.

b. Talk about a time when you felt betrayed by someone you loved. How did the fact that they were near and dear cause the betrayal to have more impact?

c. How does Jesus' willingness to wash His betrayer's feet affect you?

d. What attitude do you think He would like you to have toward the one who betrayed you?

9. The Lord came down to human level when He humbled Himself to wash the disciples' feet. However, when He finished, He was elevated to His proper place. Journal about a time when you recognized Jesus as the exalted King of heaven or as the lowly Lord on earth.

10. a. The disciples called Jesus "Master" in times of trouble. List some of the names you call the Lord.

b. Which are your favorites and why?

○ ○ ◆ ○ ○

It's probably safe to say that in every laundry room across the United States a variety of detergents are located near the washing machine. There might be a hot-water soap for dark clothing, bleach for whites, and a stain stick to get out the spaghetti sauce that accidentally dripped on our husband's new shirt. Inevitably, while taking the clothes out of the dryer, we all find one piece of clothing with the stain set in. "Urggggh," we murmur under our breaths, "I thought I stain-sticked this! Why didn't it come out?" The only thing to do is to consign the guilty piece of clothing to the dust rags or the trash heap. Sadly, some things just refuse to be washed clean.

Jesus made His point that not all the disciples were clean. We'll go into this truth in more depth tomorrow. But eleven of the disciples were willing to allow Jesus to go through the laundering process. They even said they understood the process of putting their feet in the bath. It's likely that they had no more insight into what Jesus was talking about than a stained shirt does when a diligent housewife scrubs it with her stain stick. Nevertheless, they submitted to the Master's hand and allowed Him to show them the way. One day they would understand and follow His example. Let's follow His example as well and gladly wash the tired and dirty feet of the fellow pilgrims we meet on our life's journey.

LISTEN TO ...

To say the truth, so Judas kiss'd his Master, And cried, "All hail," whereas he meant all harm.

—William Shakespeare

DAY 5

Changing Expectations

The disciples needed to change their expectations at Christ's first coming—He was the humble Savior instead of a heralded Sovereign. They also needed to adjust their own expectations, becoming servant leaders not lofty lords.

What about you? Do you expect to reach the top instead of seeking the bottom? We, too, are called to follow our Savior's humble example. Perhaps, like the poet, you need to encounter the Savior face-to-face.

> I had walked life's path with an easy tread,
> Had followed where comfort and pleasure led;
> And then by chance in a quiet place—
> I met my Master face to face.
>
> With station and rank and wealth for goal,
> Much thought for body but none for soul,
> I had entered to win this life's mad race—
> When I met my Master face to face.
>
> I had built my castles, reared them high,
> Till their towers had pierced the blue of the sky;
> I had sworn to rule with an iron mace—
> When I met my Master face to face.
>
> I met Him and knew Him, and blushed to see
> That His eyes full of sorrow were fixed on me;
> And I faltered, and fell at His feet that day
> While my castles vanished and melted away.
>
> Melted and vanished; and in their place
> I saw naught else but my Master's face;

And I cried aloud: "Oh, make me meet
To follow the marks of Thy wounded feet."

My thought is now for the souls of men;
I have lost my life to find it again
Ever since alone in that holy place
My Master and I stood face to face.[7]

LIFT UP ...

Lord, I have to admit that washing feet was not what I had in mind when I became a
Christian. It's awe inspiring to see Your humble example. Lord, I surrender my lofty plans.
Let me do what You have done and serve others. Amen.

LOOK AT ...

Yesterday's lesson left us hanging on a question. Jesus wanted to know if the disciples understood His humble actions. You can almost picture the Twelve nodding their heads in
affirmation while mumbling, "Uh huh." But, in truth, they had no clue what to make of
the situation. Jesus had given them a riddle to ponder. And now He would answer it.

The debate among Christians is whether the Lord literally meant to institute a new
sacrament of foot washing. Most agree that what Jesus intended to teach His disciples
and all Christians was the lesson of "servant leadership." Jesus was using foot washing as
a type of parable to illustrate a spiritual truth—if the Master lowered Himself to the level
of a servant, where does that place His followers? Lower than low? How low are you
willing to go?

READ JOHN 13:14–17.

*"If I then, your Lord and Teacher, have washed your feet, you also ought to wash one
another's feet. For I have given you an example, that you should do as I have done to you.*

Most assuredly, I say to you, a servant is not greater than his master; nor is he who is sent greater than he who sent him. If you know these things, blessed are you if you do them." John 13:14–17

LEARN ABOUT ...

2 Your Lord

The title "Lord" here is *Kurios.* Its Old Testament counterpart is *Adonai.* This name of God means one in supreme authority, controller, or master. To call Jesus "Lord" was to offer Him the respect of saying "Sir" or "Mr." In your Bible, when "LORD" is spelled with small capital letters, it's the Hebrew name Yahweh. A capital L with lowercase "-ord" is *Kurios* or *Adonai.*

3 Your Example

Jesus didn't ask His disciples to do something He had not done Himself. Jesus led by example. True leaders are first doers. The apostle Paul understood this principle: "Brethren, join in following my example, and note those who so walk, as you have us for a pattern" (Phil. 3:17).

6 Your Blessing

Blessed means happy. It can also be translated "supremely blest, fortunate, or well off."[8] Happiness comes from holiness. Many mistakenly believe that happiness comes from being ministered to rather than ministering to others. Jesus turns the table. "Blessed are those who keep His testimonies, Who seek Him with the whole heart!" (Ps. 119:2).

1. Jesus offered His disciples an example to follow. "If" He did something, then they should respond accordingly. In your own words, describe what He told them.

2. In giving this instruction, what title did He give Himself?

3. According to Jesus, why should the disciples wash one another's feet?

4. The phrase "most assuredly" means Jesus wanted to drive home something important. What was the first thing He wanted the disciples to "most assuredly" know?

5. What was the second thing He wanted them to know? Why is this important for us to know?

6. Jesus ended this teaching with another "if" and "then" promise. Describe what He promised "if" His disciples followed His example.

LIVE OUT...

7. Today Jesus was given the title Lord, implying one of supreme authority. Using LORD as an acrostic, list some areas in your life that you've surrendered authority to Him.

L

O

R

D

8. a.   Jesus led by example. Read 1 Thessalonians 1:5–8. In what ways was the gospel preached to the Thessalonians (see v. 5)?

b.   Whose lifestyle did the Thessalonians try to imitate (see v. 6)?

c.   What in turn did the Thessalonians become and to whom (see vv. 7–8)?

d.   Explain in your own words why they didn't need to use words to share the gospel (see v. 8).

9.   Holiness leads to happiness. Is that true in your experience? Place a ☺ beside the activities that make you happy and a ☹ next to those don't make you holy.

___Prayer	___Fellowship	___Good works
___Gossip	___Stretching the truth	___Praise
___Overspending	___Witnessing	___Selfishness
___Scripture	___Apathy	___Other_____

Jesus initiated a new style of leadership titled servant leadership. Today, corporations have incorporated this management style into their business model. Whether you work in an office, at home, or volunteering at church, as a follower of Christ you are called to be a leader. Ask yourself if you display the characteristics of a servant leader.

LEARN ABOUT …

7 Lord of All

It's been said, "If Jesus is not Lord of all, He's not Lord at all." You can't surrender control of your life incrementally. It would be like selling a car and handing over only the tires. When you give your life to Christ, don't hold anything back: "He is Lord of all" (Acts 10:36).

8 Imitation

Francis of Assisi reportedly said, "Preach the gospel. If necessary, use words." It really is true. Most people judge Christians to see if their lives line up with their lectures. Jesus practiced what He preached, and so should we: "Your godly lives will speak to them without any words. They will be won over" (1 Peter 3:1 NLT).

- Do people believe you are willing to sacrifice your self-interest for the kingdom of God?

- Do people believe that you want to hear their ideas and value them?

- Do people believe that you understand what is happening in their lives and how it affects them?

- Do people come to you when something traumatic has happened in their lives?

- Do others believe that you have a strong awareness for what is going on?

- Do others follow your requests because they want to as opposed to because they "have to"?

- Do others communicate their ideas and vision for the organization when you are around?

- Do others have confidence in your ability to anticipate the future and its consequences?

- Do others believe you are preparing the organization to advance the kingdom of God?

- Do people believe that you are committed to helping them develop and grow?

- Do people feel a strong sense of community in the organization that you lead?[9]

When you take on the role of a servant leader, you are following in the footsteps of the greatest leader of all, Jesus Christ.

LISTEN TO ...

The servant of God has a good master.

—Blaise Pascal

All for One and One for All

John 13:18–38

"All for one and one for all" first sprang from the lips of the king's musketeers in Alexander Dumas's novel *The Three Musketeers*. Athos, Pathos, and Aramis solemnly swore to abide by this vow before any clash of swords. It was a pledge of loyalty to one another and to their king through thick and thin.

This oath still represents solidarity among comrades. Its Latin version, *Unus pro omnibus, omnes pro uno,* is the traditional motto of Switzerland. The infamous motorcycle gang, the Hell's Angels, adopted the phrase to pledge allegiance to their tightly knit brotherhood. Children mimic these words on playgrounds and in sports huddles.

The twelve apostles comprised the inner circle of the King of Kings—they were His comrades and His brotherhood. The Upper Room Discourse opens the clubhouse door so we can eavesdrop on the secrets Jesus divulged to them. He also gave His disciples a noble call to solidarity: "A new commandment I give to you, that you love one another.… By this all will know that you are My disciples, if you have love for one another" (John 13:34–35). Sadly, these men would fail their King during His darkest hour: One would betray Him, another would deny Him, and the rest would desert Him.

This week we'll focus on the one who would betray His King and comrades. As we've learned, someone from the inner circle would play the role of deceiver. Although Judas's departure was not a surprise to Jesus, it must have been a shock to his cohorts. It would be the same if you made the choice to leave the Lord's Table. Your dear friends would shudder.

DAY 1
The King's Warning

LIFT UP ...

Father, help me to be one with You and my Savior. And help me to be united to Your body, the church. Let me live in love so that the world sees and believes that I belong to You. Amen.

LOOK AT ...

Today's lesson begins with Jesus warning His disciples that not all of His followers were sincere. One from among their ranks was a traitor. This deeply disturbed our Savior; after all, He was flesh and blood. Though Scripture had prophesied that one of the Messiah's followers would strike out against Him, the truth still stung. Imagine how difficult this meal must have been for Jesus. Judas was plotting evil while the Lord washed his feet and offered him bread. And Jesus was painfully aware of what was happening.

How do you treat those who willfully wrong you? The Bible says, "Bless those who persecute you; bless and do not curse" (Rom. 12:14). If you want to be like Jesus, then love both the lovely *and* the unlovable. That's what makes you different from sinners. "If you are kind only to your friends, how are you different from anyone else? Even pagans do that" (Matt. 5:47 NLT). Perhaps your next party should include a couple of irregular people. Jesus made sure His did.

READ JOHN 13:18–21.

"I do not speak concerning all of you. I know whom I have chosen; but that the Scripture may be fulfilled, 'He who eats bread with Me has lifted up his heel against Me.' Now I tell you before it comes, that when it does come to pass, you may believe that I am He. Most assuredly, I say to you, he who receives whomever I send receives Me; and he who receives Me receives Him who sent Me."

LEARN ABOUT ...

1 All But

The word "all" refers to the whole quantity as in wholly, completely, and entirely. Judas revealed that he was not *all* for the One; therefore, he was not one of the all. "Love the LORD your God with *all* your heart, with *all* your soul, and with *all* your mind" (Matt. 22:37 emphasis added).

3 Above All

The focus of all prophetic truth is Jesus Christ. As the embodiment of truth, Christ fully radiated the brilliance of God that the earlier prophets reflected only partially.[10] Jesus said, "You search the Scriptures because you think they give you eternal life. But the Scriptures point to me!" (John 5:39 NLT).

5 All Inclusive

To receive means to take hold, obtain, or seize. It's one thing to be offered a gift. It's an entirely different matter to receive it and take hold of it for oneself. Jesus implied that His gifts are a package deal—if you receive Him, you receive the Father as well. If you receive a believer, you get Jesus, too.

When Jesus had said these things, He was troubled in spirit, and testified and said, "Most assuredly, I say to you, one of you will betray Me." John 13:18–21

1. Look back to the last lesson and find the phrase "all of you" repeated by Jesus today. To whom was Jesus referring?

2. The Upper Room Discourse includes another key word, reminding us that Jesus "knew" many things. What further knowledge did Jesus reveal in our text?

3. Next Jesus quoted Psalm 41. Read the psalm and explain how this Scripture was fulfilled in Jesus' life.

4. Looking back at our text, describe the effect that fulfilled prophecy should have in the life of the believer.

5. Circle the word *receives* in our text each time it is used. Explain who receives whom and why.

6. Elaborate on Jesus' emotions and explain what caused them.

LIVE OUT...

7. Jesus implied that some people were chosen, while others, like Judas, were not. Fill in the following chart to discover some God has chosen.

SCRIPTURE	GOD'S CHOSEN
Psalm 33:12	
Psalm 89:3	
Psalm 105:26	

SCRIPTURE

Matthew 20:16

Acts 9:15

1 Peter 2:9–10

GOD'S CHOSEN

LEARN ABOUT …

8 All Glory

The worldly wise seek diplomas, the high and mighty seek trophies, the prideful nobility seek titles to receive accolades and self-satisfaction. But God will have no rivals. Therefore, He selects the foolish, the weak, the base, and the despised who will give Him all the glory.

_____

9 All Come

It's interesting to note that those who receive Christ are those who are chosen by God. How do you become one of His chosen? By choosing Him. "The Lord is … not willing that any should perish but that all should come to repentance" (2 Peter 3:9). What will you choose?

8. The men Jesus called were farmers, fishermen, and tax collectors. Read 1 Corinthians 1:26–31 and fill in the columns below.

UNLIKELY TO BE CALLED   **LIKELY TO BE CHOSEN**

Now in your own words explain the reasons why God chooses the unexpected (see vv. 29–31).

9. Another key word from today was "receive." Read John 1:11–13.

   a. Describe what happened when Jesus came to His own (see v. 11).

   b. Explain what happens to those who are willing to receive Him (see v. 12).

   c. Describe how these people are and are not born into God's family (see v. 13).

10. God chooses some to be His own; He is in charge. Yet we have a choice too: The choice to receive Him or not. What do these two truths tell you …

about God?

about humans?

about you?

○ ○ ● ○ ○

Jesus uttered a prophecy to reinforce His prediction that one among them would betray Him. Why did Jesus quote Psalm 41? First, He wanted to bolster the disciples' faith by preparing them for what was to come. Just imagine how they would feel when someone they had spent three years of their lives with turned on their leader. If they were not prepared, they might have lost heart.

Second, it would strengthen their faith in the Scriptures. They could be confident that "all Scripture is given by inspiration of God" (2 Tim. 3:16). When Jesus quoted the psalm and it turned out to be true, they would realize that God's Word is flawless. Fulfilled prophecy helps us to believe in the infallibility of Scripture.

Last, the disciples saw more clearly that Christ was the Messiah. We know that Jesus fulfilled over three hundred prophecies during His first coming. Peter Stoner in *Science Speaks* says that by using the modern science of probability in reference to only eight prophecies, "we find that the chance that any man might have lived down to the present time and fulfilled all eight prophecies is 1 in 10^{17}." To comprehend this staggering probability, Stoner uses an imaginary exercise: 10^{17} silver dollars would cover Texas two feet deep. Now pretend we marked one of these silver dollars, then threw it randomly into the pile. Then blindfold a man and ask him to pick up one silver dollar. If he chose the marked one, he would have matched the odds of Jesus fulfilling eight prophecies—1 in 10^{17}.[11]

When you read God's Word, it should do the same things: build you up, increase your confidence in the truth of Scripture, and point you to Christ as the Messiah.

LISTEN TO ...

In God there is no was or will be, but a continuous and unbroken is. In him history and prophecy are one and the same.

—A. W. Tozer

DAY 2

The Inner Circle

Proximity equals power. In Washington, D.C., influence and power are measured in direct proportion to physical proximity to the Oval Office. Hugh Sidey of the White House Historical Association wrote, "If the West Wing stands for anything, it's power. Former denizens contend that the placement of offices around the president's Oval forms a power chart similar to the old Kremlin reviewing stand, where Stalin's rankings of his politburo members were measured by how close to him they stood during parades." He went on to report:

> About 250 benignly obsessed people cram into the West Wing's 75 rooms, which are mostly small (some lack windows), badly ventilated, poorly sound-proofed but coveted beyond measure by people in the power business. A successful term in the West Wing can mean a couple of million dollars a year more in salary and consulting fees, an insider estimates.[12]

The inner circle of the West Wing provides information and access that can carry ambitious people to new heights.

At every dinner party, seating arrangements reveal the power of the host's inner circle. Think about it: When you move from the kid's table to the adult table, you know you've arrived. At a wedding, sitting at the bride's table means you're in the inner circle. At the Passover Feast, those who sat closest to the master of the feast were given a place of honor and thus prestige. The two most important seats were to the right and left of the host. Let's see who made up the inner circle during the Passover evening in the upper room.

LIFT UP ...

Jesus, I know that You don't play favorites. Thank You that You've made me a part of Your inner circle and share all of Your secrets with me. Amen.

LOOK AT ...

LEARN ABOUT ...

1 Reaction

John's gospel tells us that the disciples were "perplexed." This means they were doubting or at a loss, feeling as if they had no way out. The comparable passage in Matthew tells us that "they were exceedingly sorrowful" (Matt. 26:22).

---

2 Recumbent

This disciple clearly had a comfortable relationship with Jesus. Unlike Da Vinci's painting where the disciples sat in chairs, they probably reclined on several *triclinia*, couches arranged around three sides of a square. The fourth side was left open for bringing in food or tables. There were usually three people per *triclinium*.

At the end of yesterday's passage we saw that Jesus was troubled in spirit, knowing a turncoat was in their midst. The disciples began to respond to the pressure by asking some difficult questions.

For a few moments place yourself in the upper room. You've been taken by surprise. Jesus has thrown you off guard by washing your feet. Already you're humbled by His actions. Then He stuns you with news you just can't comprehend. One of your very best friends—someone you've eaten with, joked with, walked miles and miles with—will do the unthinkable. Then you start to look at your friends with suspicion. Maybe you look into your own heart with doubt. *Is it him? Or him? What if it's me? Am I capable of that?* So Peter, being Peter, asked the obvious.

READ JOHN 13:22–26.

Then the disciples looked at one another, perplexed about whom He spoke.

Now there was leaning on Jesus' bosom one of His disciples, whom Jesus loved. Simon Peter therefore motioned to him to ask who it was of whom He spoke.

Then, leaning back on Jesus' breast, he said to Him, "Lord, who is it?"

Jesus answered, "It is he to whom I shall give a piece of bread when I have dipped it." And having dipped the bread, He gave it to Judas Iscariot, the son of Simon. John 13:22–26

1. "Then" brings us from yesterday's lesson to today. Describe how the disciples acted and felt about the Lord's prediction.

2. Who was leaning on Jesus, and how was he described? Who do you think this unnamed disciple was, and why do you think he chose to remain anonymous?

3. What was Peter's reaction to Jesus' statement?

4. How did the unnamed disciple respond?

5. How did Jesus say He would reveal the betrayer?

6. How can we tell that Judas wasn't seated far from Jesus?

LIVE OUT...

7. It was perplexing to the disciples that one among them would leave the Lord's Table.

   a. Journal about a friend or family member who has turned their back on faith.

   b. Now journal a prayer asking God to draw that person to Himself.

8. We met an unnamed disciple leaning on Jesus who was described as the one "whom Jesus loved." Fill in the chart to discover other times we find this phrase in Scripture.

SCRIPTURE	CIRCUMSTANCES	WHO JESUS WAS WITH
John 20:1–3		
John 21:4–7		
John 21:15–21		

9. Although Judas treated Jesus like an enemy, Jesus treated Judas like a beloved friend. With that in mind read Romans 12:17–20.

   a. Does Scripture allow believers to retaliate (v. 17)? Why, or why not?

LEARN ABOUT ...

5 Revealed

Jesus bestowed special honors on Judas in two ways: 1) He seated him at His left hand; 2) He offered Judas bread from His hand. To receive the bread was to make a pledge of loyalty. The bread revealed who would betray Jesus, but it also revealed that Jesus made every gesture of love toward Judas.

7 Redeemed

The Bible has a term for believers who walk away from the Lord: backsliding. But there is hope for prodigals, backsliders, and rebels. Jesus, the Good Shepherd, will follow them and bring them home: "There will be more joy in heaven over one sinner who repents than over ninety-nine just persons who need no repentance" (Luke 15:7).

8 Repeated

Did you notice that "the disciple whom Jesus loved" was always with Peter? In John 21 we find that this unnamed disciple was John, the author of the gospel: "This is the disciple who testifies of these things" (John 21:24). It's lovely that John was so confident in His Savior's love. You can be too.

b. How then should we live (v. 18)?

c. Describe how God responds to our efforts (v. 19).

d. Rather than retaliate, how should we treat our enemies and what will be the outcome (v. 20)? How did you see this played out in today's lesson?

○ ○ ● ○ ○

Let's face it, we've all been in one or wished we were. Cliques are sophisticated, complicated, and multifaceted. Although there are different positions in cliques, we can change positions depending upon our circumstances. Rosalind Wiseman, author of *Queen Bees and Wannabes* elaborated on the "7 Common Roles Girls Play in Cliques":

1. *The Queen Bee:* Through charisma, resources, and manipulation, she reigns supreme. Through weakening friendships, she strengthens her power.

2. *The Side Kick:* She does everything the Queen Bee says. The Queen Bee makes her feel popular and included.

3. *The Floater:* She has friends in different groups and moves freely among them. She doesn't make other girls feel bad.

4. *The Torn Bystander:* She's conflicted about doing the right thing and her allegiance to the clique. She's the one most likely to be caught in the middle of a conflict.

5. *The Pleaser/Wannabe:* She will do anything to be in the good graces of the Queen Bee and the Sidekick. When two powerful girls fight, she is the go-between, but they eventually turn on her.

6. *The Banker:* Girls trust her when she pumps them for information because it doesn't seem like gossip; instead, she does it in an "I'm trying to be your friend" way.

7. *The Target:* She's the victim, set up by the other girls to be humiliated, made fun of, excluded. She feels isolated and alone.[13]

The disciples all played different roles as they grouped around Jesus. Throughout His ministry, they vied for position, as all humans are prone to do. Today, Peter played the role of "Banker" and asked the "Sidekick" for information. Judas was the "Floater" and made the choice to change allegiance.

LISTEN TO ...

O holy trust! O endless sense of rest! Like the beloved John, To lay his head upon the Savior's breast, And thus to journey on!

—*Henry Wadsworth Longfellow*

DAY 3

The Double Agent

You've probably heard of FBI agent Robert Hanssen, the most diabolical double agent in United States history. He was finally caught in 2001 after fifteen years of selling top-secret information to Russia. He reportedly did enormous damage. He sold to the KGB the names of three "moles" or double agents who were secretly working for the FBI. He also revealed an expensive U.S. secret tunnel under the Russian embassy for the purpose of eavesdropping. Hanssen sold the Russians a list of all American double agents who were passing misinformation to the Russians. Hanssen's payments from cash and gems totaled more than $1.4 million.

Surprisingly, Hanssen was an ultrareligious Catholic and a member of the secret group Opus Dei, which means "God's Work." Hanssen seldom missed daily Mass, defended family values, and was a father of six children who attended parochial schools. But he had a dark side. He had a profane sense of humor, frequented strip clubs, and even taped intimate encounters with his wife and sent them to friends.[14]

Just like Hanssen, Judas probably appeared very religious. He had witnessed Jesus perform miracles. He had helped to feed the five thousand. He had seen demons exorcised. He was included in the inner circle and was entrusted with the role of treasurer. But today we'll see his dark side and watch him become the worst double agent the Bible has ever known.

LIFT UP ...

Lord, help me to stay faithful and true to You all the days of my life. And thank You that You promise never to leave or forsake me. Amen.

LOOK AT ...

Judas had displayed a pattern of deception before this scene in the upper room. For instance, Jesus had taught many lessons about money and covetousness. Yet when Mary washed Jesus' feet, Judas rebuked her about the cost of the spikenard. John gave insight into Judas's heart, saying, "This he said, not that he cared for the poor, but because he was a thief, and had the money box; and he used to take what was put in it" (John 12:6). Soon after, Judas went to meet with the Jewish leaders to name his fee and arrange a time and place to inform on Jesus' movements. "Judas Iscariot, went to the chief priests and said, 'What are you willing to give me if I deliver Him to you?' And they counted out to him thirty pieces of silver" (Matt. 26:14–15).

As you read today's lesson, ask yourself if you've allowed a pattern of deception to creep in. Are you hiding something from those around you? Remember, God sees everything. There's nothing you can conceal from Him. It's not too late to have a change of heart.

LEARN ABOUT ...

2 Satan

Most commentators agree that Satan could not have entered Judas without his permission. Matthew Henry wrote, "Christ knew that Satan had entered into him, and had peaceable possession; and now he gives him up as hopeless.... When the evil spirit is willingly admitted, the good Spirit justly withdraws."[15]

---

5 Silver

Was it about the silver? Not likely. Thirty pieces of silver was a relatively small amount. Was it about the sword? Theologians suggest that Judas hoped to force Jesus into asserting His power and overthrowing Rome. Was it about the Savior? Commentators write that perhaps Judas thought Jesus was a false Messiah.

READ JOHN 13:27–30.

Now after the piece of bread, Satan entered him. Then Jesus said to him, "What you do, do quickly." But no one at the table knew for what reason He said this to him. For some thought, because Judas had the money box, that Jesus had said to him, "Buy those things we need for the feast," or that he should give something to the poor.

Having received the piece of bread, he then went out immediately. And it was night. John 13:27–30

1. *Now* is a connecting word linking us to the prior verse. Look back to yesterday's lesson and explain what piece of bread John is referring to here.

2. Describe what happened to Judas at this point during the meal.

3. What did Jesus ask of Judas? Why do you think Jesus included a time reference?

4. How many of the disciples understood Jesus' request?

LEARN ABOUT ...

6 Sunset

The book of John uses light and dark, night and day, as spiritual imagery. Since Jesus is the Light of the World, the fact that Judas rejected Him and went into the night makes a profound statement. It was a dark night for Judas's soul: "The way of the wicked is like darkness" (Prov. 4:19).

7 Schemer

Satan is the superhuman Enemy of God, man, and good. His other names include "the Devil," "the tempter," "the Wicked One," "the prince of the power of the air," and "the accuser of our brethren." Warning—his names depict his activities! "Lest Satan should take advantage of us; for we are not ignorant of his devices" (2 Cor. 2:11).

8 Stuff

Covetousness is an intense desire to possess something that belongs to another person. Covetousness springs from a greedy self-centeredness and an arrogant disregard of God's law.[16] "Watch out! Be on your guard against all kinds of greed; a man's life does not consist in the abundance of his possessions" (Luke 12:15 NIV).

5. What reasons did they give for Judas's departure?

6. When and how did Judas leave?

LIVE OUT...

7. Today we witnessed satanic activity in the life of Judas. Fill in the following chart to discover others who encountered the Enemy.

SCRIPTURE	THOSE SATAN ATTACKED
1 Chronicles 21:1	
Matthew 4:8–11	
Luke 22:31	
Acts 5:1–3	

8. Judas held the money box, but sadly the box held him captive. Don't let your possessions possess you. List the things you treasure most. Circle the things that belong in your treasure box and cross out the ones that do not.

9. Light and dark, night and day carry spiritual significance throughout Scripture. While Jesus was the light, Judas turned to the night. Rewrite the following passage into a personal prayer:

Walk while you have the light, lest darkness overtake you; he who walks in darkness does not know where he is going. While you have the light, believe in the light, that you may become sons of light. (John 12:35–36)

○ ○ ● ○ ○

Everything we have learned about Judas indicates that he made a cognitive decision to deny Christ. Commentator James Boice Montgomery wrote, "Judas, I am convinced, was not just a mistaken individual. He was a deceiver, a devil, a hypocrite *par excellance.* Judas lived with the others and pretended that he was one with them, while deep in his heart he was rebelling against everything that Jesus taught." One can't help but shudder at the blasphemous role he played.

Equally startling is a new phenomenon on the Web. A highly organized and vitriolic group of atheists is encouraging people to deny Christ and blaspheme the Holy Spirit. According to their Web site: "We want your soul! It's simple. You just have to record a short message damning yourself to Hell, you upload it to YouTube…. It's that easy.

> INSTRUCTIONS:
>
> You may damn yourself to Hell however you would like, but somewhere in your video you must say this phrase: 'I deny the Holy Spirit.'
>
> Why? Because, according to Mark 3:29 in the Holy Bible, "Whoever blasphemes against the Holy Spirit will never be forgiven; he is guilty of an eternal sin." Jesus will forgive you for just about anything, but he *won't* forgive you for denying the existence of the Holy Spirit. Ever. This is a one-way road you're taking here.[17]

Over eight hundred people, largely young people in their twenties, have taken the challenge. Their testimonials are gut wrenching to watch. What can we do? Pray for their souls, practice good works, and preach the good news. May God deliver them from darkness into the light!

LISTEN TO …

Fortune does not change men; it unmasks them.

—Madame Necker

DAY 4

The Sacred Oath

Throughout the ages, people from knights to nuns have taken a sacred oath of allegiance to a king, creed, or calling. During the 1800s in the United States, the Knights of Labor adopted a sacred oath that relied heavily on religious underpinnings. They believed that all that was worthy in society was derived from human labor. Hundreds of thousands of workers pledged to improve the conditions of all working people everywhere with the following promises:

> In the beginning, God ordained that man should labor, not as a curse, but as a blessing; not as a punishment, but as means of development, physically, mentally, morally, and has set thereunto his seal of approval in the rich increase and reward. By labor is brought forward the kindly fruits of the earth in rich abundance for our sustenance and comfort; by labor (not exhaustive) is promoted health of the body and strength of mind, labor garners the priceless stores of wisdom and knowledge. It is the "Philosopher's Stone," everything it touches turns to wealth. "Labor is noble and holy." To glorify God in its exercise, to defend it from degradation, to divest it of the evils to body, mind, and estate, which ignorance and greed have imposed; to rescue the toiler from the grasp of the selfish is a work worthy of the noblest and best of our race.[18]

In the upper room, Jesus was initiating His disciples into a special calling. He washed their feet, shared a meal, and then offered the most holy creed: *Love one another; as I have loved you.* In doing so, the whole world would know that they were knights of His sacred oath.

LIFT UP ...

Jesus, as part of Your inner circle I want to spread Your love to those around me. Please help me to love others as You have loved me. Amen.

LOOK AT ...

Judas's betrayal cast a long shadow over the gathering in the upper room. Jesus felt great sorrow. The disciples became suspicious. And ultimately they would all reel from the shockwaves that emanated from Judas's Satan-inspired scheme.

However, once Judas abruptly departed, the atmosphere transitioned from gloom to glory. Jesus turned to the remaining disciples to challenge them with a new commandment, a new creed to live by. He was teaching them that with every privilege comes responsibility. It had to be quite an honor, even prestigious, to be among Jesus' inner circle. Yet the Lord required something in return. The Bible instructs, "To whom much is given, from him much will be required" (Luke 12:48). Do you consider yourself a member of the Lord's inner circle? If you've pledged allegiance to the Lord, then you are considered His nearest and dearest. Now it's up to you to fulfill the sacred oath.

READ JOHN 13:31–35.

So, when he had gone out, Jesus said, "Now the Son of Man is glorified, and God is glorified in Him. If God is glorified in Him, God will also glorify Him in Himself, and glorify Him immediately. Little children, I shall be with you a little while longer. You will seek Me; and as I said to the Jews, 'Where I am going, you cannot come,' so now I say to you. A new commandment I give to you, that you love one another; as I have loved you, that you also love one another. By this all will know that you are My disciples, if you have love for one another." John 13:31–35

1. Again we must go backward to move forward. The word *so* connects us to yesterday's passage. Explain who had gone out and why.

2. *Now,* another key word, is introduced. Circle the various forms of the word *glorify,* then explain who is glorified and why.

3. What term of endearment did Jesus use for the disciples, and what information did He link with this term?

LEARN ABOUT …

2 Glorify

Jesus spoke of His glorification in the present tense. The moment Judas left, Jesus turned to the disciples and said: "*Now* the Son of Man is glorified." The unstoppable events were set in motion for His crucifixion. Jesus would glorify His Father through His perfect obedience and sacrificial death on our behalf.

---

4 God's Children

John, the author of this gospel, adopted Jesus' term of endearment. *New Unger's Bible Dictionary* records, "When all capacity to work and teach was gone—when there was no strength even to stand—he [John] directed himself to be carried to the assemblage of believers, and simply said, with a feeble voice, 'Little children, love one another.'"19

---

6 God's Commandment

The word *new* does not mean it was "brand-new." Even the Old Testament had commanded, "You shall love your neighbor as yourself" (Lev. 19:18). The word implied that this love would be fresh, regenerate, and youthful. In other words, as believers they would experience love anew.

4. How would this term of endearment make you feel? What reasons might Jesus have for using it?

5. Jesus issued a new commandment using a repeated word. Circle the key word and explain the new commandment.

6. What will be the outcome of the new commandment?

7. After reading this commandment, give your definition of a disciple.

LIVE OUT…

8. The Lord's glorification was tied to His obedience to the Father even to the point of death on a cross. Christ's disciples follow a similar path in bringing glory to their Lord: "If anyone desires to come after Me, let him deny himself, and take up his cross, and follow Me" (Matt. 16:24).

With this in mind, in the appropriate column list some things you need to deny and some ways you must follow the Lord.

DENY YOURSELF	FOLLOW HIM

9. Today we saw Jesus address His disciples as "little children."

   a. List other terms of endearment found in Scripture for God's children.

   b. What is your favorite term of endearment and why?

10. Jesus challenged His disciples to love one another in the way that He had loved them. Use LOVE as an acrostic and write some words to describe the type of love Jesus displayed throughout His life and ministry.

L

O

V

E

LEARN ABOUT …

8 Obedience

Obedience is difficult when we're asked to suffer or sacrifice. Yet Jesus is our example. The writer of Hebrews said, "Though He was a Son, yet He learned obedience by the things which He suffered. And having been perfected, He became the author of eternal salvation to all who obey Him" (Heb. 5:8–9).

10 Love

In English there is more than definition for the word love. The Greek language has several variations for the word love: *Eros* refers to erotic love. *Philia* speaks of brotherly love and affection. And *agape* "is the antithesis of selfishness. Luther calls it 'the shortest and longest divinity.' It is active, and dissatisfied if not blessing others."[20]

∘ ∘ • ∘ ∘

Let's spend some time getting to know John. Scripture tells us that he was one of the sons of Zebedee. Most people believe his mother's name was Salome. John and his brother James were partners in a fishing business with their father before their calling to follow Christ. He and James apparently had fiery personalities because Jesus nicknamed them the "sons of thunder." John stood with Mary as one of the last at the cross and with Peter as one of the first at the tomb.

It's amazing that the hotheaded young man became the tenderhearted church elder. Church tradition says that as an old man John would say, "Little children, love one another!" It tells us that people got tired of the repetition and asked, "Master, why do you always say that?"

He replied, "It is the Lord's command. And if this alone be done, it is enough!"

Obviously the Upper Room Discourse had an abiding impact on John. The Master's endearment of calling the flock "little children" and command to love one another stayed with John throughout his life.

It is said that John faced martyrdom by being boiled in oil during the Roman persecution. However, he miraculously survived and was exiled to the island of Patmos. There he wrote the book of Revelation. He died peacefully as an old man in Ephesus. John's brother James was the first of the apostles to die, while John was the last.

John lived out the oath of love he took in the upper room. As a result, the world has come to know him as the apostle of love. If, like John, you are a woman who speaks thundering words, it's not too late to change your ways—live love.

LISTEN TO ...

They are the true disciples of Christ, not who know most, but who love most.

—*Frederich Spanheim the Elder*

DAY 5

The Coming Crucible

A crucible is a container to melt metals at temperatures above 500°C. Crucibles can resist temperatures over 1600°C. A crucible is filled with metal, then placed into a furnace until the substance becomes liquid. The crucible is removed from the furnace so the molten metal can be poured into a mold. Symbolically, the term *crucible* is used for circumstances that are extremely difficult and refine or reshape the person.

War can serve as a crucible of souls. *The Crucible of War,* a documentary that interviewed victims of the war in the Balkans, included an interview with Franciscan priest Ivo Markovic in July 1999. He said: "I had an actual case with forgiveness when my father was killed. He was an unbelievably good person, a peacemaker. And for that man to be killed—a person who defended against this atmosphere of revenge. I didn't have a problem with overcoming that. If a man has at least a little bit of soul and wisdom, he would see that my father was killed as a victim of peace—on that road. This is the path of Jesus. Maybe I will meet the same fate. On that path, any kind of devastation—and even death!—in a certain sense, this is a victory over evil.… But when you experience difficulties and troubles, man always comes out stronger as a result."[21]

Fra Ivo faced a crucible and was refined into a gracious and godly man.

Conflict can also serve as a crucible. As we'll see, Peter was unprepared for the coming crucible. How will you face the fire of life's crucibles?

LIFT UP ...

Sometimes the fires of life seem too hot to bear. Help me, Lord, to withstand the heat and to be molded into Your image. Amen.

LOOK AT ...

We saw yesterday that Jesus gave the disciples a new commandment and told them that He

2 Afterward

"Afterward" was an enigmatic reply. It probably carried several layers of meaning. One day Peter *would* follow Jesus to the cross. This meant Peter would also follow His Savior to heaven. Tradition tells us that Peter was crucified upside down because he did not feel worthy to die in the same manner as Jesus.

---

4 Ironic

Though we can't hear His tone of voice, Jesus' question to Peter seems ironic. After all, Jesus was preparing to go to the cross to lay down His life for Peter: "I lay down My life that I may take it again…. I have power to lay it down, and I have power to take it again. This command I have received from My Father" (John 10:17–18).

was going somewhere they could not go. Today we see Peter's response to Jesus' revelation and Jesus' prediction that Peter would deny Him.

The main characters in John 13 have been Jesus, Peter, John, and Judas. Some may think Judas's betrayal and Peter's denial were equally grave. But that could not be further from the truth. As we have noted before, Judas's treachery was premeditated and callous. However, Peter was carried away in the heat of the moment. Because his heart was pure, he would eventually be restored and return stronger than ever. Don't we all have just a bit of Peter in us? He seemed to have good intentions but poor follow-through. When the crucible comes—and it will—remember that the Lord is burning away the impurities from your life so you can shine like pure gold.

READ JOHN 13:36–38.

Simon Peter said to Him, "Lord, where are You going?"

Jesus answered him, "Where I am going you cannot follow Me now, but you shall follow Me afterward."

Peter said to Him, "Lord, why can I not follow You now? I will lay down my life for Your sake."

Jesus answered him, "Will you lay down your life for My sake? Most assuredly, I say to you, the rooster shall not crow till you have denied Me three times." John 13:36–38

1. Look back to yesterday's text and explain what prompted Peter's question.

2. What truth did Jesus reiterate, and what new revelation did He add? What do you think Jesus meant by this?

3. Recount Peter's follow-up question and try to explain his reasoning.

4. What rhetorical question did Jesus ask?

5. Luke records a parallel account of these events. Read
   Luke 22:31–34.

   a. What did Jesus warn Peter about (see v. 31)?

   b. How did Jesus encourage Peter (see v. 32)?

   c. What promise did Peter repeat from the John passage, and how
      did he embellish it in Luke (see v. 33)?

   d. What parallel prediction did Jesus make (see v. 34)?

LIVE OUT...

6. Jesus often talked about following Him. Fill in the following chart
   to discover more about following the Lord.

SCRIPTURE	WHAT DO YOU LEARN ABOUT FOLLOWING JESUS?
Matthew 4:19	
Matthew 19:21	
John 10:27–28	
John 12:26	

7. Jesus affirmed that He would lay down His life for His followers.
   Read 1 John 3:16–18.

   a. How should we reflect Christ's love to one another (see v. 16)?

   b. In what ways might we show or stifle God's love (see v. 17)?

LEARN ABOUT ...

5 Denial

To deny means to disown, forsake, or renounce. One definition adds that to deny is to prove oneself false or to act unlike oneself. "Peter remembered the word of Jesus who had said to him, 'Before the rooster crows, you will deny Me three times.' So he went out and wept bitterly" (Matt. 26:75).

6 Follow

What did Jesus mean when He said that where He was going they could not follow *now?* Jesus was headed to the cross to redeem mankind from death and hell. After the resurrection He would provide access to heaven. Without the crucifixion there would be no way for the disciples to follow Him to heaven.

LEARN ABOUT ...

8 Lesson Learned

Peter learned a lot from failing this test. He wrote later that Christians can rejoice in trials that test their faith by fire (see I Peter 1:6–7), that those who suffer for doing right are blessed (see I Peter 3:14), and that it's an honor to share in Christ's sufferings (see I Peter 4:12–19).

c. Explain why actions speak louder than words (see v. 18).

8. Danger and suffering are crucibles that test our faith. The heat of interrogation under the danger of arrest burned away Peter's pride. Has danger or suffering ever tested your faith? If so, journal about that experience and how you responded.

∘ ∘ • ∘ ∘

Jesus had predicted that within twenty-four hours Peter would deny Him three times. It's doubtful that Peter believed this prophecy. After all, he had boasted that he would die with Christ. Sadly, we know the outcome. Before the rooster crowed, Peter would disown his Savior. Mark records this tragic episode, "Then he [Peter] began to curse and swear, 'I do not know this Man of whom you speak!'" (Mark 14:71).

It is likely that Peter's lapse in faith was the direct result of fear. Fear can be seen as the opposite of faith. But there were other mitigating factors, a downward cycle that brought Peter to the place of denial. We've already mentioned the first step, self-reliance. Peter thought too highly of Peter. Pride truly comes before a fall!

The next two steps are found in Mark 14:54: "But Peter followed Him at a distance, right into the courtyard of the high priest. And he sat with the servants and warmed himself at the fire." Step two reveals that Peter followed Jesus *at a distance*. He was pulling away from the inner circle. Scripture tells us, "Let us not neglect our meeting together" (Heb. 10:25 NLT). Distance leads to denial.

Step three found Peter warming up to unbelievers and joining the company of skeptics. The psalmist warns, "Blessed is the man who does not ... sit in the seat of mockers" (Ps. 1:1 NIV). Bad company can corrupt good morals. There are some places Christians must avoid.

These missteps led to Peter's fall when he denied even knowing Jesus not once, not twice, but three times. Thankfully, though it was devastating, it was not permanent. Eventually Jesus restored Peter and he went on to be a leader of the early church and the author of two books in the Bible. It's comforting to know that the Savior not only redeems sinners, He restores fallen saints! Jesus is able to ensure that believers remain *One for All and All for One!*

LISTEN TO ...

There is a time when we must firmly choose the course we will follow, or the relentless drift of events will make the decision.

—*Herbert V. Prochnow*

Father Knows Best
John 14:1–14

Father Knows Best, the beloved family sitcom from the 1950s, featured an idealized middle-class family in society where moms stayed at home and wore dresses and high heels, kids were free to roam the neighborhood with their friends, and fathers supposedly knew best. The Anderson family was made up of Jim, the father who worked as an insurance salesman; Margaret, the wise and patient housewife; Bud, the teenage son; Betty, the daughter better known as Princess; and Kathy, the baby of the family. The underlying theme of the show was that father might think he knew best, but mother really ruled the roost.

The series was based on the experiences Robert Young and his good friend and producer, Eugene B. Rodney, had with their wives and children. To them, the show represented "reality." Critics felt it sidestepped real life social problems such as substance abuse and avoided "the other America" altogether. Perhaps it is more important for what it has come to represent than for what it actually was.[22]

As Jesus continued talking during the Last Supper, He gave the disciples some insight into His heavenly home and His heavenly Father. Throughout the Upper Room Discourse, the word *Father* is used almost fifty times. In today's passage Jesus informs the disciples that heaven is His Father's house. God sometimes uses the earthly realm to mirror the spiritual realm, but unlike the earthly realms, which are less than perfect, our heavenly Father is perfect in every way. He really does know what's best.

Day 1: John 14:1–3	THE FATHER'S HOUSE
Day 2: John 14:4–6	THE FATHER'S ACCESS
Day 3: John 14:7–9	THE FATHER'S LIKENESS
Day 4: John 14:10–11	THE FATHER'S BUSINESS
Day 5: John 14:12–14	THE FATHER'S BLESSING

DAY 1
The Father's House

LIFT UP ...

Father, so many things trouble my heart. Help me to put my confidence in You, the faithful One. I look forward to living with You in the place You have prepared for me. Amen.

LOOK AT ...

In one night over one meal we've seen Jesus humble Himself by washing His disciples' feet, reveal a traitor among them, and warn of Peter's upcoming betrayal of Him. Jesus commanded His disciples to love one another to glorify the Father. Emotions ran the gamut that night. Acknowledging their anxiety, Jesus comforted His friends by giving them the heavenly assurance that one day He and they would be together forever. In the coming days and years, this assurance would carry these disciples through many trials.

This heavenly assurance can be ours, too, if we believe. John said that "as many as received Him, to them He gave the right to become children of God, to those who believe in His name" (John 1:12). To be invited to live in the Father's house, you must be part of the family. Aren't you glad there's always room for one more?

READ JOHN 14:1–3.

"Let not your heart be troubled; you believe in God, believe also in Me. In My Father's house are many mansions; if it were not so, I would have told you. I go to prepare a place for you. And if I go and prepare a place for you, I will come again and receive you to Myself; that where I am, there you may be also." John 14:1–3

1. Look back to yesterday's passage and review the last verse in chapter 13. What circumstances had Jesus predicted for Peter?

2. Describe what you think the mood was that night as Jesus revealed Judas's betrayal and Peter's denial.

3. Sensing the disciples' sorrow and confusion, how did Jesus comfort them?

4. Next, Jesus drew their attention to a heavenly future. Explain what He revealed about the Father's resources.

5. a. What was Jesus' reason for leaving them?

   b. How do you think this made the disciples feel?

6. What three aspects of their eventual reunion did Jesus promise?

LIVE OUT...

7. Troubles come our way for a variety of reasons. List some of the troubles we may experience in the appropriate columns.

SELF-INFLICTED	SITUATIONAL	SPIRITUAL

8. Jesus asked His followers to believe in Him as they believed in the heavenly Father. Look up the following verses, then draw a line to the objects of our belief. How do you think these are aligned with believing in the Father?

Mark 1:15	in God
John 1:12	the light
John 12:36	His name
1 Peter 1:21	the gospel

LEARN ABOUT ...

2 Heart Trouble

To be troubled means to be stirred up or agitated like churning water. Jesus was "troubled in spirit" by the events of that evening. The disciples probably picked up on their Lord's distress. Prior to this He had been the calm in their storms. In addition, Jesus predicted His imminent departure.

---

3 Believe in God

Jesus was asking the disciples to transfer the confidence they had in the Father to Him. Since the Father is faithful and in control, they could trust that Jesus would exhibit the same characteristics. In Revelation, Jesus is described as "the Faithful and True Witness, the Beginning of the creation of God" (Rev. 3:14).

---

4 Many Mansions

The Greek word translated as "mansions" means rooms or abiding places, not different dwellings. The disciples had given up their homes to follow Jesus. The idea of spending eternity in a permanent home with Jesus in a place He personally prepared must have been very appealing and comforting.

LEARN ABOUT ...

7 Heart

In the Bible, the heart stands for our entire mental and moral activity, both the rational and the emotional elements. The heart is used figuratively for the hidden springs of the personal life. "Blessed are the pure in heart, For they shall see God" (Matt. 5:8).[23]

8 Believe

To believe means to be persuaded of, to place confidence in, or to trust. It also signifies a strong reliance upon rather than mere acceptance. *Believe* is most frequently used in John's writings, especially his gospel. Of the gospel writers, Matthew uses the verb ten times, Mark ten, Luke nine, John ninety-nine.[24]

9. We know that there are many mansions in the Father's house, but some people haven't found the way. Inside the house, write the name of someone who is not a member of God's family. Then write a prayer asking Jesus to guide this person to His home.

○ ○ ● ○ ○

The carpenter who walked the earth is constructing a castle in the heavenlies. The tragedy is that some folks don't want to live in His home. One of my dearest family members even refused to discuss heaven. When I'd bring it up, he'd reply, "Lenya, stop praying for me. I don't want to go to heaven. Most of my friends are in hell and I plan on joining them."

Tearfully I'd say, "You don't understand what you're saying. Heaven is not saints playing harps on puffy clouds, and hell is not a party with your friends."

Glen Eyrie in Colorado Springs is a startling example of an earthly mansion that someone failed to inhabit. General William Jackson Palmer built a grand home for his wife, Mary Lincoln Mellen, nicknamed "Queen." The magnificent mansion sat on two thousand acres near the Garden of the Gods. Built in the 1800s, the estate boasted every modern convenience: electric gates, greenhouses, a laundry, a bowling alley, telephones, and horse stables.

Before it was completed, young Queen suffered a mild heart attack and was advised to move to a lower altitude. She moved to the East Coast and later to England where she died at the age of forty-four. Many stories circulated about what had transpired. Some say she found life in the West lacking in culture. Others claim marital strife. Whatever the reason, Mary never enjoyed living in the mansion built for a queen.

Don't you want to enjoy the magnificence of the Father's home? Jesus has gone to prepare *your* place. When you believe in the Son, you will dwell with God forever.

LISTEN TO ...

The tests of life are to make, not break us. Trouble may demolish a man's business but build up his character. The blow at the outward man may be the greatest blessing to the inner man. If God, then, puts or permits anything hard in our lives, be sure that the real peril, the real trouble, is that we shall lose if we flinch or rebel.

—Maltbie D. Babcock

DAY 2

The Father's Access

Every Sunday afternoon, Pastor John and his eleven-year-old son, Daniel, combed the neighborhood and handed out gospel tracts. One drizzling Sunday, the child bundled up in his waterproof clothes and said, "Let's go, Dad!"

His father hesitated. "But it's raining."

Daniel replied, "People still need Jesus."

Pastor John suggested, "Well … you go and I'll stay and pray."

After going door to door and getting soaked to the bone, Daniel had one tract left. He rang the last doorbell in the neighborhood, but no one answered. So he knocked loudly. Then he rang again. Finally an elderly woman opened the door and said, "Hello, sweetie."

The boy handed out the tract and said, "JESUS REALLY LOVES YOU!" Pleased, he headed home.

The following Sunday, Pastor John began the service asking, "Who has a testimony they'd like to share?"

To Daniel's surprise the elderly lady walked forward and said, "Last Sunday I felt depressed enough to end my life. I was writing my farewell note. Before I could finish, my doorbell rang. Then I heard a knock. I thought, *I'll wait a minute, and whoever it is will go away.* But when the bell rang again I decided to open the door, and there stood Daniel, the pastor's son. He handed me a tract and said, 'JESUS REALLY LOVES YOU!' It made me think life's worth living. So here I am."

This desperate woman gained access to the heavenly Father through the hands of the pastor's son. In truth, Jesus the Son offers us access to God the Father. And He really does love us.

LIFT UP …

Jesus, thank You for being so clear about how to get to the Father. You gave Your life so I could have fellowship with the Father and spend eternity with Him. I am so grateful for You. Amen.

LOOK AT ...

At the end of yesterday's passage we saw Jesus reveal that He was leaving His disciples to prepare a place for them. Today we'll hear Him disclose the secret about how to access the Father.

The disciples must have been confused about the things that had happened that evening. What began as a celebration had turned into a dissolution. One of their members had left for good. Jesus predicted that He, too, would be leaving His friends for a while. Having heard the good news about heaven, they didn't understand how they would be able to follow Jesus there. Perhaps you've wondered if there are alternate ways to get to heaven. Maybe you even doubt if you're worthy of a place in heaven. The statements Jesus made to the disciples can be applied to our lives today. Are you unsure about your eternal future? Jesus didn't leave much doubt when He spoke about getting to heaven. Let's listen closely to His straightforward words.

READ JOHN 14:4–6.

"And where I go you know, and the way you know."

Thomas said to Him, "Lord, we do not know where You are going, and how can we know the way?"

Jesus said to him, "I am the way, the truth, and the life. No one comes to the Father except through Me." John 14:4–6

1. "And" is a connecting word. Look back to yesterday's lesson "and" recount where Jesus was going.

2. What two things did Jesus assure the disciples they already knew? If someone asked you where Jesus is and how to get there, what would you say?

LEARN ABOUT ...

2 Do You Know?

In Greek there are many words for "to know." In this verse *eido* expresses knowledge that comes from observation. Alternately, *horao* means to stare at or know clearly. *Theoreo* means to study or have an experiential knowledge.[25] *Ginosko* means to recognize or come to understand, and sometimes to know personally. Perhaps Thomas wanted to know that he knew.

LEARN ABOUT ...

4 Who Was Thomas?

Thomas was one of the twelve apostles. He's best known for his inability to believe that Jesus had risen, forever earning the name "doubting Thomas."[26] However, he offered to die with Christ: "Thomas, who is called the Twin, said to his fellow disciples, 'Let us also go, that we may die with Him'" (John 11:16).

7 Who Has Access?

In John 14:6, Jesus makes one of the most exclusive claims in Christianity. It has saved lives and offended others. There is no confusion about who Jesus says He is—God—and what He claims to do—forgive sin. He is the remedy to the alienation from the Father caused by sin: "There is salvation in no one else!" (Acts 4:12 NLT).

9 Any Questions?

There's a big difference between asking God questions and questioning God. True seekers ask Jesus honest questions with the intent to understand and obey. To those He gives a ready answer. However, those who question Him with impure motives are often rebuked: "After that no one dared question Him." (Mark 12:34).

3. In your own words describe what confused Thomas.

4. Do you think Thomas was the only one who didn't understand what Jesus meant? What makes you say that?

5. What do you think this question revealed about Thomas?

6. What profound statement did Jesus make about Himself? How would you explain the meaning of this statement in your own words?

7. What did Jesus reveal about the path to the Father?

LIVE OUT...

8. We learned today that there are many forms of knowledge: 1) to look, 2) to learn, and 3) to live. As Christians we are to progress from being hearers of God's Word, to learning more about what God's Word means, to becoming doers of it. From the following list of topics write three biblical commands that you really *know* (that is, you understand it and you do it): salvation, repentance, righteousness, love, patience, kindness, goodness, forgiveness, prayerfulness, evangelism, purity, self-denial, worship, other.

9. Thomas was willing to ask Jesus questions when he didn't understand what the Lord meant. Fill in the following chart to discover others who questioned God and why.

SCRIPTURE	WHO ASKED?	WHAT WAS ASKED?
Matthew 18:21–22		
Luke 1:34–35		
Luke 18:18–23		

Scripture	Who asked?	What was asked?
John 3:4–5		
Acts 9:3–6		

10. Today we saw Jesus proclaim that He is *the* way, *the* truth, and *the* life, implying exclusivity. Notice that He did not use the word "a" to describe Himself. Journal about a time in your life when Jesus replaced a way, truth, or source of life with the correct one.

° ° • ° °

Jesus' exclusive claims present problems for those who would reduce Him to a mere moral teacher. When Jesus made His "I AM" statements, the religious Jews understood that He was claiming to be God. After one such proclamation, "They took up stones to throw at Him" (John 8:59). In those days, stoning was the punishment for blasphemy.

C. S. Lewis, in his book *Mere Christianity*, wrote, "A man who was merely a man and said the sort of things Jesus said would not be a great moral teacher. He would either be a lunatic—on the level with a man who says he is a poached egg—or he would be the devil of hell. You must take your choice. Either this was, and is, the Son of God, or else a madman or something worse. You can shut Him up for a fool or you can fall at His feet and call Him Lord and God. But let us not come with any patronizing nonsense about His being a great human teacher. He has not left that open to us."

Lewis's logic presents a trilemma, a term philosophers use to describe a choice between options that are or seem equally unfavorable or mutually exclusive. Josh McDowell encapsulated Lewis's logic into the "Liar, Lunatic, or Lord" trilemma. Here is the premise:

Learn about …

10 Who Is He?

Jesus made extraordinary claims regarding Himself, making it impossible to marginalize Him to one of many ways. Throughout John's gospel Jesus made several "I am" statements. Three are in this verse. The others include I am the living bread (see 6:51), the light (see 8:12), the door (see 10:9), the good shepherd (see 10:11), the resurrection (see 11:25), and the vine (see 15:5).

If Jesus was not God but He believed He was, He's a *Lunatic*.

If Jesus was not God, knew it, but said so anyway, He's a *Liar*.

If Jesus is who He said He is—God—then He is *Lord*.[27]

Theologians believe that this is the most important argument in Christian apologetics for the deity of Christ. Truly, it's more logical to believe in the divinity of Jesus than to suppose He was only an admirable man. Who is Jesus to you? Is He the *only* way, the *only* truth, and the *only* life?

LISTEN TO ...

Follow me: I am the way, the truth, and the life.

Without the Way there is no going;

Without the Truth there is no knowing;

Without the Life there is no living.

—*Thomas À Kempis*

DAY 3

The Father's Likeness

What could beat winning an Olympic medal? Toby Dawson found that meeting his biological father surpassed any prize. The U.S. Olympic skier, known as "Awesome Dawson," was reunited with his birth father from Korea in March of 2007 after twenty-six years. "This will be a day that I will remember for the rest of my life," Dawson said during a press conference in downtown Seoul.

Dawson's first words were uttered in broken Korean. "I've been waiting a long time, Father." Dawson bore a striking resemblance to his father and younger brother, who also attended the reunion. Besides bearing the same facial structure, all three had an affinity for sideburns. Though time, distance, and culture separated them, it was clear that Dawson looked just like his long-lost dad.[28]

For those of us who love God, one of the longings in our hearts is to look at our Lord face-to-face. Job wrote, "How my heart yearns within me!" (Job 19:27) to see God. It makes sense, doesn't it? A pregnant mother can't wait to see the face of the baby in her womb. A couple separated by distance craves the sight of their beloved. So it is with us. We want to see the object of our affection. To behold His beauty. To spend time in His presence. To get to know Him better and better so we can love Him more.

As the disciples spent time with Jesus on this final evening, they would learn that having seen Jesus, they had, indeed, beheld the Father.

LIFT UP ...

Lord, I want to know You more. Please reveal Yourself to me through Your Word and help me to see You at work in my life. Thank You for Jesus, who has revealed the Father. Amen.

LOOK AT ...

Yesterday we saw Jesus point the way to the Father. Today we will see Him initiate a conversation with His disciples to help them understand His relationship to the Father. Every

LEARN ABOUT …

2 Knowing Him

There are four kinds of knowing: 1) to know a fact; 2) to know the truth behind the fact; 3) to know a person through relationship; 4) to know a person through deep relationship.[29] Jesus focused on the last two kinds of knowing, in essence saying, "If you have a relationship with Me, you would have a deep relationship with my Father."

3 Seeing Him

Seeing is not believing; believing is seeing. When we believe, we see with new, spiritual eyes. Philip wanted a demonstration—to see God with his eyes. What he needed was comprehension—to see with his heart. Jesus told Martha, "Did I not say to you that if you would believe you would see the glory of God?" (John 11:40).

Christian should long to see the Father. For Philip this desire was very literal. But there were limitations to "seeing" the Father. Surely Philip had heard the story of Moses, who had hidden in the cleft of the rock because God told Moses, "You cannot see My face; for no man shall see Me, and live" (Ex. 33:20). But Jesus explained that knowing and seeing Him was the same as knowing and seeing the Father, because He bore the Father's likeness.

Have you longed to see God? "Knowing" and "seeing" Him are achieved by reading His Word, experiencing His presence, and communicating with Him through prayer. You don't have to wait until you get to heaven—Jesus is ready to reveal the Father to you if you'll take the time.

READ JOHN 14:7–9.

"If you had known Me, you would have known My Father also; and from now on you know Him and have seen Him."

Philip said to Him, "Lord, show us the Father, and it is sufficient for us."

Jesus said to him, "Have I been with you so long, and yet you have not known Me, Philip? He who has seen Me has seen the Father; so how can you say, 'Show us the Father'?" John 14:7–9

1. Jesus began a conversation with Philip by making a conditional statement: "If" something happened, it would result in something else. What was this conditional statement?

2. What two things did Jesus promise for the future?

3. What request did Philip make of Jesus? Why do you think he asked this?

4. What rhetorical question did Jesus ask Philip in response to his request? What do you think Jesus was trying to tell Philip?

5. Do you think Philip was the only one intended to hear Jesus' response? Why?

6. What connection did Jesus again make between Himself and the Father? Why do you think He felt it was necessary to repeat this truth?

LIVE OUT...

7. a. We spent time today focusing on knowing the Father. Fill in the following chart to discover some benefits of knowing God.

SCRIPTURE	BENEFITS OF KNOWING GOD
Hosea 6:6	
Romans 11:33	
Ephesians 1:17–18	
Philippians 1:9–10	
Colossians 1:9–10	

b. Journal about how you have personally benefited from knowing God.

8. Philip asked to see the Father. Which of the following verses talk about seeing in the sense of physical eyesight? Which are talking about insight? Do any of them talk about both?

JOB 33:28—He will redeem his soul from going down to the Pit, And his life shall see the light.

MATTHEW 15:31—The multitude marveled when they saw the mute speaking.

LEARN ABOUT ...

6 Comprehending Him

To know Jesus is to know the Father. To see Jesus is to see the Father. This is one of the great mysteries of the Bible. The invisible God was made visible through the Son. John wrote at the beginning of his gospel: "No one has seen God at any time. The only begotten Son, who is in the bosom of the Father, *He* has declared Him" (John 1:18 emphasis added).

7 Seeking Knowledge

The highest knowledge is the knowledge of God. Though we can't know everything about Him, we can know God as He has revealed Himself through creation, His Word, and Jesus Christ who reveals Him to us: "No one knows the Father except the Son and those to whom the Son chooses to reveal him" (Matt. 11:27 NIV).

8 Seeing Clearly

God is "seen" through His Word, nature, miracles, circumstances, the deeds of others, and His people, to name a few. In the Old Testament, God would sometimes manifest Himself in person. This is called a theophany, where God would take on a human form to deliver a message. In the New Testament, Jesus is the physical expression of God.

MARK 4:12—Seeing they may see and not perceive.

MARK 16:14—He appeared to the Eleven as they sat at the table; and He rebuked their unbelief and hardness of heart, because they did not believe those who had seen Him after He had risen.

ROMANS 1:20—Since the creation of the world His invisible attributes are clearly seen, being understood by the things that are made, even His eternal power and Godhead.

9. a. Today's lesson has focused on seeing and knowing God. Read 1 Corinthians 13:12 and describe how we see things now and how we will see things when Christ returns.

   b. How does knowing this make you feel?

° ° • ° °

Spending time in the upper room has offered us insight into Jesus and His followers. Now let's spend some time gaining deeper insight into Thomas and Philip because sometimes, in knowing others, we get to know ourselves.

Thomas was a fisherman from Galilee. He was apparently absent when the resurrected Lord appeared. Hearing the news he said, "Unless I see in His hands the print of the nails, and put my finger into the print of the nails, and put my hand into His side, I will not believe" (John 20:25). When Jesus appeared and told Thomas to put his hands into his sword-pierced side, doubting Thomas finally believed. Jesus' words echo with the moral of our lesson, "Thomas, because you have seen Me, you have believed. Blessed are those who have not seen and yet have believed" (John 20:29). Thankfully, it *is* possible to "see" Jesus without gazing upon Him with the physical eye.

Philip met Jesus during John the Baptist's ministry. Jesus tested Philip before He fed the five thousand, asking him how to feed the people. Philip tried to calculate the cost. After the miraculous feeding, "those men, when they had seen the sign that Jesus did, said,

'This is truly the Prophet who is to come into the world'" (John 6:14). Philip actually *saw* a miracle and proclaimed Jesus as a prophet. Philip followed Him as a disciple from the beginning, yet today's lesson shows he wanted to see more. How much have you seen? What will it take before you believe?

LISTEN TO ...

Jesus departed from our sight that he might return to our heart. He departed, and behold, he is here.

—*Augustine of Hippo*

DAY 4

The Father's Business

A family business is a company owned, controlled, and operated by family members. Some of the oldest businesses in the Unites States began as family-owned and family-operated ventures. They include Ford Motor Company, DuPont, Colgate, Seth Thomas Clockmakers, Brooks Brothers Clothiers, and Baldwin Pianos.

Family participation often strengthens companies since family members are more loyal—after all, blood is thicker than water. In addition, since relatives have a vested interest in the enterprise, they are dedicated to long hours and sacrifice. However, managing a family business is a juggling act, particularly when an underperforming family member remains in a position that hurts the company's bottom line.

A story about Stew Leonard's Supermarket in Connecticut perfectly illustrates this dilemma. A supervisor concluded that the owner's son's performance was unsatisfactory. After analyzing the data, the father assured the supervisor that he'd handle the situation. That night Dad invited his son to come to the house for a talk in the hot tub. While basking in the bubbling hot water, the father placed a hat that read "Boss" on his head. He then informed his son that he was fired. Next, he removed the hat and put on another hat embroidered "Father." Looking at his surprised offspring, he said, "Son, I'm very sorry to hear that you lost your job. Is there anything I can do for you?"[30]

Our heavenly Father employed His only begotten Son when the job of redemption needed to be done righteously. As a result, Jesus was promoted to a heavenly position and given a name above all names. His works glorified the Father's business, making it possible for the rest of God's children to enter their venture of faith.

LIFT UP ...

Lord, thank You for the Bible. In it I find Your words and Your works to build up my faith. Teach me to trust You as I study the Scriptures. Amen.

LOOK AT ...

Jesus took the time to show many different connections between He and His Father. The conversation originated with Philip's request to see the Father and developed into an explanation of how Jesus went about the Father's business. Jesus continued to expand on the subject of "seeing" God. We begin to comprehend that to see God is to believe that Jesus and the Father are one. This belief takes place on levels; one is to believe Jesus' words and the other is to believe in Jesus' works. As our belief in God grows, so will our faith.

What about your faith? Is it growing? Jesus wants you to trust His Word and the works He has already completed, and to trust that He will continue to work in your life.

READ JOHN 14:10–11.

"Do you not believe that I am in the Father, and the Father in Me? The words that I speak to you I do not speak on My own authority; but the Father who dwells in Me does the works. Believe Me that I am in the Father and the Father in Me, or else believe Me for the sake of the works themselves." John 14:10–11

1. Review yesterday's lesson and summarize to whom Jesus was talking and the essence of their conversation.

2. What question did Jesus ask them concerning His relationship to the Father?

3. How did Jesus explain the source and basis of His speech?

4. Explain how the Father accomplished His work through Jesus.

5. What fact did Jesus state and ask the disciples to believe?

LEARN ABOUT ...

2 In the Father

Although they are two different persons, Jesus here claims that He and the Father are one—intermeshed, intermingled, integrated. Matthew Henry wrote, "In Christ we behold more of the glory of God than Moses did at Mount Horeb." Jesus had previously proclaimed, "I and My Father are one" (John 10:30).[31]

4 Father in Him

The word *dwell* carries the idea of continually abiding, enduring, and remaining. Christ was the Father's dwelling place just as the Christian's heart becomes Christ's home: "That Christ may dwell in your hearts through faith; that you, being rooted and grounded in love" (Eph. 3:17).

5 Believe in Them

Warren Wiersbe wrote, "The 'believe' in verse 10 is singular, for Jesus was addressing Philip; but in verse 11, it is plural and He addresses all of the disciples. The tense of both is 'go on believing.' Let your faith grow!" May we pray, "Lord, I believe; help my unbelief!" (Mark 9:24).[32]

LEARN ABOUT ...

8 Trinity

The doctrine of the Trinity means that within the being and activity of the one God there are three distinct persons: Father, Son, and Holy Spirit. Although the word *Trinity* does not appear in the Bible, the "trinitarian formula" is mentioned: "Baptizing them in the name of the Father and of the Son and of the Holy Spirit" (Matt. 28:19).[33]

---

9 Word and Works

Jesus said that His works were evidence of His deity. His works ratified His words. It is the same for Christians; our works must back up our words. Jesus said, "Let your light so shine before men, that they may see your good works and glorify your Father in heaven" (Matt. 5:16).

6. a. If the disciples had a hard time taking Jesus at His word, what evidence did Jesus tell them to look to?

   b. Have you ever had a hard time believing? How does this evidence bolster your beliefs?

7. a. Reread today's text. What key words are repeated? How many times are they used?

   b. What does this repetition say about the points Jesus wanted to stress?

LIVE OUT...

8. Jesus told His disciples that He and the Father were one. Many scholars call John 14—16 Jesus' Trinitarian teaching because it reveals the unity of the Father, Son, and Holy Spirit. Fill in the following chart to discover more about the Trinity.

SCRIPTURE	TRINITARIAN TEACHING
Matthew 12:28	
Luke 1:30–35	
Luke 3:21–22	
Luke 10:21–22	
2 Corinthians 13:14	

9. Today Jesus asked us to believe in Him because of His works. In John 5:31–47, you read how Jesus revealed "the fourfold witness" to His deity. Read the text and then write down these four witnesses.

1)

2)

3)

4)

10. Jesus asks us to believe that He is who He says He is based on concrete evidence: His works. Likewise, the world will believe that you are His disciple based on your words and good works. Using WORD and WORK as an acrostic, list some ways that your speech and service have or should testify of your faith.

W   W

O   O

R   R

D   K

° ° • ° °

A Gallup poll conducted some years ago revealed that 60 percent of Americans do not know who the "Holy Trinity" is.[34] Many Christians believe in the Trinity without completely understanding the doctrine. The Web site Christian Research & Apologetic Ministry published a comprehensive article on the Trinity:

> God is a trinity of persons: the Father, the Son, and the Holy Spirit. The Father is not the same person as the Son; the Son is not the same person as the Holy Spirit; and the Holy Spirit is not the same person as Father. They are not three gods and not three beings. They are three distinct persons; yet, they are all the

one God. Each has a will, can speak, can love, etc., and these are demonstrations of personhood. They are in absolute perfect harmony consisting of one substance. They are coeternal, coequal, and co-powerful. If any one of the three were removed, there would be no God.

Jesus, the Son, is one person with two natures: Divine and Human. This is called the Hypostatic Union. The Holy Spirit is also divine in nature and is self aware, the third person of the Trinity.

There is, though, an apparent separation of some functions among the members of the Godhead. For example, the Father chooses who will be saved (Eph. 1:4); the Son redeems them (Eph. 1:7); and the Holy Spirit seals them, (Eph. 1:13).

The word "person" is used to describe the three members of the Godhead because the word "person" is appropriate. A person is self aware, can speak, love, hate, say "you," "yours," "me," "mine," etc. Each of the three persons in the Trinity demonstrate[s] these qualities."[35]

Now if you are interviewed by the Gallup poll you can say, "Yes, I know who the Holy Trinity is personally."

LISTEN TO ...

The Trinity is a mystery which my faith embraces as revealed in the Word, but my reason cannot fathom.

—John Arrowsmith

DAY 5

The Father's Blessing

What do you most want to know when one of your friends is moving away? How to stay in touch! We want to know our friend's new address and phone number so we can stay connected.

It was finally beginning to sink in that Jesus was going away and that the disciples would not see Him for a period of time. Jesus redirected the conversation to how the disciples could stay in touch with Him—through prayer. He also explained the reason for staying in touch: to continue the work.

Evangelist Luis Palau describes five ways God answers prayer and reminds us that "whatever the answer, your best interest is always in mind."

NUMBER ONE: "No, I love you too much." The Lord of the universe isn't under obligation to say yes to every prayer.

NUMBER TWO: "Yes, but you'll have to wait." Immediate answers to prayer: You want them. I want them. But God simply does not always work that way. And to get His best, we must be patient.

NUMBER THREE: "Yes, but not what you expected." Have you ever asked God to use you? If so, expect the unexpected!

NUMBER FOUR: "Yes, and here's more!" Don't ever wonder if the Lord really knows what you want and need.

NUMBER FIVE: "Yes, I thought you'd never ask." Many people think prayer is complicated. Actually, the simplest prayer can bring you the miracle you need, when you need it.[36]

LIFT UP ...

Father, I want to glorify You with my life and the works I do for You. Help me to be an example of Your love and mercy to others. I ask You in Jesus' name. Amen.

LEARN ABOUT ...

3 Greater

Jesus wasn't predicting more stupendous or miraculous works; He was predicting a greater number of works. In other words, He was predicting a greater quantity rather than quality of works. While the disciples did perform miracles, their main mission was to spread the gospel and give glory to God. This occurred when they were dispersed.

LOOK AT ...

We saw yesterday that Jesus taught the disciples to believe in Him based on what He said and did as well as who He was—God Himself. He knew that this belief was crucial. The disciples would need unwavering faith to carry out the ministry of spreading the gospel. Today we'll see Jesus give His close friends the assurance that they would have the Father's blessing when they came to the Father in the name of the Son.

Before Christ's atoning death, the priests served as mediators between God and man. But Christ was now preparing the disciples for a new type of relationship. Because of their personal relationship with Jesus, they could make their own requests of the Father. Jesus promised to answer their prayers with the goal of glorifying the Father. Jesus didn't offer a magic wand that they could wave. Rather He taught them the conditions under which their prayers would be answered. If you want to learn to pray with power, then pay attention to Jesus' words to the disciples. You, too, will have your prayers answered in God's perfect time and God's perfect way.

READ JOHN 14:12–14.

"Most assuredly, I say to you, he who believes in Me, the works that I do he will do also; and greater works than these he will do, because I go to My Father. And whatever you ask in My name, that I will do, that the Father may be glorified in the Son. If you ask anything in My name, I will do it." John 14:12–14

1. What phrase emphasized the importance of the statement Jesus was about to make?

2. Describe what comparable works those who believed in Jesus would do. What kinds of works do you think He was talking about?

3. What could the disciples expect as a result of Jesus going to the Father? What do you think He meant by this?

4. a. Recount what Jesus promised those who prayed in His name.

   b. What do you think He meant by praying in His name? Was it just a matter of saying, "In Jesus' name"?

   c. Describe your practice of prayer. When? How often? For what? How do you know you honestly pray in His name for His purposes?

5. Why would prayers prayed in Christ's name be answered?

6. Jesus uttered another conditional statement beginning with "if." What was this statement?

7. Keeping in mind what you've learned about "whatever" and "anything," talk about what you would pray for right now and why.

LIVE OUT...

8. Jesus told the disciples to pray to the Father in His name. Read Matthew 6:5–8 and list the Dos and Don'ts of prayer:

   Dos   **Don'ts**

9. Jesus promised that the disciples would do "greater works than these." Fill in the following chart to see some of the "Acts" of the Holy Spirit through the lives of the disciples.

LEARN ABOUT ...

5 Glorifying

By linking "whatever" and "anything" with His name, Jesus showed that the provisional nature of our prayers should be to want *whatever* Christ wants; to seek *whatever* gives Christ the most glory. If our prayers don't align with that goal, then the Father is not constrained to honor them.

7 Getting

Jesus told us when we pray to "ask in His name." It's helpful to use the acronym ASK as a prayer help: **A**sk, **S**eek, **K**nock. Jesus urged us to, "Ask, and it will be given to you; seek, and you will find; knock, and it will be opened to you" (Matt. 7:7). Prayer should be fervent and diligent.

8 Greedy

Included in God's prayer dos and don'ts is motive. When asking with impure motives such as greed, we won't receive. "You lust and do not have.... Yet you do not have because you do not ask. You ask and do not receive, because you ask amiss, that you may spend it on your pleasures" (James 4:2–3).

LEARN ABOUT ...

10 Glorify

To glorify means to display God's worthiness by praising Him and honoring His commandments. Jesus also glorified His Father through His perfect obedience and His sacrificial death on our behalf.[37] "I will praise You, O Lord my God, with all my heart, And I will glorify Your name forevermore" (Ps. 86:12).

SCRIPTURE

Acts 2:43

Acts 8:26–29

Acts 9:17–18

Acts 16:6–10

GREAT WORKS OF THE APOSTLES

10. a. Jesus revealed that answered prayer in His name brought glory to the Father. Journal about some of the answered prayers you've experienced. How did they glorify the Lord?

b. Spend time raising your voice to glorify His name in praise and thanksgiving.

○ ○ ● ○ ○

Jesus promised His followers that they would do "greater works" as He answered their prayer based on three prerequisites: 1) Jesus must depart and return to the Father. This was accomplished through His death and resurrection. 2) They must make their request in His name. To make a request in someone's name implies that the prayer is in accordance with that person's character. Jesus will not answer a prayer that is ungodly. 3) Their motives must be to glorify the Lord. God does not answer prayers that are for selfish gain or sinful pursuits.

A wonderful example of a prayer that possessed all these prerequisites comes from Martin Luther. In 1540 Luther's good friend and assistant, Friedrich Myconius, became sick and was expected to die within a short time. From his bed he wrote a tender farewell letter to Luther. When Luther received the message, he immediately sent back a reply: "I command thee in the name of God to live because I still have need of thee in the work of reforming the church—the Lord will never let me hear that thou art dead, but will permit thee to survive me. For this I am praying, this is my will, and may my will be done, because I seek only to glorify the name of God."[38]

To some this prayer may seem presumptuous. However, it must have been God's will, for Myconius soon recovered. He lived six more years and died two months after Luther. Just imagine what God can do in answer to your prayer in Christ's name for His glory.

LISTEN TO ...

In commanding us to glorify him, God is inviting us to enjoy him.

—*C. S. Lewis*

LESSON FOUR

The Invisible Man
John 14:15–31

Imagine possessing the power to become invisible. Where would you go? On whose conversations would you eavesdrop? The thought of a vanishing act is intriguing, perhaps even intoxicating. But what temptations would accompany this trick?

H. G. Wells's book *The Invisible Man* grapples with this elusive concept. The story begins with a scientist named Griffin who develops a theory that supposes a person's refractive index could be changed to exactly that of the air, making the body incapable of absorbing or reflecting light. As a result, the person would no longer be visible.

One day Griffin successfully performs the experiment on himself but discovers that he is unable to become visible again. Ultimately, the isolation and power cause him to become mentally unstable. He commits arson, harassment, and robbery with his newfound anonymity. Fellow scientist Dr. Kemp discovers Griffin's secret and reports him to the authorities. So Griffin plots to murder the doctor. A chase scene occurs in which Griffin is apprehended by a mob and brutally beaten. Dr. Kemp survives to witness the naked and battered body of Griffin slowly reappear as he dies.

The moral of the story? Humans are not intended to be invisible. However, God the Holy Spirit is both invisible and incorruptible. He uses His unseen ability to come to the aid of God's people. He is known as the Helper, the Healer, the Unseen Hand of God at work in our lives. Before Jesus' departure, He assured His disciples that the invisible Holy Spirit would stay by their sides.

Day 1: John 14:15–18   **THE UNSEEN SPIRIT**

Day 2: John 14:19–21   **NOW YOU SEE ME, NOW YOU DON'T**

Day 3: John 14:22–24   **EYES OF FAITH**

Day 4: John 14:25–28   **SPIRIT OF PEACE**

Day 5: John 14:29–31   **INTO THIN AIR**

DAY 1

The Unseen Spirit

LIFT UP ...

Father, thank You for showing me that the way to You is through Jesus Christ. Please give me the desire to show my love for You through obedience as I rely on the Holy Spirit, my Helper. Amen.

LOOK AT ...

Last week we saw Jesus reassure the disciples that He was going to prepare a place for them. He comforted them with His pledge that He would one day return. Then they heard His claim that He was the only way to the Father.

Today we continue with Jesus and His disciples at their last private gathering. He reminded them that obedience was an expression of love. You might say Jesus understood that actions speak louder than words. It's not easy to obey Christ's commands in the power of the flesh. So Jesus turned His teaching to the One who could truly empower His followers to be obedient: the Holy Spirit. Apart from the work of the Spirit in the believers' lives, we humans cannot live up to God's commands.

Have you been trying to obey the Lord and found yourself faltering instead? Perhaps you've been relying on self rather than the Spirit's power. Jesus' instructions on the Comforter can bring you hope and help. If you run to His side and seek His help, surely He will tuck you under His wing and teach you to soar!

READ JOHN 14:15–18

"If you love Me, keep My commandments. And I will pray the Father, and He will give you another Helper, that He may abide with you forever—the Spirit of truth, whom the world cannot receive, because it neither sees Him nor knows Him; but you know Him, for He

dwells with you and will be in you. I will not leave you orphans; I will come to you." John 14:15–18

1. At the beginning of our text we encounter another conditional phrase. "If" Jesus' followers did something, there would be a result. Describe this cause-and-effect condition.

2. a. The word *will* is one of the key words in this passage. Underline the word *will* in the text and record how many times Jesus used this word. In your mind, what does the word *will* convey?

   b. How would you feel if Jesus said He *will* do things in *your* life?

3. Look for the first two *wills* in this passage and recount what Jesus promised He *will* do and what the Father *will* do as a result.

   What Jesus will do:

   What the Father will do:

4. a. Jesus also called the Helper the Spirit of truth. How did Jesus predict the world would acknowledge this Helper?

   b. In what ways do you think this holds true today?

5. Jesus was clear that the disciples would know the Helper. Describe how they would personally experience the Holy Spirit's presence.

6. Jesus made personal promises to the disciples of the things He will do. What two things did He promise to do?

LEARN ABOUT …

1 Commandment

A commandment is an authoritative prescription. It is a law, edict, or statute specifically given by God. Therefore a commandment is not optional, it is compulsory. At the same time the commandments are a litmus test. When we keep God's commands, we are expressing our love to God.

---

4 Comforter

Helper comes from two Greek roots: *para* meaning "beside" and *keleo* meaning "to call." The Holy Spirit has been called alongside the believer. *Strong's Greek Dictionary* defines *Helper* as comforter, advocate, or intercessor.[39] "The love of God has been poured out in our hearts by the Holy Spirit who was given to us" (Rom. 5:5).

---

6 Comfortless

The Greek word *orphanos* means "bereaved" or "parentless." The King James Bible translates this passage, "I will not leave you comfortless." As Christians, we are never abandoned since He sent One just like Him to dwell in our hearts: "He Himself has said, 'I will never leave you nor forsake you'" (Heb. 13:5).

LEARN ABOUT ...

7 Charity

Jesus used the Greek word *agapao* for love. It means to dote upon, to breathe after, or to have charity toward. If we dote upon Jesus, then we'll eagerly do the things He asks. This type of love "bears all things, believes all things, hopes all things, endures all things." (I Cor. 13:7).

---

9 Christ's Helper

Two prepositions are used in conjunction with the Holy Spirit's work in the believer's life: "in" and "with." Previously the Spirit had been with the disciples in the person of Jesus Christ. Now Jesus would send "another Helper" just like Himself to dwell in them forever. Have you received His help?

LIVE OUT...

7. a. Have you ever used or implied the "if ... then" equation when asking someone to demonstrate their love to you? If so, what are some of your "if ... then" love equations? (Example: "If you love me, then you'll be faithful to me.") Do you think your requests were reasonable and righteous.

   b. Jesus said, "If you love Me, keep My commandments." What is one specific thing you think the Lord wants you to do to express your love this week? Cite Scripture to back up your belief.

8. Today we've learned that Jesus sent the Holy Spirit to be our Helper. Rewrite the following verse into a personal prayer asking God to comfort you:

   "So we say with confidence, 'The Lord is my helper; I will not be afraid. What can man do to me?'" (Hebrews 13:6 NIV).

9. The world "cannot receive" the Holy Spirit, because they neither know nor see Him. Read John 3:1–8.

   a. Describe Nicodemus and what he knew about Jesus (see vv. 1–2).

   b. Who did Jesus say could "see" God's kingdom (see v. 3)?

   c. How did Nicodemus respond to this information (see v. 4)?

   d. What analogies did Jesus use to describe the kingdom of heaven (see vv. 5–8)?

   e. What do you think Jesus meant by this teaching? Have you experienced this spiritual birth?

∘ ∘ • ∘ ∘

Unseen things are hard to comprehend. Most of us have a need to quantify or verify with one of our five senses. We're a lot like the no-nonsense folks from Missouri, whose state motto is, "Show Me." But the Bible teaches us to "walk by faith, not by sight" (2 Cor. 5:7).

Jesus understood that it was difficult for us to grasp lofty "spiritual" concepts, so He used common imagery to enlighten us. When Nicodemus did not understand how a man could be born again, Jesus used the wind to describe the Spirit's regenerating work. We can't see the wind; we don't know where it begins or where it will end, but we can witness its effect in the rustling leaves or crashing waves.

How else can we describe the Spirit's indescribable power? You can't see or touch the Spirit—He's a nontangible entity. Perhaps electricity would be a helpful analogy in understanding this magnificent person. We can't see the current of electricity, but when it is channeled through the proper conduits, a room can be illuminated; sights and sounds can emerge from a box of glass, wires, and plastic. So, too, the Spirit is unseen, but that does not mean He is inactive. We can see His dynamic work flowing through the lives of His people. Like the disciples, you can experience the Spirit's power coursing through you when you ask Him into your heart.

LISTEN TO ...

Wicked men obey from fear; good men, from love.

—*Augustine of Hippo*

Now You See Me, Now You Don't

In September 2006, news of an astonishing breakthrough circulated quickly. A team at Duke University in North Carolina built a device that seemed to spring more from the pages of a science-fiction novel than from a real lab. "First demonstration of a working invisibility cloak," the press release boasted. As might be expected, the headlines were filled with references to *Star Wars* and Klingon cloaking devices.

However, inquiries into this extraordinary discovery proved more pedestrian. "David Smith's team at Duke had indeed built a device that could hide an object from view, but only from the eyes of a microwave detector—and then only at a very specific microwave frequency. What's more, the device would only work for 'flatliners' living in two dimensions, and was hardly a cloak; it was more like a small invisibility barrel. Nevertheless, the teams' work is not to be sniffed at. Hiding anything at any frequency is an impressive feat."[40]

Scientists, illusionists, and novelists seem to be the only ones who can accomplish a "now you see me, now you don't" trick. How can something physical and tangible shift back and forth between the seen and unseen, the here and then not here? During the Upper Room Discourse, Jesus seemed to give His disciples a mixed message: He'd be absent *and* present simultaneously. He told them that the world wouldn't see Him, but they would. To some He would be manifest, while to others He would be masked. The secret is not some microwave frequency or a Klingon cloaking device, but the supernatural ability of an omnipresent and omniscient God!

Lift up ...

Lord, thank You for coming to dwell in my heart. I thank You that my love for You will be returned with love from my heavenly Father. Amen.

LOOK AT ...

Yesterday we saw Jesus assure the disciples that He would send a Helper like Him to be with them. He wanted them to know that while He was calling them to obedience, they would not have to accomplish the task alone.

Today we see Jesus reaffirm that His time on earth was short. In an intricately worded text, Jesus spoke to the disciples about the resurrection life. Like a jewel that has many facets, the resurrection life is a multifaceted concept. One way to look at it is that the world would not see Him because He would literally die. Yet they could anticipate His literal resurrection from the dead. Another facet is that He promised that they, too, would experience a future resurrection from the dead, because He had conquered sin and death. The third facet is what Christians call "resurrection life," which begins at salvation. This is a life that is synonymous with eternal life. But eternal life is not merely a quantity of life, as in living forever (although we will live forever with Christ in heaven). Eternal life is also a quality of life for the here and now. Jesus said, "I have come that they may have life, and that they may have it more abundantly" (John 10:10). Are you living the abundant life now? Your resurrection life began the instant you asked Jesus into your heart. Don't wait another second to start really living this life that shines like a jewel and is more valuable than rubies.

READ JOHN 14:19–21.

"A little while longer and the world will see Me no more, but you will see Me. Because I live, you will live also. At that day you will know that I am in My Father, and you in Me, and I in you. He who has My commandments and keeps them, it is he who loves Me. And he who loves Me will be loved by My Father, and I will love him and manifest Myself to him."
John 14:19–21

1. Jesus began with the time reference "a little while longer." Explain why you think He started that way.

2. After that time, who would no longer see Him and who would see Him? What event do you think this statement points to?

LEARN ABOUT ...

2 The World

The term *world* in the Bible is often associated with humanity. Christ said that His disciples were "the light of the world" (Matt. 5:14). Frequently, unbelieving people are referred to as "the world" not simply because they compose the greater part of the world's population but because they pursue and cherish the things of this world.[41]

3 That Day

"That day" has a dual application: 1) the Lord's death and resurrection; 2) the great resurrection day when Christians are raised up. "But if the Spirit of Him who raised Jesus from the dead dwells in you, He who raised Christ from the dead will also give life to your mortal bodies" (Rom. 8:11).

6 The Beloved

Two of the most fundamental needs we possess as humans are to love and to be loved. "To love" satisfies our innate desire to nurture—someone needs me. "To be loved" fulfills our basic craving for significance—I matter to someone else. In Christ we both offer love and are the beloved of God.

3. List the three things the disciples would know "at that day." What do you think "that day" refers to?

4. What command did Jesus repeat from Day 1? Why would He repeat this command?

5. Describe the other type of love those who love Jesus experience.

6. In return, how did Jesus promise to reciprocate?

LIVE OUT...

7. Today we discovered that the word *world* refers to humanity. Fill in the following chart to learn more about the world.

SCRIPTURE	LESSONS ABOUT THE WORLD
Matthew 4:8–9	
John 1:10	
John 3:16–19	
Romans 5:12–13	

8. Jesus offered the disciples hope with His promise of resurrection life. Read Romans 6:3–11.

   a. Explain what scriptural ritual Paul likened to the death and resurrection of Jesus and why (see vv. 3–4).

   b. How do our lives parallel "the likeness of His resurrection" (see vv. 5–7)?

   c. Explain how you are a part of the "living dead" (see vv. 8–11).

9. Today the Lord shared two truths that stem from two key words in the text: "in" and "love."

a. Circle these key words in today's text.

b. "In" points to the deepest possible connections of intimacy: A is in B, and B is in C, yet C is at the same time in B. According to our text, who is in whom?

c. What do you think it means for you to be "in" Christ? In what ways do you experience this?

d. The repeated word *love* points to a chain reaction of love. Trace that chain reaction: Who loves whom? Then who will be loved? And then who? How might this chain continue?

° ° ● ° °

When I (Lenya) was growing up on the shores of Lake Michigan and its tributaries, two things were abundant: rocks and water. To entertain ourselves, my siblings and I would gather on the coastline to skip pebbles across the still water. We'd gleefully watch the chain reaction of concentric circles collide into one another. Each solitary stone would break through the surface of the water. We'd watch the water form a pattern of ever-increasing intersecting rings.

Today Jesus seemed to use concentric circles to describe how obedience begins a ripple effect of love that spreads outward from His followers through Jesus toward God the Father. In a sense, our obedience to Jesus' commands acts like a pebble in water that spreads outward, broadening the Father's love.

Have you initiated the ripple effect by expressing your love through obedience? James Montgomery Boice said, "Many Christians would be

LEARN ABOUT …

7 Not the World

Our priorities reveal our passions. Those passionate about Christ are recipients of the Father's love. Those passionate about worldly pursuits won't find favor with the Father: "Do not love the world or the things in the world. If anyone loves the world, the love of the Father is not in him" (I John 2:15).

8 Living Dead

Only God could give life to the dead. "I have been crucified with Christ; it is no longer I who live, but Christ lives in me; and the life which I now live in the flesh I live by faith in the Son of God, who loved me and gave Himself for me" (Gal. 2:20).

willing to do spectacular things if by that means they could come to know Christ better. But they are unwilling to do the commonplace things that are involved in simple obedience. Will you do them? If you will, you will most certainly grow in God's grace. If you obey, Christ will increasingly unveil his heart to you. You will come to know him and not just about him. On the other hand, if you fail to obey, he will cease to reveal himself to you, and your own love for him will weaken."[42]

Listen to …

To love God is the greatest of virtues; to be loved by God is the greatest of blessings.

—*Author Unknown*

DAY 3

Eyes of Faith

At birth, the sense of sight is the least developed of the five senses because babies don't see much inside the womb. The baby can only see bright light filtering through the abdominal wall and amniotic fluid. "It might be like looking at the world through frosted glass, the image is all diffused," says Carla Shatz, PhD, professor of neurobiology at the University of California, Berkeley. After birth, babies like looking at human faces more than anything. By the first month, a baby can pick out familiar faces. By the second month, the baby's vision is more fine-tuned. By about eight months, a baby can see almost as well as an adult. However, the normal development of vision depends greatly on children getting enough practice using their eyes during the first two years of life.[43]

When we are born again, we receive eyes of faith. We first see Jesus as the light—our Lord and Savior: "The people who sat in darkness have seen a great light" (Matt. 4:16). Next, we see Him through His Word, the Scriptures. Jesus said, "These are they which testify of Me" (John 5:39). Through the power of the indwelling God, we begin to grow and mature, to develop eyes of faith as we "do not look at the things which are seen, but at the things which are not seen" (2 Cor. 4:18). Let your faith grow and develop so you can see Him more deeply as He continually reveals Himself to you.

LIFT UP ...

Lord, I want my heart to be Your home. Thank You that You have promised to dwell in my heart forever. Amen.

LOOK AT ...

Yesterday we saw Jesus reaffirm His love relationship with His followers based on obedience to His commands. Clearly, Jesus had a wonderful give-and-take relationship with His disciples. Throughout the evening several of the disciples raised questions about the

LEARN ABOUT ...

I Manifest

Manifest literally means "to make visible, uncover, or appear." There are levels of manifestations. The disciples would literally see Jesus during His resurrection appearances. All believers see God spiritually through His Word, His people, spiritual revelation, and providential circumstances. One day we'll all see Jesus when He comes again.

3 Made at Home

We see God when He opens our spiritual eyes. He does this by coming to live inside our hearts. This is called the "indwelling" of God. Here, Jesus reveals that both the Father and the Son come and take up residence in the believer's heart. Earlier we learned the Holy Spirit also takes up residence.

6 Message

Jesus made it clear that what He was saying came straight from the Father's mouth and was, therefore, completely trustworthy. The living Word was sharing the Word of the Father. The listener could absolutely believe they would see Jesus because the Father said so. "The word of the LORD is proven" (Ps. 18:30).

enigmatic things He was saying. They would later have the Holy Spirit's help to bring His teachings to their remembrance.

In today's text a disciple named Judas (not the traitor) asked a question about something confusing: How could Jesus reveal Himself to them but not to the world? Jesus offered insight into the secret of seeing into the spiritual realm: love and obedience. Don't you want to see into the secret things of God? The answer is to make your heart a special habitation for Him. When you do that, He will allow you to see things His way.

READ JOHN 14:22–24.

Judas (not Iscariot) said to Him, "Lord, how is it that You will manifest Yourself to us, and not to the world?"

Jesus answered and said to him, "If anyone loves Me, he will keep My word; and My Father will love him, and We will come to him and make Our home with him. He who does not love Me does not keep My words; and the word which you hear is not Mine but the Father's who sent Me." John 14:22–24

1. What question did Judas ask? Restate it in your own words.

2. Which part of Jesus' answer reaffirmed the "new commandment"?

3. Describe what Jesus promised those who love and obey Him.

4. How would those who do not love God show themselves?

5. Why do you suppose it's impossible to love Jesus without obeying Him?

6. What did Jesus reveal about the words He spoke?

7. How would you react if someone brought words directly from the Father to you?

LIVE OUT...

8. Judas (not Iscariot) was confused about seeing Jesus again. In the following chart describe whether Jesus literally or metaphorically kept or will keep His promise to manifest Himself to believers.

SCRIPTURE	LITERALLY OR METAPHORICALLY?
Job 19:25–26	
Matthew 5:8	
Matthew 18:20	
Mark 13:26	
Luke 24:13–35	

9. Jesus made a promise to the church at Laodicea similar to the one made in today's lesson.

a. Read Revelation 3:20 and compare this promise to today's passage.

b. Do you experience this "indwelling"? If so, describe what it's like for you. If this kind of intimacy isn't part of your experience of Christ, now is the perfect time to start! Jesus is standing at the door and knocking. Simply open your heart to Him and ask His forgiveness for the things that have distanced you from Him. Pray a prayer that says something like this: *Lord, I know I'm a sinner. I need a Savior. You died and rose from the dead to pay for my sin. I want to love and obey You. Please help me do those things. I want to live in You and You in me. Please be my Lord, and make me aware of Your life blazing inside me! Thank You for forgiving me for my sin! Amen.*

LEARN ABOUT ...

8 Metaphor

Arthur Pink wrote, "Faith is frequently represented in Scripture under the metaphor of bodily sight. Our Lord said of the great patriarch, 'Your father Abraham rejoiced to see My day, and he saw it and was glad' (John 8:56), meaning that his faith looked forward to the day of Christ's humiliation and exaltation."[44]

9 Mansion

Jesus not only promised to build a mansion in heaven for those who turn from their sin and turn to Him; He promised to make the believer's heart a mansion for God. God did not come to indwell believers during Old Testament times. James Montgomery Boice said, "The presence of the Lord within his people is the glorious distinctive of the present time."[45]

10. We learned that Jesus eagerly spoke the Father's words.

    a. According to Proverbs 30:5–6, what makes speaking God's Word safe? What might happen if you are not faithful to His Word?

    b. Have you ever found yourself in a situation when you relied on God's Word rather than your own? If so, describe how it helped you.

° ° • ° °

We've met many of the "major" apostles during our study of the Upper Room Discourse. Today we encountered Judas, one of the lesser-known followers of Christ. Our text parenthetically referred to him as (not Iscariot). Who was this man who bore the same name as the betrayer? Not much is known about him. The gospel of Luke tells us he was "the son of James" (Luke 6:16). Most commentators agree he can be identified as "Lebbaeus, whose surname was Thaddaeus" (Matt. 10:3). Tradition says he preached in Assyria and Persia and died as a martyr like the other apostles.

Jesus didn't treat him as an interruption or with impatience. He responded to this Judas with as much respect as He did Peter, James, or John. Judas's question has helped open our eyes to the spiritual world. When Christ spoke of His disciples seeing Him again, He wasn't merely talking about the here and now. He was talking about a time soon to come (the resurrection) and a time far in the future (the second coming). He also gave us new insight into the indwelling God. Aren't you glad Judas asked the question?

You may relate to Judas (not Iscariot). Maybe you're more quiet and reserved than some of your Christian friends. Maybe others get more attention than you. You should know that Jesus sees and hears you. He listens to all of your questions and will talk to you as He talks to a friend. No one is "lesser" in the kingdom of God.

LISTEN TO ...

Unless he obeys, a man cannot believe.

—Dietrich Bonhoeffer

DAY 4

Spirit of Peace

God initiated the first peace talks shortly after Cain slew his brother Abel. However, the consequences of the fall escalated from conflict between family members to war between tribes and nations. In the earth's short history, humans have experienced very few sustained seasons of peace.

Society eventually developed folklore that envisioned an earthly place where people achieved complete harmony. Sir Thomas More imagined an idyllic country called *Utopia* that was made ideal by laws, government, and society with perfect conditions. British novelist James Hilton's book *Lost Horizon* conjured up Shangri-la. Situated in a mystical, harmonious valley hidden in the Himalayas, it promised to keep its residents permanently happy by isolating them from the outside world. Buddhists describe this perfect place as Shambhala, their version of paradise where enlightened inhabitants possess the appropriate karma.

Modern nonfiction incarnations arose with these same lofty ideals. They include the Hague Confederation of States, which initiated the League of Nations, which evolved into the United Nations. Their intended goals were to encourage disarmament, prevent war through sanctions, settle disputes between factious countries through diplomacy, and improve global welfare. They initially enjoyed some notable successes as well as a few early disappointments. But by the onset of World War II the League of Nations had failed to meet its primary purpose—avoiding any future world war. Benito Mussolini stated, "The League is very well when sparrows shout, but no good at all when eagles fall out."

Failure was inevitable because these imaginations and organizations never dealt with the core issue—humanity's fallen nature. True peace can only come from a person—Jesus Christ, the Prince of Peace. In the upper room, Jesus promised that His followers would enjoy the Spirit of Peace, who promises a type of peace unlike anything the world has to offer.

LIFT UP ...

Lord, thank You for being my Prince of Peace. Help me to turn away from the false peace this world offers and turn toward the true peace that only You provide. Amen.

LEARN ABOUT ...

2 Peace

Shalom, the Hebrew word for peace, is one of the most frequently used words among the Israelites. Like the Hawaiians' *aloha,* it serves as both a greeting and farewell wish. However, *shalom* implies much more than peace. It embraces a sense of wholeness, completeness, security, health, and prosperity.

LOOK AT ...

The Upper Room Discourse was an intimate conversation between close friends. As they shared a meal, they enjoyed the warm approachability of their leader. Several in their turn came to Jesus to ask follow-up questions that arose from the lessons He'd shared. We've seen Peter, John, Thomas, and Judas (not Iscariot) probe Jesus for clarity when they were confused. The Lord proved to be a patient teacher.

Today's text introduces a topic change as it records the first mention of peace. We see that Jesus understood the disciples' state of unrest. He wanted them to rest assured that the Spirit He was sending was one of peace—His peace. This was the legacy He would leave them. It is the legacy He gives to you. When you struggle, do you turn to the Spirit of Peace for comfort? Like the disciples in the upper room, don't be afraid to ask!

READ JOHN 14:25–28.

"These things I have spoken to you while being present with you. But the Helper, the Holy Spirit, whom the Father will send in My name, He will teach you all things, and bring to your remembrance all things that I said to you. Peace I leave with you, My peace I give to you; not as the world gives do I give to you. Let not your heart be troubled, neither let it be afraid. You have heard Me say to you, 'I am going away and coming back to you.' If you loved Me, you would rejoice because I said, 'I am going to the Father,' for My Father is greater than I." John 14:25–28

1. Today starts with the phrase "these things." Look back to yesterday's lesson and summarize "these things" Jesus spoke about.

2. a. Jesus referred to the Helper who was coming in His place. Describe the things the Helper would do for the disciples.

b. Tell about a time when you experienced this help in your life.

3. What would Jesus leave them with? How would you explain this in your own words?

4. Jesus personalized this gift as coming from Him. Describe how you feel knowing this is not a generalized gift of peace, but that it comes from the Savior.

5. Jesus commanded the disciples not to let their hearts be troubled or afraid. Why do you think this is a significant command? How does it minister to you in your present situation?

6. Because they loved Him, what reaction should the disciples have had to Jesus' departure? Why?

7. Explain the emotions you might experience knowing you were going to the Father.

LIVE OUT...

8. a. Jesus promised that His followers could experience a peace unlike anything the world could offer. Based on your personal experience, fill in the columns with some earthly and heavenly paths to peace.

EARTHLY PEACE   **HEAVENLY PEACE**

b. Which path has brought you the most peace? How?

LEARN ABOUT ...

9 Presence

Two biblical phrases are often united: 1) "Do not be afraid"; 2) "I am with you." Fear flees from God's powerful presence: "Fear not, for I am with you; Be not dismayed, for I am your God. I will strengthen you, Yes, I will help you, I will uphold you with My righteous right hand" (Isa. 41:10).

10 Partners

It's a lovely thing to observe how the members of the Trinity function. As in a dance, sometimes one leads while the others follow. Jesus yielded to the Father at the incarnation. The Father, in turn, elevated Jesus above all in heaven and earth. The Holy Spirit serves to glorify the Son. We could all learn from their harmonious union.

9. a. We've learned that to be afraid embraces both fear and intimidation. Jesus assured that His peace conquers both. Fill in the following chart to discover what we should not be afraid of and why.

SCRIPTURE	WHAT NOT TO FEAR AND WHY?
Deuteronomy 20:1–4	
Proverbs 3:25–26	
Jeremiah 1:8	
Luke 12:4–5	
1 Peter 3:14–15	

b. What are you afraid of?

c. Which of the passages above offer you the most comfort? Reword the passage into a personal prayer asking God to help conquer the fear.

10. Although He is an equal member of the Trinity, Jesus declared that the Father was greater than Himself. Read Colossians 1:15–18.

a. Recount Paul's description of Jesus (see v. 15).

b. Describe Jesus' role in creation and list the areas in which He was involved (see vv. 16–17).

c. Explain why Jesus is preeminent (see v. 18).

d. In what specific ways do you give Him preeminence in your life? Or in what ways do you need to give Him preeminence?

○ ○ ● ○ ○

Dance creates a fluid form of communication between partners, one who leads and one who follows. A perfectly synchronous couple can convey an unspoken language as they glide across the dance floor keeping time to the music. The leader guides the overall dance, deciding which moves will be incorporated and how the couple will use the dance floor. The leader also sets the stylistic mood and initiates the moves. The follower must complement and complete the leader's suggested movement. "The most accomplished dancers use connection as a line of communication which allows the leader to incorporate the follower's ideas, abilities and creative suggestions into their own styling and selection of moves."[46] The music introduces the rhythm, flow, and style of dance.

It's easy to visualize the Trinity's harmonious interaction as a dance. The Father leads expansively while the Son follows effortlessly. And God the Holy Spirit acts as the gentle music floating through the air. Author C. S. Lewis used this poetic language to describe the Godhead. "In Christianity God is not a static thing—not even a person—but a dynamic, pulsating activity, a life, almost a kind of drama. Almost, if you will not think me irreverent, a kind of dance. The union between the Father and Son is such a live concrete thing that this union itself is a Person.… What grows out of the joint life of the Father and Son is a real Person, is, in fact, the Third of the three Persons who are God."[47] Tenderhearted John, of all the gospel writers, seemed most in tune with the Trinity's lovely dance.

LISTEN TO …

To be of a peaceable spirit brings peace along with it.

—*Thomas Watson*

DAY 5

Into Thin Air

Have you heard of a place where battleships and bombers vanish into thin air? During a hundred-year period, it is believed that over fifty ships and twenty planes were spirited away while cruising through the Bermuda Triangle. Also known as the Devil's Triangle, its three corners extend across the Atlantic Ocean from Bermuda to Miami, Florida, to San Juan, Puerto Rico.

One of the most famous disappearances was Flight 19. On December 5, 1945, five US Navy Avenger bombers mysteriously vanished while on a routine training mission. Lieutenant Charles Taylor, who kept in contact on the radio until nothing could be heard, led the mission. Astonishingly, the rescue plane sent to recover the squadron never returned either. It vanished into thin air.

Many conspiracy theories have evolved. Could the lost city of Atlantis be buried beneath the waves? Are aliens abducting humans in the triangle? Or is it the Devil himself snatching lost souls? Experts dismiss folklore with more scientific explanations. The deepest point in the Atlantic lies beneath the Bermuda Triangle. Therefore, some believe the depth and water temperatures cause broken vessels to sink precipitously. It's also one of the most trafficked stretches of ocean, naturally increasing the odds for accidents. Additionally, weather and strong currents account for many tragedies.

Like the Bermuda Triangle, great mystery surrounds the death and resurrection of Jesus. Unbelievers try to explain it away as fantasy or fallacy. The truth is that God ordained this supernatural occurrence to redeem our souls from sin. There is no mystery. The Bible is clear. Souls would be lost to the power of the world, the flesh, and the Devil unless He came to the rescue. To do so, the Savior would seemingly vanish into a garden tomb for three days. And when He returned, the world would be astonished and the Enemy would be vanquished.

LIFT UP ...

Lord, I am thankful that Satan has no hold over You. Help me to break the bonds of sin as I walk in this world. Amen.

Look at ...

In our lesson yesterday, Jesus spoke to the disciples about God's supernatural peace. The world bases its peace on the absence of war or the presence of prosperity. But the Bible reveals two true paths to peace: 1) peace with God; 2) the peace of God. Before salvation the human heart is a battleground with the flesh waging war against the spirit. At salvation a person makes peace with God through spiritual birth: "Therefore, having been justified by faith, we have peace with God through our Lord Jesus Christ" (Rom. 5:1). After salvation the Christian is invited to enjoy the peace of God. We're promised that "the peace of God, which surpasses all understanding, will guard your hearts and minds through Christ Jesus" (Phil. 4:7).

Today we'll see Jesus warn of two great adversaries to believers: the world and Satan. Jesus gave the disciples a powerful reminder that, though Satan is the ruler of this world, he holds no power over Jesus, who is sinless. Jesus concludes by calling the disciples to arise and follow Him just as He beckons us all. Do you take comfort knowing that you have a Savior who is willing to lead you rather than let you wander on your own?

Learn about ...

❙ Before

Foreknowledge is God's unique ability to know all events, including the free acts of humans, before they happen.[48] The crucifixion came as no surprise to the Savior. Jesus was "delivered by the determined purpose and foreknowledge of God" (Acts 2:23) into His killers' hands.

Read John 14:29–31.

"And now I have told you before it comes, that when it does come to pass, you may believe. I will no longer talk much with you, for the ruler of this world is coming, and he has nothing in Me. But that the world may know that I love the Father, and as the Father gave Me commandment, so I do. Arise, let us go from here." John 14:29–31

1. Our text begins with "and" to connect one thought to another. Review yesterday's lesson and recount what Jesus had told the disciples before it came to pass.

LEARN ABOUT ...

3 Be Quiet

Jesus would have much more to say in chapters 15 and 16. He was likely implying that because of the imminent approach of His enemy and death, He would have to quicken His pace. The advancing enemy was likely the Satan-inspired betrayal by Judas, which was probably taking place at that precise moment.

4 Beyond

"He has nothing in Me" means that Jesus was beyond Satan's influence. Matthew Henry explains: "There was no corruption in Christ, to give advantage to the prince of this world in his temptations. He could not crush his undertaking by drawing him to sin, because there was nothing sinful in him, nothing irregular for his temptations to fasten upon." [49]

7 Behold!

David told us to behold the vast knowledge that God possesses regarding His people. He described the enormity of this information as lofty and "too wonderful for me." God knows our every thought, step, word, and path. Therefore, to know ourselves better, we must get to know God!

2. Jesus told the disciples of the things to come. What would this promote in their lives?

3. Why would Jesus not talk with the disciples much longer?

4. a. What do you think "he has nothing in Me" means?

   b. Why is this important for us to know?

5. a. Explain what Jesus would do to show the world His love for the Father.

   b. How do you think this is different from the way the world acts?

6. How did Jesus conclude this conversation?

LIVE OUT...

7. Throughout the Upper Room Discourse Jesus revealed His accurate foreknowledge of coming events. Psalm 139 records the intricate details of God's foreknowledge regarding individuals, including you and me.

   a. How does the psalmist describe God's foreknowledge of you (see Ps. 139:1–6)?

   b. Record the extent to which God's presence can find you (see vv. 7–12)?

   c. Read 139:17–18, 23–24 and write your own psalm of praise regarding His knowledge.

8. Jesus did not fear "the ruler of this world" because He had overcome the Enemy's tactics. As Christians we, too, can be overcomers. Read 1 John 4:1–6.

LEARN ABOUT …

8 Beelzebub

"Beelzebub, the ruler of the demons" (Matt. 12:24), rules over this world until Jesus returns. At that time Jesus will lay "hold of the dragon, that serpent of old, who is the Devil and Satan, and [bind] him for a thousand years; and … cast him into the bottomless pit, and shut him up" (Rev. 20:2–3).

   a. How do you know whether someone is "of God" or of "the world" (see vv. 1–3)?

   b. Explain how God's "little children" can overcome the one who is "already in the world" (see v. 4).

   c. Note the various forms of the word *hear* in verses 5 and 6. How does someone's ability to hear reveal whether they belong to the "spirit of truth" or the "spirit of error"?

9. Jesus leads by example. He told His disciples that by obeying His commands they would express their sincere love. He modeled this by expressing His love to the Father through obedience. Using the words LOVE and OBEY as acrostics, list some ways you will express your love and obedience to the Lord.

L   O

O   B

V   E

E   Y

∘ ∘ • ∘ ∘

Nobody likes a know-it-all. A know-it-all is a person who believes that he or she possesses an enormous amount of information on most topics and eagerly offers opinions. She often boasts of her knowledge so others can hear. But if you listen closely, she knows a little about a lot, but not much about anything.

In the Old Testament story of Job, you might view Job's friends who come to counsel him through his troubles as know-it-alls. They had the audacity to speak for God. They presumed to know Job's actions and motives. Sadly, Job attempted to explain God's actions, becoming a know-it-all too. Eventually, God interrupted their conversation to ask a few probing questions: "Who is this who darkens counsel By words without knowledge? Now prepare yourself like a man; I will question you, and you shall answer Me. Where were you when I laid the foundations of the earth? Tell Me, if you have understanding. Who determined its measurements? Surely you know!" (Job 38:2–5). Only a real expert can put a know-it-all in their place.

One of God's attributes is omniscience—He knows everything about everything. A. W. Tozer said: "God knows instantly and effortlessly all matter and all matters, all mind and every mind, all spirit and all spirits, all being and every being, all creaturehood and all creatures, every plurality and all pluralities, all law and every law, all relations, all causes, all thoughts, all mysteries, all enigmas, all feeling, all desires, every unuttered secret, all thrones and dominions, all personalities, all things visible and invisible in heaven and in earth."[50]

By revealing details of His foreknowledge to His disciples, Jesus authenticated His deity. He was God and He knew it all!

LISTEN TO ...

Before God created the universe, he already had you in mind.

—*Erwin W. Lutzer*

LESSON FIVE

God's Vineyard
John 15:1–17

In chapter 15 Jesus turned His conversation to God's vineyard. In Hebrew the word for vineyard also means garden. Since Jesus' last words in chapter 14 were, "Arise, let us go from here," we can infer that the dinner party was ending and the men might have been making their way to the garden of Gethsemane. Perhaps as they walked they paused at the great golden vine that decorated the door to the Holy Place of the temple. Or it could be that the wine served with the meal or the sight of a vineyard out the window prompted Jesus' teaching.

No doubt Jesus chose the imagery of a vineyard since it was a common metaphor in the Bible. Of all the agricultural forms in the eastern lands, a vineyard was the most costly and troublesome:

- Vineyards, unlike other crops, required a permanent fence to keep out predators.

- Vineyards needed a watchtower to provide protection from thieves.

- Vineyards required large stones to be cleared, gathered, and heaped into rows beside the plants. In Israel the vines were draped upon these rows to safeguard the fruit from the damp ground.

- Vineyards had their own winepress and vat, since exporting the fruit bruised the precious grapes.

Isn't it lovely that God uses a vineyard to describe His people and the many ways He meticulously cares for us? He sets a guard around us, stands high above us, is the stone we can fall upon, and was crushed for our iniquities. He truly is the Master Gardener who provides for all our needs.

Day 1: John 15:1–3   THE GARDENER

Day 2: John 15:4–6   ABIDING IN THE VINE

Day 3: John 15:7–9   BEARING FRUIT

Day 4: John 15:10–13   RIPE FOR THE HARVEST

Day 5: John 15:14–17   GARDEN OF FRIENDS

DAY I
The Gardener

LIFT UP ...

Father, I'm grateful to be a branch connected to the true Vine who is Jesus. Though sometimes painful, please prune away what is necessary that I may always produce good fruit for Your glory. Amen.

LOOK AT ...

In last week's lesson Jesus introduced His disciples to the Holy Spirit, whose help they would need to lead the Christian life. Today Jesus describes His Father as the heavenly Gardener. He draws a picture of the believer's relationship with God using the example of the vine and the branches. While the disciples know they have the comfort of the indwelling Holy Spirit, they need to understand that they are connected to Jesus and can rely on Him to bring forth fruit even after He departs.

It's not easy to be dependent on others, is it? We're used to working hard and getting credit for our labors through praise, pay, or personal satisfaction. But following Jesus requires complete dependence on Him, just as the vine depends on the branch for the production of fruit. Would you describe yourself as dependent or independent? The answer to that question will help determine the amount of spiritual fruit in your life.

READ JOHN 15:1–3.

"I am the true vine, and My Father is the vinedresser. Every branch in Me that does not bear fruit He takes away; and every branch that bears fruit He prunes, that it may bear more fruit. You are already clean because of the word which I have spoken to you." John 15:1–3

1. How does Jesus describe Himself? Why do you think He uses this symbolism?

LEARN ABOUT ...

1 True Vine

The Old Testament portrayed the vine as Israel. Sadly, Israel proved to be an unprofitable vine that yielded bad fruit. Isaiah wrote, "When I looked for good grapes, why did it yield only bad?" (Isa. 5:4 NIV). Here, in His last "I am" statement, Jesus revealed that He is the true Vine.

---

2 The Vinedresser

A vinedresser is a farmer who tends a vineyard. Shepherding a flock and working the land were the two major occupations for the ancient Hebrews. The vinedresser would plow, plant, tend, and harvest. Both analogies were familiar and would have resonated with truth.

---

6 Clean

The pruning process is part of cleansing. A vinedresser prunes away dead wood or live growth that hinders vigorous development. For a believer, the cleansing process is achieved by reading the Word of God, which identifies any obstacle in our lives that would interfere with a fruitful harvest.

2. How does Jesus describe the Father? How does this analogy help describe God's character?

3. The branches are described as "in Me." What does it mean to you to be "in Christ"?

4. Describe in detail what happens to the branches that don't bear fruit. Why do you think this might be necessary?

5. Explain what happens to the branches that do bear fruit. What is the reason for this?

6. a. What made the disciples "already clean"?

   b. Can you be described in this way? How do you know?

LIVE OUT...

7. Today Jesus revealed He is the true Vine. Fill in the following chart to discover other things He truly is.

SCRIPTURE	TRUE WHAT?
John 1:9	
John 6:32–33	
Hebrews 8:12	

8. Jesus used a vine to allegorically describe the church. Read Isaiah 5:1–7.

   a. Who is the vinedresser tending in this passage?

   b. Describe how verse 2 relates to the introduction to this lesson.

c. What disappointing outcome did this effort produce? How do you think this made the vinedresser feel?

d Describe the future for this vineyard.

9. a. Draw a vine with three branches on it. Add fruit to each branch according to the three categories Jesus describes in today's text: does not bear fruit; bears fruit; and bears more fruit. Label the branches based upon how much fruit they bear.

b. What prompts the growth of more fruit? How have you experienced God's divine pruning in your life, and how did it promote more growth?

○ ○ ● ○ ○

It takes a master gardener to prune a grapevine. Unlike deadheading your daisies or cutting back your roses, pruning grapevines is more complicated and takes a great deal of expertise. One vinedresser said, "If you fail to prune your grapevines they will go completely berserk. It doesn't take long for a vine to reach thirty or more feet and vines can be quite unproductive at that size."[52] No wonder God compares us to grapevines.

In our text today we learned that God has the expertise of a master vinedresser. He knows which useless branches to radically lop off, which mature branches to gently trim, and which tender branches to carefully train. He does this because grapes grow only on new wood. Although it can be painful, pruning allows new wood to grow. When done correctly, pruning allows the vine to produce more fruit than before. The real secret

Learn About ...

7 True or False

When Jesus described Himself as the true Vine, this implied a comparison to a false vine. John Montgomery Boice said, "He is the one, perfect, essential and enduring vine before which all other vines are but shadows."[51] "But the LORD is the true God; He is the living God and the everlasting King" (Jer. 10:10).

9 Bear Fruit

Vine branches are not like branches on a tree. They are good for bearing fruit or burning. They are not strong enough for building. The reason a vinedresser plants grapes is to bear fruit. A barren branch is worthless. But those that bear fruit can be pruned to produce yet more fruit.

behind pruning the grapevine is to know how much to remove and how much to leave. Interestingly, it takes three years for the vine's training to be complete. How long did Jesus train His disciples? Three years.

Is God cutting off dead weight that is keeping you from bearing more fruit? Take heart! It is for your good and His glory. Or maybe He is busy training you to stay close to the vine so your fruit will not spoil. Remember, He has your best interests at heart. God prunes those He loves. And He loves *you!*

LISTEN TO ...

One of the marks of spiritual maturity is the quiet confidence that God is in control ... without the need to understand why he does what he does.

—*Charles R. Swindoll*

DAY 2

Abiding in the Vine

The analogy of branches and a vine is a good one. Like branches on a vine, some followers are fruitful and some are faltering. John MacArthur wrote, "The imperative to abide is an exhortation to unbelievers, yet it also applies to Christians. In a positional sense, we do abide in Christ—that is the character of being saved. But there's a sense in which Christians fail to abide as fully as they ought. We're always in fellowship with the Father and the Son, because fellowship means partnership, and nothing can ever break that if we're saved. However, we lose the joy and the experience of that fellowship when we temporarily cease to abide in a close relationship with Christ."[53] Gardeners tell us that fruit will fall off a tree if it fails to get the proper nutrients or if pests can get to the fruit and hinder its growth.

The same is true with believers. When we maintain a steady diet of the Word, we are more likely to abide in the Vine rather than falling short. And when we cling to Christ, He can protect us from the sinful situations that might cause us to fall away from His protective presence. Fruit trees must depend on the gardener to protect them. But believers must make some purposeful life choices to stay close to the safety of the source of their strength. Will you choose to abide in or abandon the true Vine? When you cling to God, fruit will abound in its season.

Lift up ...

Jesus, thank You for taking the responsibility of producing fruit in my life. There is nothing of eternal value that I can do outside of You. Help me to be a profitable servant. Amen.

Look at ...

Yesterday Jesus revealed that the Father is the Vinedresser who uses the technique of pruning and cleansing to protect the vine. Though these procedures may feel painful for the plant, they are necessary for growth. While pruning cuts away dead weight, cleansing purges contaminants. The Word of God is the tool that both cuts and cleanses. Hebrews reveals the

LEARN ABOUT ...

2 Rotten Fruit

The flesh cannot produce fruit. Like the Pharisees, we may try to produce fruit through religious efforts. Jesus rebuked the religious leaders of His day, calling their self-righteousness fruit bad: "Either make the tree good and its fruit good, or else make the tree bad and its fruit bad; for a tree is known by its fruit" (Matt. 12:33).

4 Real Fruit

The kind of fruit Jesus speaks about is spiritual, springing from a relationship with Him. It includes the fruit of righteousness (see James 3:18), the fruit of repentance (see Matt. 3:8), the fruit of the Spirit (see Eph. 5:9), and the fruit of our lips (see Heb. 13:15). Such fruit is nourishing to others and glorifies the Father.

Word's pruning effect: "The word of God is living and powerful, and sharper than any two-edged sword, piercing even to the division of soul and spirit" (4:12). Paul says the believer is cleansed by "the washing of water by the word" (Eph. 5:26).

Today Jesus reveals another secret to a fruitful life—abiding in Him. Branches depend on the root system for the nourishment they need. Likewise the disciples must depend on Christ to grow and spread the gospel. Choosing Jesus means being part of a great harvest. Living apart from Him means uselessness. Will you surrender your life to the Master's hand, whether painful or pleasant? Abiding in Christ has its rewards, but choosing to live apart from Him has its consequences.

READ JOHN 15:4–6.

"Abide in Me, and I in you. As the branch cannot bear fruit of itself, unless it abides in the vine, neither can you, unless you abide in Me. I am the vine, you are the branches. He who abides in Me, and I in him, bears much fruit; for without Me you can do nothing. If anyone does not abide in Me, he is cast out as a branch and is withered; and they gather them and throw them into the fire, and they are burned." John 15:4–6

1. Jesus commanded the disciples to "abide in Me."

   a. What did He promise in return?

   b. How do you know you are abiding in Him?

2. Elaborate on what the branches and the disciples would be unable to do if they did not live an abiding life.

3. Why do you think Jesus repeated the analogy, "I am the vine, you are the branches"?

4. a. What could the disciples expect if they remained in Jesus and He in them?

   b. Using farming terms, try to quantify the amount of fruit in your life: pint, flat, basket, bushel, etc.

5. Explain what the disciples could expect to accomplish without Jesus. How have you found this to be true in your life?

6. Describe what happens to the "branches" that choose to remain apart from Christ.

LIVE OUT...

7. Today we learned that rotten fruit comes from the flesh, while real fruit springs from the Spirit. Read Galatians 5:16–26, then place the attributes in the appropriate column.

   REAL FRUIT   **ROTTEN FRUIT**

8. Jesus likened the disciples to branches of the true Vine. In other texts believers are portrayed as trees of righteousness. Place the types of fruit others may sample from your life in the branches of your tree.

LEARN ABOUT ...

6 Roaring Fire

The branches cut from the vine are worthless except for building rapidly burning fires. Fire means judgment. I Corinthians 3:12–13 says a believer's work will be judged to see if it is "wood, hay, straw ... it will be revealed by fire; and the fire will test each one's work, of what sort it is."

7 Abide

Warren Wiersbe explains that *abide* means "to keep in fellowship with Christ so that His life can work in and through us to produce fruit. This certainly involves the Word of God and the confession of sin so that nothing hinders our communion with Him. It also involves obeying Him because we love Him."[54]

8 Righteous Fruit

Real fruit is righteous fruit. Righteous means to have holy and upright living, in accordance with God's standard. At its root the word means "straightness." Righteousness is a moral concept. God's character is the definition and source of all righteousness. Therefore, man's righteousness is defined in terms of God's.[55]

9. Jesus told His disciples, "Without Me you can do nothing." Journal about some of the ways you have tried to produce fruit without Christ's help. Then write a prayer asking Him to help you bring forth spiritual fruit.

○ ○ ● ○ ○

My (Penny) grandfather was a gardener—but I wouldn't call him a "master" gardener. He offered to take care of my yard when I had three small kids and my husband was working overtime. One hot day he pulled up in his El Camino with giant pruning shears. A few minutes later I looked out my backdoor and called out, "Granddaddy, are you sure you want to cut back my lilac bush?"

"No problem, honey! Been doin' this my whole life!"

I watched in horror as he chopped my lush lilac bush down to nothing but a short, stubby stump. He walked up to me proudly and said, "Next year that bush will bloom like nothin' you've ever seen before."

I nodded and said, "Thanks. Want some tea?"

The next year I waited for that bush to bloom. And the next year. And the next. That bush never did recover from my granddaddy's overenthusiastic "pruning."

Thank goodness the One who does the pruning in our lives is God. He knows just what, how, and when to prune to make us fruitful and fragrant. As tools in God's hands, let's not make the mistake of taking God's Word as pruning shears to cut others—we may do more harm than good. Better to tend to the sin in our own lives and pray that the Vinedresser will tend to others in His perfect way and time.

Listen to ...

If we prune back that part of our activity which is not really fruitful in the Holy Spirit, we find that we do less, but accomplish more.

—*John Michael Talbot*

DAY 3
Bearing Fruit

In addition to abiding, bearing fruit is another major theme in John 15. The heavenly Vinedresser desires His people to increase their production from fruit to more fruit to much fruit. To make this possible He ensures favorable conditions. Let's spend a little time gaining insight into how real fruit is produced.

Fruit trees begin to bear fruit soon after they're old enough to flower. Several factors influence a mature tree's ability to produce fruit. Just one unfavorable condition may reduce the yield or prevent the tree from bearing any fruit at all.

BEARING AGE: The age when trees can be expected to bear fruit depends on the type of fruit you are growing.

TREE HEALTH: Trees must be healthy to produce good-quality fruit. Weak or diseased trees produce either poor-quality fruit or no fruit at all. It is vital to keep trees free from insects and diseases.

CLIMATE AND WEATHER: The fruit is frequently injured by frost. Injured flowers may appear to be normal, but if the pistils (center parts of the flower) are killed, no fruit will be produced.

POLLINATION: Flowers of fruit trees must be pollinated to produce fruit. Without sufficient pollination, they may blossom abundantly but will not bear fruit.

CULTURAL PRACTICES: Fruit trees need good cultural practices during the season to maintain an adequate number of good leaves for quality fruit production. These practices include correct placement in sun or shade, spacing, mulching, and weeding.[56]

As you study this lesson, spend time examining your fruitfulness. Ask God to show you how you can begin to bear even more fruit so that you can glorify Him.

LIFT UP ...

Dear Jesus, more than anything I want to abide in You and for You to abide in me. Teach me how to do that. Show me how to choose You every day in all the details of my day. Amen.

LOOK AT ...

Yesterday we saw that failing to abide caused us to fall far short of God's best for us. Yet even faithful branches require pruning in order to grow and flourish. It is a clarion call to understand the importance of abiding in the true Vine as the source of our strength and sustenance. Today Jesus continues His discussion on bearing fruit, expanding on the theme of abiding in Him.

How can you tell if you're abiding in Christ? Is it a feeling? More than a feeling, fruitfulness is the sign. So far we've seen a variety of fruit, from the fruit of the Spirit to the fruit of repentance. Today's text reveals yet another kind of fruit—answered prayer. Two different types of abiding produce this fruit: 1) abiding in Him (developing His character in our lives) and 2) His Word abiding in us—(obedience and conformity to His commands). If someone were to be a fruit inspector, would they say you were bearing this fruit?

READ JOHN 15:7–9.

"If you abide in Me, and My words abide in you, you will ask what you desire, and it shall be done for you. By this My Father is glorified, that you bear much fruit; so you will be My disciples.

"As the Father loved Me, I also have loved you; abide in My love."
John 15:7–9

1. What two types of abiding did Jesus speak of in today's text?

2. Describe the two results of abiding. Talk about an example of this in your life.

3. a. According to this passage, how is the Father glorified?

LEARN ABOUT ...

1 His Words

How does a Christian abide in God's Word? Joshua explained the secret: "The Law shall not depart from your mouth, but you shall meditate in it day and night, that you may observe to do according to all that is written in it. For then you will make your way prosperous" (Josh. 1:8).

2 His Will

What prayers does the Father answer? Those compatible with His character and commands. He transforms our desires into His own: "Delight yourself also in the LORD, And He shall give you the desires of your heart. Commit your way to the LORD, Trust also in Him, And He shall bring it to pass" (Ps. 37:4–5).

3 His Way

What types of answered prayers bring the Father glory? Those that further His kingdom. Those that benefit others. Those that build up the church. The apostle Paul wrote, "Brethren, pray for us, that the word of the Lord may run swiftly and be glorified, just as it is with you" (2 Thess. 3:1).

b. Describe how this is true in your life.

4. What title did Jesus give those who bear much fruit?

5. How did Jesus compare the love He had for the disciples?

6. a. What final command did Jesus repeat to the disciples?

   b. Based on what we've learned, how do you think this is accomplished?

LIVE OUT...

7. Jesus explained that answered prayer is one evidence of fruit in a believer's life. He modeled the way believers should pray. Read the Lord's Prayer below, and record what parts of the prayer you have seen answered in your life. Then talk about how this encourages you that you are bearing fruit in your life.

When you pray, say:
Our Father in heaven,
Hallowed be Your name.
Your kingdom come.
Your will be done
On earth as it is in heaven.
"Give us day by day our daily bread.
And forgive us our sins,
For we also forgive everyone who is indebted to us.
And do not lead us into temptation,
But deliver us from the evil one (Luke 11:2–4).

LEARN ABOUT ...

7 His Glory

We are His glory! As we abide in Christ, He develops desires in our hearts that are His own. From these desires spring prayers that the Father gladly answers. These answered prayers produce fruit. As a result, God is glorified: "We who first trusted in Christ should be to the praise of His glory" (Eph. 1:12).

8 His Harvest

The harvest occurs at the end of the growing season when crops are gathered. It's one of the happiest times of the year in Israel and is marked with celebrations. Jesus used the same metaphor for gathering together those who believe in Him.[57] "Look at the fields, for they are already white for harvest!" (John 4:35).

Answered prayer:

I know I'm bearing fruit because:

8. So far we've discovered the great variety of fruit the Christian produces as a result of abiding in the true Vine, Jesus Christ. Another type of fruit is the harvest of lost souls. Jesus told His disciples, "The harvest truly is plentiful, but the laborers are few. Therefore pray the Lord of the harvest to send out laborers into His harvest" (Matt. 9:37–38).

   a. List some of the people you know who are unsaved and ripe for harvest.

   b. Pray that "the Lord of the harvest" will send someone to share the gospel with.

   c. Ask the Lord how you can become a laborer "into His harvest." Commit to share the gospel with at least one other person this week.

9. a. Fruitfulness proves that we are Christ's disciples. Review today's lesson, then record the variety of fruit a Christian might display.

   b. Choose a "type" of fruit, then journal about how you'd like to see it evidenced in your life.

∘ ∘ • ∘ ∘

We've seen that answered prayer is one of the ways the Father is glorified. In Lenya's book *Holy Moments,* she uttered a prayer to God that was in His will without even really knowing it. Here's what she wrote:

> During my sophomore year of college Billy Graham's book *How to Be Born Again* was a top seller, so I decided to purchase a copy and go to the beach to read it. An excerpt from chapter three, "Does God Really Speak to Us?" made

me blurt out loud, "Yeah right!" Graham proposed that God was the Creator who speaks to his creatures through creation: "In its own language, nature speaks of God's existence, whether it is the cry of a baby or the song of a meadowlark ... the instincts of a bird are within his plans."[58]

Arrogantly, I decided to put Creator God to a test, challenging "If You formed the instincts within a bird and want to show me that You are sovereign over all, then influence the bird tweeting in the distance to land upon the tree I'm sitting under to sing a little tune." Fluttering out of the distance a small gray swallow lit upon the branch above my head and chirped a happy melody. Closing the book ceremoniously I thought; *Maybe God really does exist and has created me for a purpose too.* Just like that, in a holy moment, God had sprung the lock on a college co-ed's closed-mind with His unseen hand of providence.[59]

LISTEN TO ...

The disciple who abides in Jesus *is* the will of God, and his apparently free choices are God's foreordained decrees. Mysterious? Logically contradictory and absurd? Yes, but a glorious truth to a saint.

—*Oswald Chambers*

Ripe for the Harvest

This may seem obvious, but vines bear fruit for others to enjoy. In the same way, as believers we should produce fruit that nourishes others through our words and works. Fruit is a sign of maturity that blesses others.

No one enjoys eating unripe fruit, since it is usually hard, green, and sour. On the other hand, ripe fruit is soft, colorful, and sweet, having clung to the branch from blossom to bud to fruit ripe for the harvest. The ripening process has often taken the fruit through sun, wind, and storms. It has endured the pruning shears and the cleansing process.

Once the fruit ripens, its mission is to spread the seed. When fruit ripens, it becomes overwhelmingly desirable so that it will be carried away and eaten, and so that the seeds can spread and more fruit can grow.

Just as real fruit shows signs of ripeness, the fruit we bear is a sign of spiritual maturity. It has aroma—a full, fruity scent: "We are to God the fragrance of Christ" (2 Cor. 2:15). It has tender texture—the fruit becomes softer: "Love as brothers, be tenderhearted, be courteous" (1 Peter 3:8). It is heavy—weight is an indicator of maturity: "Our light afflic-tion, which is but for a moment, is working for us a far more exceeding and eternal weight of glory" (2 Cor. 4:17).

The analogy of fruit is a picture of the cycle of life, death, and new birth. The fruit grows ripe and sacrifices its seed so that a new crop can be planted. So, too, Jesus laid down His life to offer new life to all who believe.

LIFT UP ...

Lord, thank You for the Word. In it I learn to live a life that is willing to sacrifice my will and my way for others. Amen.

LOOK AT ...

We've seen that the abiding life is a fruitful life that glorifies the Father. Spiritual fruit contains the seeds required to reproduce even more fruit. Man-made or artificial fruit is lifeless and cannot reproduce. However, in order for seed to be spread, the fruit must die. Using another agricultural allegory, Jesus said, "Most assuredly, I say to you, unless a grain of wheat falls into the ground and dies, it remains alone; but if it dies, it produces much grain" (John 12:24).

The Christian life is a life spent dying—dying to self, dying to the flesh, and dying to our will. It is in dying that we truly live. Paul wrote, "If you live according to the flesh you will die; but if by the Spirit you put to death the deeds of the body, you will live" (Rom. 8:13). Today Jesus teaches the disciples the joy of laying down one's life for another. May you find the joy Jesus offers.

LEARN ABOUT ...

2 Role Model

Jesus didn't simply tell us what to do; He gave us an example to follow. The best leaders are those who show the way rather than simply give instruction. The psalmist prayed, "Show me Your ways, O LORD; Teach me Your paths" (Ps. 25:4). Christ's life was a template for all believers to follow.

READ JOHN 15:10–13.

"If you keep My commandments, you will abide in My love, just as I have kept My Father's commandments and abide in His love.

"These things I have spoken to you, that My joy may remain in you, and that your joy may be full.

"This is My commandment, that you love one another as I have loved you. Greater love has no one than this, than to lay down one's life for his friends." John 15:10–13

1. By keeping Christ's commandments, of what could the disciples be assured? In your own words describe what this means to you.

2. What example had Jesus given the disciples to follow?

3. Can you think of a time when you failed to keep the commandments and didn't feel like you were abiding? Or can you talk about a time when you did keep the commandments and knew you were abiding? Describe what happened.

Learn about ...

5 Man of Joy

There are many indications that Jesus was a man of joy. He described Himself as a bridegroom; He performed His first miracle at a wedding (see John 2:1–9); He defended His disciples when they were accused of failing to fast (see Mark 2:18–20); He "rejoiced in the Spirit" (Luke 10:21). No wonder He wants His people to be full of joy.[60]

---

7 Love for Friends

Love is not passive; love is active to the point of pain. Love willingly puts itself in vulnerable situations so that the object of love might prosper. Jesus was preparing His disciples for the ultimate act of love—laying down His life on a cross. Down the road, most of them would become martyrs for the faith.

---

8 Full of Love

Love, the Christian kind of love, is not so much a feeling as it is a choice to obey God's command to exhibit love toward others. Any love we have, whether it is directed toward God or others, finds its foundation in God since "love is of God" (1 John 4:7).

4. a. Briefly review this week's lesson. Summarize what Jesus referred to as "these things."

   b. Talk about which of "these things" is most significant to you and why.

5. Jesus spoke so that His joy might remain in His followers. Describe the other type of joy Jesus spoke of. Explain how, if at all, these two types of joy are linked in your experience.

6. Jesus repeated the commandment to love one another as He had loved them. Why do you think He repeated this commandment here?

7. According to Jesus, what is the greatest demonstration of love?

Live out...

8. Jesus told the disciples to abide in His love as He abided in the Father's love, showing Himself to be the perfect role model.

   a. Talk about some of the role models you have had in your life. Who were they and what made them tick?

   b. As believers, we are to set an example for others to follow. With this in mind, reword the following passage into a personal prayer: "Be an example to the believers in word, in conduct, in love, in spirit, in faith, in purity" (1 Tim. 4:12).

9. Jesus wanted His followers to be full of joy. John spoke about this concept again in 1 John 1:1–4.

a. Read the passage and describe the things John wrote about so the reader would be full of joy.

b. Now link these elements to your level of joy. How has what John described made you a more joyful person?

10. Jesus described true love as sacrificial. On the vertical bar of the cross write some things you're willing to sacrifice to show your love for God. On the horizontal bar write some things you're willing to lay down to show your love for others.

° ° • ° °

What more can we say about love than what Jesus has said? Perhaps this poem can capture the beauty of sacrificial love:

> Love is the filling from one's own,
> Another's cup,
> Love is the daily laying down
> And taking up;
> A choosing of the stony path
> Through each new day,
> That other feet may tread with ease
> A smoother way.
> Love is not blind, but looks abroad
> Through other's eyes;

LEARN ABOUT ...

9 Full of Joy

Full of joy is a "metaphor taken from a vessel, into which water or any other thing is poured, until it is full to the brim. The religion of Christ expels all misery from the hearts of those who receive it in its fullness. It was to drive wretchedness out of the world that Jesus came into it."[61]

And asks not, "Must I give?"
But, "May I sacrifice?"
Love hides its grief, that other hearts
And lips may sing;
And burdened walks, that other lives
May buoyant wing.
Hast thou a love like this?
Within thy soul?
'Twill crown thy life with bliss
When thou dost reach the goal.

—*Anonymous*

LISTEN TO ...

Give me a pure heart—that I may see thee, A humble heart—that I may hear thee, A heart of love—that I may serve thee, A heart of faith—that I may abide in thee.

—*Dag Hammarskjöld*

DAY 5
Garden of Friends

Jesus was the perfect friend. He laid down His life to plant a garden of His friends so that they could spread His message on earth. One Web site offered some tips on what makes a good friend:

- Focus on what you can give rather than what you can get out of a friendship.

- Encourage your friends to be the best they can be.

- Appreciate your friends. Be sure to thank them when they have done something for you.

- Be willing to forgive. Don't let hurts turn to grudges.

- Tactfully point out mistakes. But realize that nobody is perfect.

- Be reliable. Be where you say you'll be.

- Don't try to control your friends. Real friendship does not mean you always have to be together.

- Be there for good and bad times. Most of the time, what friends really need is a sympathetic ear.

- Accept your friends as they are and don't take their behavior personally.

- Don't reveal secrets. Nothing is worse than if your friends find out that you have leaked intimate details.

- Don't let an argument destroy a friendship. Your desire to win the argument may ruin your friendship.[62]

Friendship with Christ is on a different level than friendship with human beings. Christ is so superior that being His friend is an honor and a blessing.

LIFT UP ...

Father, thank You for the privilege of calling me Your friend. Help me to bear fruit that remains. Amen.

LOOK AT ...

Abraham was "called the friend of God" (James 2:23); also, "the LORD spoke to Moses face to face, as a man speaks to his friend" (Ex. 33:11). What gave these Old Testament patriarchs the distinction of being God's friend? 1) They listened to God's voice. Abraham heard God's call from the time he left Ur of the Chaldees to the time God made a covenant with him to the time God asked Abraham to sacrifice his son Isaac. 2) They were obedient to God's commands. Moses led a group of complaining people for forty years through a wilderness wasteland. 3) They had a personal relationship with Him. Both men looked to God for their present needs and future hopes. If you want to be God's friend, follow Moses' and Abraham's example: Listen to His voice, obey His commands, and develop a personal relationship with Him. Now let's learn what Jesus said about becoming His close friend.

READ JOHN 15:14–17.

"You are My friends if you do whatever I command you. No longer do I call you servants, for a servant does not know what his master is doing; but I have called you friends, for all things that I heard from My Father I have made known to you. You did not choose Me, but I chose you and appointed you that you should go and bear fruit, and that your fruit should remain, that whatever you ask the Father in My name He may give you. These things I command you, that you love one another." John 15:14–17

1. What does Jesus expect of His friends? Talk about how you could be a better friend to Him.

2. Explain why Jesus called the disciples *friends* rather than *servants*.

3. Who chose whom? Why does that matter?

4. Explain why Jesus chose and appointed the disciples.

5. What did He promise concerning their prayers? What have you learned about prayer that helps you better understand this promise?

6. a. What did Jesus command?

   b. How many times has Jesus repeated this command? Why do you think He keeps emphasizing it?

LIVE OUT...

7. a. Jesus faithfully told His friends everything His Father had told Him. Fill in the following chart to discover more about the Father's wisdom.

SCRIPTURE	THE FATHER'S WISDOM
Matthew 6:31–34	
Matthew 18:12–14	
Matthew 24:35–37	

   b. What part of the Father's wisdom do you need for your life right now?

8. We were chosen in order to bear fruit. Read 1 Corinthians 1:27–29 and describe the type of people God chooses and why He chooses them.

LEARN ABOUT ...

1 Comrades

Friend is a term of endearment toward a loved one. It refers to a person one trusts, a close companion or comrade. The best example of human friendship in the Bible was between Jonathan and David. "The soul of Jonathan was knit to the soul of David, and Jonathan loved him as his own soul" (1 Sam. 18:1).

3 Chosen

To choose means to pick out or select. It does not imply the rejection of what is not chosen. Rather, it means making a choice with kindness, favor, and love. Regarding salvation, Christ initiates a relationship with His people, wooing them to Himself. He chooses those who will choose Him: "Many are called, but few chosen" (Matt. 20:16).

6 Command

Is it possible to command love from one's friends? James Montgomery Boice said, "The answer is in the nature of the friendship involved.... We are God's friends—by grace. But that does not mean that we can approach God as his equal or dictate the terms of the friendship. It means that we must approach him in gratitude."[63]

9. Jesus encouraged the disciples to pray to bear fruit that remains. With this in mind, journal Colossians 1:10 into a personal prayer: "That you may walk worthy of the Lord, fully pleasing Him, being fruitful in every good work and increasing in the knowledge of God."

° ° • ° °

Aesop told the fable about an old crow in the wilderness. The crow had not had anything to drink in a long time and became very thirsty. He came upon a jug that had a small amount of water in the bottom. The old crow desperately poked his beak into the jug trying to reach the water. Sadly, his beak couldn't reach the bottom of the jug. But the wise old crow thought long and hard and came up with a brilliant idea. He started picking up pebbles, and one by one he dropped them into the jug. As the pebbles accumulated in the bottom of the jug, the water rose in the container. Finally the old crow was able to quench his thirst.

This fable can help us understand the way God works out His plan in our world. If each of us would drop our own little pebble into the vessel and use the gifts God has given to us, God's kingdom would spread throughout the earth. We could obey His command to love one another by reaching out to at-risk youth, serving on a committee, or visiting our lonely neighbors. And God would get the glory.

LISTEN TO ...

The elect are whosoever will; the non-elect are whosoever won't.

—*Henry Ward Beecher*

LEARN ABOUT ...

7 No Condemnation

One mark of friendship is seen when a friend lets you in on secrets. Jesus is the best friend you can ever have. Not only has He revealed His secrets through the Word, but He will listen to your secrets when you go to Him in prayer. There is no condemnation in Him (see Rom. 8:1), only love and forgiveness.

8 Collaboration

It's amazing enough that God chooses us. But He also graciously bestows upon us the free will to choose to follow Him. Then He condescends to allow us to work with Him to represent Him and spread the gospel message. What a gracious God we serve.

Warning Labels
John 15:18—16:4

Warning labels advertise impending dangers. They let people know that the contents may be toxic, flammable, or poisonous. Do people actually read warning labels? More importantly, do they heed them? Astonishingly, millions of people still smoke cigarettes even though they must first tear through the small print warning of hazardous health alerts. Many also ignore the symbol that has long symbolized danger: the skull and crossbones. Dating back to European cemeteries, this warning label served as a harbinger of death. By 1829, the state of New York legislated that the skull and crossbones be placed on all poisonous substances. In the 1870s, this practice became ubiquitous throughout the world.

Imagine if this symbol were not employed. Children might mistake bright-colored cough syrup for Kool-Aid. Foreigners might inadvertently sprinkle their waffles with Comet instead of powdered sugar. Countless lives have been saved because of the skull and crossbones. Did you know that some crucifixes feature the skull and crossbones beneath the depiction of Jesus' body? Historians believe that this is related to the New Testament passages that refer to Golgotha as the "Place of a Skull" (Matt. 27:33).

You might say that the Bible comes with some warning labels of its own. Sin is poisonous and deadly! Those who partake of it will surely die. The only antidote is the cross of Christ. Through His death and resurrection, Jesus has rescued humanity from its eternal consequences. In today's text we'll read about another one of the Bible's warning labels: Hate is contagious. Those who hate Jesus will seek to destroy both Him and His followers. Be warned, Christian, the world is deadly!

Day 1: John 15:18–20   **MAY CAUSE IRRITATION**

Day 2: John 15:21–23   **HIGHLY CONTAGIOUS**

Day 3: John 15:24–25   **READ INSTRUCTIONS CAREFULLY**

Day 4: John 15:26–27   **HIGH VOLTAGE**

Day 5: John 16:1–4   **DANGEROUS CURVE AHEAD**

DAY I

May Cause Irritation

LIFT UP ...

Lord, thank You for taking ownership of my life and my heart. I would rather belong in Your kingdom than in this world. Help me in times of persecution to know that my life is securely in Your hand. Amen.

LOOK AT ...

Last week we saw Jesus liken believers to branches on a vine. He revealed that He was the root and that those who abide in Him would bear fruit. God, the Vinedresser, would prune the branches so they would become more fruitful. The life-giving sap flowing throughout causes a believer to blossom in love.

Today the topic radically changes from love to hate. It's hard to comprehend that God, who is love, could be hated by the world. But Jesus made it clear that the world would hate Him. And He predicted that the world would also hate the disciples who Jesus loved. In other words, the world would consider them guilty by association. You might see hate as a litmus test for love. To love the world is to hate God. Therefore, those who love the world cannot love God. These forces are mutually exclusive. In his first epistle, John wrote, "If anyone loves the world, the love of the Father is not in him" (1 John 2:15). As you study this week's lesson, ask yourself how you pass the love/hate litmus test.

READ JOHN 15:18–20.

"If the world hates you, you know that it hated Me before it hated you. If you were of the world, the world would love its own. Yet because you are not of the world, but I chose you out of the world, therefore the world hates you. Remember the word that I said to you, 'A servant is

LEARN ABOUT ...

I Hate

Hate in Hebrew carries the idea of ugliness or deformity. Hate includes feelings contrary to love. It can also mean to abhor or to loathe.[64] "Blessed are you when men hate you, And when they exclude you, And revile you, and cast out your name as evil, For the Son of Man's sake" (Luke 6:22).

3 World

The Greek word for world is *kosmos* as in "cosmopolitan." It originally meant an ornament like a decorative object that had fine proportions of beauty. It possesses three distinct meanings: 1) the created world that "was made through Him" (see John 1:10); 2) the world of humanity that God loves (see John 3:16); 3) the world system in rebellion against God (see I John 4:10).

5 Persecution

Persecution is the pain or affliction that one person purposefully inflicts upon another. There are three possible methods of persecution: 1) mental, when a person malignantly torments another; 2) verbal, using cruel words and criticism; 3) physical, harming the person's body.[65]

not greater than his master.' If they persecuted Me, they will also persecute you. If they kept My word, they will keep yours also." John 15:18–20

1. Circle the various uses of the word *hate* in today's text. In your own words, explain why the world hates Christians.

2. How does the world treat its own? Why do you think this is the case?

3. Underline the phrase "of the world." What do you learn about those who are no longer included in this group?

4. a. Jesus asked the disciples to "remember" something. Reflecting on previous lessons, cite the text and situation Jesus was talking about.

   b. Why do you think He wanted them to think about this particular instance at this point in time?

5. Jesus warned the disciples that they would also be persecuted as He was. Based on your knowledge of church history, list some of the parallels you've noticed between how the Savior and His servants were persecuted.

6. Explain who might keep God's Word and how they would respond to the disciples if they did.

LIVE OUT...

7. Today we learned that the world hates Christians. Fill in the following chart to discover who else is hated and why.

Scripture	Who is hated?	Why?
Proverbs 9:8		
Proverbs 29:10		
Amos 5:10		
Matthew 24:9–10		

8. Most of us long to be loved and accepted. But what price would we be willing to pay? To gain the affection of this world is to lose God's love. Fill in the following columns with things you've discovered that God loves and the things the ungodly love.

Things that God Loves	Things the Ungodly Love

Journal about a time the world hated you and how it related to your love for God.

9. Jesus asserted that since He was persecuted, His followers would be too. We must follow our Master's example in experiencing pain. But we should also have His heart toward those who inflict it. Read Matthew 5:43–48.

a. Compare how Jesus told the disciples to treat their enemies with how their enemies would treat them.

b. What are Jesus' reasons for treating our enemies differently?

c. Describe the benefits for those who love their enemies.

10. Does anybody hate (or strongly dislike) you? If so, are they reacting against your godliness, or something else? How do you treat them?

Learn about …

7 Hated

There are three reasons the world might hate true believers: 1) because we are not like them, meaning we are not part of the world system that lives in rebellion against God; 2) because Jesus has chosen us out of the world (if some are accepted, they feel some are rejected); 3) because we are identified in Christ.

9 Enemies

It is startling to note that the greatest enemies Jesus faced came from the religious establishment—Pharisees, Sadducees, and the Sanhedrin. This tide of opposition grew from resentment, to hatred, to persecution, and finally to capital punishment: "For this reason the Jews persecuted Jesus, and sought to kill Him" (John 5:16).

o o • o o

Throughout the Upper Room Discourse, Jesus shared the promises available to His disciples—including answered prayer, a home in heaven, the Holy Spirit, fruitfulness, and access to the Father. But Jesus did not neglect to warn them either. He talked about their privileges as well as the persecution they would face. He warned them that they would be hated for His name's sake. Sadly, the persecution that the early church suffered continues today.

International Christian Concern provides this startling list of countries known for persecution or severe discrimination against Christians: Afghanistan, Bangladesh, Belarus, Bhutan, China, Cuba, Egypt, Eritrea, Ethiopia, European Union, India, Indonesia, Iran, Iraq, Jordan, North Korea, Laos, Maldives, Morocco, Myanmar, Nepal, Nigeria, Pakistan, Palestine, Saudi Arabia, Sri Lanka, Sudan, Syria, Turkey, United Arab Emirates, Uzbekistan, Vietnam, and Yemen.[66]

Voice of the Martyrs recently posted this instance of persecution in India: "On September 16, Pastor Virendra Singh (50) his wife Bhavana (45) and his daughter Rushali (14) were on their way to their church in the village of Bhadwadi when they were beaten by approximately 150 Hindu militants. The militants accused the family of forcibly converting people to Christianity. Both the pastor and his wife received minor injuries. The militants then went to Pastor Singh's church and burnt it to the ground. The 500-600 believers present fled the building. Bibles, religious books and musical instruments were destroyed."[67]

Living in the United States you may never be interrogated or incarcerated for your faith. Instead, our culture tends to persecute through isolation and intimidation. The world will label you ignorant for your beliefs and intolerant for your moral stance. Take heart, dear one, that's just how they treated Jesus.

LISTEN TO ...

It is the crushed grape that yields the wine.

—Author Unknown

DAY 2
Highly Contagious

Infectious diseases that are transmitted from one person or species to another are referred to as highly contagious. Contagious diseases are often spread through exposure to physical contact, bodily fluids, or contaminated objects. The Black Plague killed seventy-five million people worldwide through contact with diseased humans or rodents. The flu is an airborne virus transmitted through the coughs or sneezes of an infected host. Scabies, a skin condition caused by a burrowing mite, is spread through physical contact.

My (Lenya's) son Nathan led a mission trip to Jinja, Uganda. The mission team enthusiastically performed street dramas, organized soccer camps, and visited orphanages. Before arriving at one of the poorest orphanages, the students were warned to avoid physical contact with the children, since they were infected with scabies. However, one thing abandoned children crave is to be touched, tickled, and tackled. Nathan just couldn't resist gliding them like airplanes through the air and giving them piggyback rides around the play yard. Of course, he contracted a raging case of scabies. He remembered Jesus' words, "Let the children come to me. Don't stop them! For the Kingdom of Heaven belongs to those who are like these children" (Matt. 19:14 NLT). Once he applied the topical medicine offered by the missionaries, the irritating symptoms cleared.

We've seen how the religious leaders feared that the things Jesus taught were highly contagious. They didn't want the Jewish nation to be contaminated by this new doctrine. Jesus predicted that hate and persecution would be employed to quarantine the outbreak. They thought that eliminating the carriers would eradicate the epidemic. Instead Jesus revealed that they were the ones infected with the deadly virus—sin.

LIFT UP ...

Lord, I am thankful that I am able to know and have a relationship with my heavenly Father because of the sacrifice You made. Thank You for opening my eyes. You've shown me that in You I am free. Amen.

LOOK AT ...

Jesus warned the disciples that God's love would lead to the world's hatred. James Montgomery Boice wrote, "Hatred does not exist because of what Christians are in themselves; they are nothing. It does not exist because of what they have done; they are harmless (or at least they should be). Hatred exists because the world hates Jesus and because Christians are identified with him by virtue of His call."[68]

Now Jesus gave the disciples another reason for the world's hatred. The words He spoke exposed people's sinfulness despite their assertions of being righteous. The religious leaders thought righteousness could be found in rules. But God doesn't focus only on keeping our eye on the law. He also fills our hearts with love. Going through the motions without experiencing the emotions is hollow: "For the LORD does not see as man sees; for man looks at the outward appearance, but the LORD looks at the heart" (1 Sam. 16:7). What about you? Do your actions *and* attitude both glorify God?

READ JOHN 15:21–23.

"But all these things they will do to you for My name's sake, because they do not know Him who sent Me. If I had not come and spoken to them, they would have no sin, but now they have no excuse for their sin. He who hates Me hates My Father also." John 15:21–23

1. Jesus used the phrase "these things." Look back to Day 1 and recount what things would be done for His name's sake.

2. a. Why did Jesus say these things would occur?

   b. Is this true of you? Why or why not?

LEARN ABOUT ...

I Namesake

A namesake is someone named after another. The early believers were nicknamed Christians because they followed Christ. "The disciples were first called Christians in Antioch" (Acts 11:26). Namesakes inherit the perks as well as the pain of their predecessor. Christians receive the love of the Father, but they are also loathed by the world.

2 No Knowledge

The religious leaders thought they were know-it-alls. Sadly, they knew the law but not the Lord. Jesus rebuked them for their ignorance: "You search the Scriptures, for in them you think you have eternal life; and these are they which testify of Me" (John 5:39). We must know God with our hearts, not just our heads.

3. What activities did Jesus engage in on earth?

4. Based on this, what responsibility do people now have?

5. Jesus was the example of a perfect life. He came humbly, spoke in love, and was without sin. To someone who thought he lived a "good" life, describe how Jesus' example could have made him feel.

6. What phrase lets you know that Jesus and the Father are both God? What else do you learn about them?

LIVE OUT...

7. We learned today that believers are Christ's namesakes. Therefore we are to be Christlike. Journal about some of the ways you would like to be Christlike. What kind of namesake do you think you are?

8. Although many of the religious leaders knew *about* Jesus, they did not actually *know* Him. Read Matthew 7:21–23.

   a. Describe the types of people who will and will not go to heaven.

   b. What do you think Jesus meant when He said, "I never knew you"?

   c. How do you think those listening to Jesus' teaching might have responded to this information?

9. Christians will be hated because the world hates Christ. People

LEARN ABOUT ...

4 No Excuses

Humans are notorious for justifying or rationalizing their own sins. We do this by comparing ourselves with others worse than us. Somehow their bad behavior makes us look good. But according to God's standard of righteousness, no human being is good enough: "There is none who does good, no, not one" (Rom. 3:12).

8 Knowing Personally

There's a big difference between knowing *about* a person and knowing them personally. You may know a great deal about a person without ever being introduced. The religious leaders proved that they had intellectual knowledge of God but did not have an intimate relationship with Him. Paul affirmed, "I know whom I have believed" (2 Tim. 1:12).

9 No Son, No Father

Jesus said that hating Him was equivalent to hating the Father. The religious leaders boasted in their relationship to God. However, Jesus challenged that without the Son you do not have the Father. Previously He said, "You know neither Me nor My Father. If you had known Me, you would have known My Father also" (John 8:19).

harbor prejudice that is unfounded. What about you? Do you possess any prejudices (even secretly)? Check the box and fill in the blank that represents people you may treat as guilty by association.

❒ People of another race. List who _____

❒ People of another economic status. List who _____

❒ People of another religion. List who _____

❒ People of another denomination. List who _____

❒ People of another background. List who _____

❒ People who look different from me. List who _____

❒ People who associate with those I don't like. List who _____

Rewrite James 3:17 into a personal prayer asking God to help you live a life that is impartial and unprejudiced: "The wisdom that is from above is first pure, then peaceable, gentle, willing to yield, full of mercy and good fruits, without partiality and without hypocrisy."

° ° • ° °

Brigitte Gabriel knows what it's like to be persecuted for righteousness' sake. As a Christian living in Lebanon, her childhood was lost to Islamic extremists. In her book *Because They Hate* she recalls:

When Lebanese Muslims and Palestinians declared jihad on Christians in 1975, we didn't even know what that word meant. We had taken the Palestinians in, giving them refuge in our country, allowing them to study side by side with us in our schools and universities. We gave them jobs and shared our way of life with them. What started as political war spiraled very fast into religious war between Muslims and Christians.... We didn't realize the depth of their hatred and resentment toward us as infidels.[69]

For seven years Brigitte lived in a bomb shelter with her mother and father as they endured relentless attacks. Eventually she escaped war-torn Lebanon, finding refuge in her adopted nation, the United States. But on 9/11 her haunted past reemerged. While watching the carnage on television, she found herself mouthing the words, "Now they are here." Her book serves to awaken Americans to our very real threat.

America has failed to recognize this hatred throughout all the attacks launched against it, beginning with the marine barracks bombing in Beirut in 1983 all the way up to September 11, 2001. It was that horrible day that made Americans finally ask, "What is jihad? And why do they hate us?" I have a very simple answer for them: because you are "infidels."[70]

Listen to ...

If the world doesn't hate you, you are not like Jesus.

—Author Unknown

DAY 3

Read Instructions Carefully

Sometimes if you read instructions carefully, you might just get a laugh. The following are actual instructions written on product labels:

- On a Sears hairdryer: Do not use while sleeping.
- On a Rowenta iron: Do not iron clothes on body.
- On a Boeing 757: Fragile. Do not drop.
- On Sainsbury's peanuts: Warning: contains nuts.
- On a Superman costume: Wearing of this garment does not enable you to fly.

Although some labels seem ridiculous, they must never be ignored. One wintry Michigan day, my (Lenya's) teenage sister and I found a sunlamp tucked deep inside the hall closet. It prompted dreams of a coveted California tan. The instructions cautioned that we hold the lamp two feet away from our skin for no more than three to five minutes. Foolishly, we sat under that sunlamp suspended just six inches from our faces for nearly twenty minutes. Instead of sun-kissed faces, we woke up looking like we had third-degree burns! Mom insisted that we go to school to caution others to *read instructions carefully* or else pay the consequences. It was a humiliating lesson.

Even from a young age Jesus studied God's instruction book: "Now so it was that after three days they found [Jesus] in the temple, sitting in the midst of the teachers, both listening to them and asking them questions" (Luke 2:46). Continually in this discourse, Jesus has referred to the Scriptures, the commandments, and the law. At this point in the discourse, He reminded the disciples of something else written in the Word. If the Messiah diligently searched the Scriptures, don't you think His followers should too?

LIFT UP ...

Lord, thank You for the works You have completed in my life. Please reveal the areas in my faith walk that are not pleasing to You. Help me to exhibit works of true faith and not false motives. Amen.

LOOK AT ...

Yesterday we saw Jesus caution His disciples that the world would hate them because of His words. He knew the world would bristle when His words exposed their deceptive hearts.

Now we'll see Jesus make the connection between His words and His works. This twofold assault exposes those who excuse their sinfulness with self-righteous attitudes as Christ's words expose the hypocrites who claim to do works for God. As a result their hatred spreads from Christ to the heavenly Father. Hatred creates darkness just as surely as God's love breaks forth into light. And darkness always flees from the light. So, too, these sinners are fleeing from Jesus, the Light of the World. Think about a time when the light of Jesus' words or works revealed darkness in your heart. Did you fight back, or fall to your knees for cleansing?

READ JOHN 15:24–25.

"If I had not done among them the works which no one else did, they would have no sin; but now they have seen and also hated both Me and My Father. But this happened that the word might be fulfilled which is written in their law, 'They hated Me without a cause.'" John 15:24–25

1. a. Based on this passage, describe the kind of works Jesus did.

   b. Based on your knowledge of Scripture, give some examples of such works.

2. Where did Jesus do His works?

3. If Jesus had not performed these works, how would things have been different for the world? Why do you think this would be the case?

LEARN ABOUT ...

1 Works

The Jews believed certain works would accompany the Messiah. When John the Baptist heard of Christ's works, he inquired as to whether Jesus was the One. Jesus said, "Tell John ... the blind see and the lame walk; the lepers are cleansed and the deaf hear; the dead are raised up and the poor have the gospel preached to them" (Matt. 11:4–5).

---

3 Without Sin

Jesus wasn't saying that prior to His works people were without sin. However, it was His works that brought their sin into light. They simply didn't take His works to their logical conclusion. If they'd admitted they'd seen a miracle, they'd also have to admit He was the Messiah. They refused to face their sin honestly.

LEARN ABOUT ...

5 Words

Fulfilled prophecy is one of the greatest proofs of Christ's deity and the Bible's veracity. Several Old Testament passages predicted that the Jewish nation would not accept Jesus as its Messiah. "Let them not rejoice over me who are wrongfully my enemies; Nor let them wink with the eye who hate me without a cause" (Ps. 35:19).

---

7 Words and Works

John's gospel often connects Jesus' words and works (see John 5:36–38; 10:24–27; 14:10–11), because one ratifies the other. Nicodemus was converted by their tandem effect. He said, "Rabbi, we know that You are a teacher come from God; for no one can do these signs that You do unless God is with him" (John 3:2).

---

8 Written Before

Jesus was not hated because of anything He had done, but because it was prophesied. When you are persecuted, you can take comfort in knowing it's not personal; it's been predicted. "Be happy when you are insulted for being a Christian, for then the glorious Spirit of God rests upon you" (1 Peter 4:14 NLT).

4. How did the world respond to what they'd witnessed?

5. Why did this happen?

6. Read Psalm 69:4. What might it have felt like to be David or Jesus, who so many people hated without cause?

LIVE OUT...

7. Sadly, the people of Jesus' day did not believe that Jesus was the Messiah despite His miraculous works. Read Luke 16:19–31.

   a. In your own words summarize the lives and destinies of the rich man and poor Lazarus.

   b. While in Abraham's bosom, what two things did the rich man ask Lazarus to do?

   c. What reason did Abraham give for denying these requests?

   d. How does Jesus connect believing God's words and His works in this story?

8. Truly Jesus was hated without a cause. Have you encountered people who hate Jesus for no apparent reason? If so, journal about a time you witnessed prejudice against the Lord. How did it make you feel? How did you respond?

9. Jesus performed works that no one else could do. Fill in the following charts to discover some of these miraculous works.

SCRIPTURE	MIRACULOUS WORK
John 2:1–11	
John 4:46–54	
John 5:1–9	
John 6:10–14	
John 6:16–21	

° ° • ° °

Sadly, the prediction Jesus gave regarding the persecution and hatred of Christians was fulfilled quickly after His death. Letters have been preserved that were written to a man named Diognetus during the second century AD. He was a kindly pagan man who wanted to understand the Christian religion. An unknown person sent him Christian letters to educate him. He elaborated on the hatred that early Christians endured:

> They live in their own countries, but only as aliens. They have a share in everything as citizens, and endure everything as foreigners. Every foreign land is their fatherland, and yet for them every fatherland is a foreign land. They marry, like everyone else, and they beget children, but they do not cast out their offspring. They share their board with each other, but not their marriage bed. It is true they are "in the flesh," but they do not live "according to the flesh." They busy themselves on earth, but their citizenship is in heaven. They obey the established laws, but in their own lives they go far beyond what the laws require. They love all men, and by all men are persecuted. They are unknown, and still they are condemned; they are put to death, and yet they are brought to life. They are poor, and yet they make many rich; they are completely destitute, and yet they enjoy complete abundance. They are dishonored, and in their very dishonor are glorified; they are defamed, and are vindicated. They are reviled, and yet they bless; when they are affronted, they still pay due respect. When they do good, they are punished as evildoers; undergoing punishment, they rejoice because they are brought to life. They are treated by the Jews as foreigners and enemies, and are hunted down by

the Greeks; and all the time those who hate them find it impossible to justify their enmity.[71]

Christians can possess faith that overcomes all circumstances. Despite persecution, they have peace. In the face of death, they find new life. Paul boasted, "We who live are always delivered to death for Jesus' sake, that the life of Jesus also may be manifested in our mortal flesh. So then death is working in us, but life in you" (2 Cor. 4:11–12).

LISTEN TO ...

Folks never understand the folks they hate.

—James Russell Lowell

DAY 4

High Voltage

It's easy to take some things for granted. For instance, each morning when you put your car key into the ignition you expect the battery to ignite the engine. When nothing happens you feel betrayed. *What? It's always worked before. Why now? Why me?* A dead battery sucks the life out of your plans.

The top three causes for dead batteries are: 1) forgetting to turn off your lights; 2) neglecting battery maintenance (specifically fluid levels); 3) corrosion between the cables and battery. But none of this matters when you're stranded without the high voltage boost to get your car started. At times like these, you need a jump start. And when help arrives, you hope they've come equipped with the proper cables and the knowledge of how to use them.

Jesus knew that His death would drain the life out of His followers. Their faith would temporarily stall. The crucifixion shattered the disciples' faith. But after a jolt of high voltage from the Holy Spirit, Jesus knew the disciples would testify of Him. Following His resurrection, Jesus told the disciples, "Behold, I send the Promise of My Father upon you; but tarry in the city of Jerusalem until you are endued with power from on high" (Luke 24:49). The Spirit would get the disciples going again!

LIFT UP ...

Lord, I am thankful that Your truth testifies of Your grace and love. Show me all of the ways I can testify of Your love in this world. Amen.

LOOK AT ...

Yesterday we learned that the world initiated a chain reaction of hate. James Montgomery Boice sums up this multifaceted hatred in his commentary: "In the final analysis, the hatred of the world for Christ's followers may be reduced to this. The world hates Christ's followers because it hates Christ, and the world hates Christ because it hates God the Father."[72]

LEARN ABOUT ...

1 Comforter

Helper can be translated "Comforter." Sometimes the help we most need is to be comforted. *Help* portrays something tangible, while *comfort* implies something tender. The Spirit comes to help us in every way: physically, spiritually, and emotionally. "You received the Spirit of adoption by whom we cry out, 'Abba, Father'" (Rom. 8:15).

3 Counselor

John uses the term "Spirit of truth" four times to describe the Holy Spirit. The KJV translates *Helper* as "Comforter." However, the NIV uses the word *Counselor.* The Spirit acts as our lawyer, counseling us to testify truthfully. "God is Spirit, and those who worship Him must worship in spirit and truth" (John 4:24).

5 Companion

The furtherance of the gospel was dependent upon those who had been with Jesus "from the beginning." Their eyewitness account brought validity to their claims. Peter testified, "We did not follow cunningly devised fables when we made known to you the power and coming of our Lord Jesus Christ, but were eyewitnesses of His majesty" (2 Peter 1:16).

Today we see that, although there were many who would testify falsely against Jesus, there is One who testifies in truth. Webster's Dictionary defines *testify* as "to prove or demonstrate; to be clear evidence of something." Today, those testifying in a court of law must swear to "tell the truth, the whole truth, and nothing but the truth, so help you God." The purpose of the Helper is to tell the whole truth about Jesus. Jesus promised that with the Spirit's help the disciples would be empowered to do the same.

READ JOHN 15:26–27.

"But when the Helper comes, whom I shall send to you from the Father, the Spirit of truth who proceeds from the Father, He will testify of Me. And you also will bear witness, because you have been with Me from the beginning." John 15:26–27

1. Jesus referred to the Helper as one who would come in His place. Look back to Lesson Four and record some things you've learned about this Helper.

2. In your own words, describe how the Spirit is sent. What does this teach you about the Trinity?

3. Jesus described the Spirit as "the Spirit of truth." How does this term help define the Spirit as God?

4. What would the Spirit do on behalf of Jesus? Why do you think this is important?

5. Describe what the disciples would do and why.

LIVE OUT...

6. Jesus sent the Holy Spirit to help us be witnesses of the truth. In other words, He testifies so that you can testify. What is your testimony?

7. We must not only possess a testimony of salvation, but also bear witness to the gospel through evangelism.

   a. List three people with whom you *have* shared the gospel. What was the result?

   Name: _____ Result? _____

   Name: _____ Result? _____

   Name: _____ Result? _____

   b. Now list three people with whom you *will* share the gospel. When will you do it?

   Name: _____ When? _____

   Name: _____ When? _____

   Name: _____ When? _____

   c. Take the time to pray for these people. Ask the Spirit to open their eyes and lead them to the truth. Ask Him to give you the perfect opportunity to share the good news with them.

LEARN ABOUT ...

6 Commission

The Father sent the Son into the world to do His works. Likewise, the Son sent the Holy Spirit. Jesus also "appointed twelve, that they might be with Him and that He might send them out to preach" (Mark 3:14). All Christians must "go into all the world and preach the gospel" (Mark 16:15).

7 Coworkers

It's astounding to realize that God is looking for coworkers. God uses women like us. However, there is a prerequisite. First, the Spirit must bear witness. We must not try to do our part until we've received the Spirit's enabling. We are powerless without the presence and supernatural activity of the Spirit.

8. The Spirit helps us as a comforter and a counselor. Using the word HELP as an acrostic, list some of the ways the Spirit has accomplished these purposes in your life.

H

E

L

P

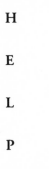

A startling new trend is being hyped by the hip-hop culture—don't be a snitch. Understandably, nobody likes a tattletale. The common definition for a snitch is someone who becomes an informant for money. We all know that money corrupts. But this is not what hip-hoppers mean when they say, "Don't snitch."

In an interview with *60 Minutes,* rapper Cam'ron boasted, "I wouldn't tell if a serial killer lived next door to me!" But he's not the only one on the antisnitch crusade. Busta Rhymes witnessed his own bodyguard being gunned down right in front of him. Yet he has refused to cooperate with investigators. These cowardly examples are creating tragic consequences.

Journalist Sherri Jackson reported that in Birmingham, Alabama, Rodreckus Johnson was gunned down in cold blood in front of several witnesses. But three years later not one person has cooperated with the police department.

His mother, Carolyn, said, "Even adults were out there. Also in the house and nobody would come forward with any information. It's been real hard to deal with." So Johnson is taking matters into her own hands, starting the Who Killed My Child campaign. She said, "Eleven of my members, their cases have not been solved. We started billboards and flyers."[73]

Justice is being thwarted because people are unwilling to testify about the things they've witnessed. Killers roam free. But there is an even greater injustice when Christians refuse to share the good news with people destined for death and destruction. If people tell the truth, lives can be changed. Who will you tell?

LISTEN TO ...

Witnessing is not a spare-time occupation or a once-a-week activity. It must be a quality of life. You don't go witnessing; you are a witness.

—Dan Greene

DAY 5

Dangerous Curve Ahead

My (Lenya's) husband, Skip, has been riding Harley Davidson motorcycles since he was eighteen years old without incident. On the other hand, my brief dalliance with motorbikes ended abruptly when I crashed my brother's Honda-90 into a brick wall. I walked away with a brake lever protruding from my left hand. Afterward I vowed never to mount a motorcycle again. I kept that promise until Skip's fortieth birthday. The only thing he wanted was me on the back of his bike. As a good wife, I complied and went for a Harley ride.

Everything was uneventful until he yelled back, "Dangerous curves ahead: Make sure you don't try to counterbalance the bend in the road!" Thankfully, we arrived at our destination unscathed.

Sadly, that's not how things ended for a Canadian couple vacationing in Alaska. The State Troopers responded to a motorcycle collision report that "a 57-year-old Canadian resident lost control of the 2005 Harley Davidson he was operating while negotiating the curve. He was traveling northbound and was carrying his wife as a passenger. According to the driver, he could not get the motorcycle to respond while cornering due to his wife leaning in the wrong direction. The motorcycle left the roadway on the north bound side and traveled 77 feet along the shoulder before coming to rest in the ditch. The passenger was transported to Ketchikan General Hospital via ambulance with an injured leg and other cuts and bruises."[74]

It's one thing to know that there are dangerous curves ahead, it's quite another to know how to negotiate them. Therefore, Jesus offered His disciples both the warning and the wisdom to navigate the coming obstacles. Disaster awaits those who lean one way when Jesus is leading the other. We must keep in sync with the Savior in order not to stumble.

LIFT UP ...

Lord, Your words of encouragement keep me upright instead of stumbling. Thank You for continually reminding me of all of the wonderful gifts. Your love is the greatest gift of all! Amen.

LOOK AT ...

Yesterday we saw Jesus inform the disciples that the Spirit of truth was coming to testify about Him. As a result, they would be empowered to testify about Him to the world. Their witness would eventually change the world.

Now we see Jesus again warn His followers about the future threats they would face. They would no longer be welcome in their places of worship because of their association with Christ. In addition to providing religious standing, synagogue worship affected one's financial and social status. Business transactions and relationships were cultivated at the synagogue. Excommunication meant financial disaster for the disciples. Although the disciples risked worldly ruin, they gained a heavenly reward.

Can you imagine what it would be like to be banned from your church for doing what is right? It would feel terrible to be shunned by people you had once loved and trusted. You may find yourself tempted to compromise to regain relationships or respect. But the Bible is clear, "We ought to obey God rather than men" (Acts 5:29).

READ JOHN 16:1–4.

"These things I have spoken to you, that you should not be made to stumble. They will put you out of the synagogues; yes, the time is coming that whoever kills you will think that he offers God service. And these things they will do to you because they have not known the Father nor Me. But these things I have told you, that when the time comes, you may remember that I told you of them.

"And these things I did not say to you at the beginning, because I was with you." John 16:1–4

1. We begin again with the phrase "these things." Quickly review Days 1–4 and note below what things Jesus is referring to.

2. Explain why Jesus spoke about these things.

3. What did Jesus predict would happen to the disciples?

4. How would the persecutors view themselves? Can you think of any parallels in today's headlines?

5. Rather than doing God a service, why were they really persecuting believers?

6. a. Saul of Tarsus also believed he was doing service to God by persecuting believers.

   Read Acts 9:1–9. What did Saul of Tarsus want to do with believers he found?

   b. Describe what happened to Saul (see v. 3).

   c. Who spoke to Saul, and what did He ask?

   d. How did Saul respond?

   e. What do you learn from this about persecution?

7. Explain Jesus' decision about when to tell the disciples about the persecution to come.

LIVE OUT...

8. Jesus was aware that certain events could potentially weaken the disciples' faith. Therefore, He prepared them in advance for what was to come. Fill in the following chart to discover some things we have been told in advance.

SCRIPTURE

Mark 13:5–27

1 Thessalonians 3:3–4

2 Thessalonians 2:1–5

Jude 17–19

THINGS TOLD IN ADVANCE

9. Early in His ministry Jesus predicted persecution. Read Matthew 5:11–12 to discover what He said.

   a. According to this passage, how should we view persecution?

   b. Whose footsteps are we following when we're persecuted?

   c. What does Jesus promise those who are persecuted?

   d. Does this passage help you endure the disdain of your friends and family who don't understand your commitment to Christ?

10. On a personal level, Christians must be careful not to become like those who hate them. We must not retaliate but allow God to right the wrongs inflicted upon us.

   Journal about a situation where you were treated unjustly for righteousness' sake. How did it make you feel? How did you treat the perpetrators? How could you handle this situation better in the future?

° ° • ° °

Jesus understood that to be forewarned was to be forearmed. The Jews who converted to Christianity would pay a heavy price. They would be cast out of their synagogues. Modern Christians find it difficult to understand the severe consequences that would follow excommunication. For modern Christians to be expelled from their church, the greatest pain is emotional trauma. In modern America, many people have the freedom to switch churches or denominations.

In addition to emotional duress, excommunication for the Jew impacted almost every area of life. First, it would be the end of spiritual life. He had no place else to go. He could no longer worship or make sacrifices. There would be no Scripture since the Old Testament had not been published for the masses. He could only hear it when it was read aloud by the priests.

Secondly, he would be ostracized relationally. Friends would spurn him, deeming him worse than a pagan. Family members would be forced to shun their own relatives who converted. Some Orthodox Jews would actually "sit shiva" in symbolic mourning for the death of a family member who stopped practicing Judaism or married outside the faith.

Thirdly, he would suffer financially. He would lose his job. If the person was a business owner or self-employed, he would lose his customer base. Many business transactions took place around the synagogue. Therefore, he would not have access to negotiations.

Those who bore the consequences of conversion might think it was a fate worse than death. But Jesus also warned that they could face martyrdom as well. The early converts had to count the cost of discipleship. That's why Jesus said, "If anyone desires to come after Me, let him deny himself, and take up his cross, and follow Me. For whoever desires to save his life will lose it, but whoever loses his life for My sake will find it. For what profit is it to a man if he gains the whole world, and loses his own soul? Or what will a man give in exchange for his soul?" (Matt. 16:24–26).

LISTEN TO ...

A Christian is someone who shares the sufferings of God in the world.

—Dietrich Bonhoeffer

Coming and Going
John 16:5–24

Many parents of young children have experienced a phenomenon known as separation anxiety. The symptoms are easy to recognize. When a child is left with a caregiver, there are emotional good-byes, lots of tears, and temper tantrums. Child development experts report that separation anxiety is normal. But it can be very disturbing to both parent and child. So what makes the sweet-tempered baby suddenly become a temperamental tot? The answer is that the child has developed what is called a sense of "object permanence." The baby has learned that things exist even when they can't be seen. That's why playing "dropsy" becomes so fascinating to the child. If you drop an object, the child knows it's gone and wants you to pick it up and return it—immediately. This is a wonderful development, but it also has a flipside. The baby realizes it has only one mother or father, and if that parent leaves the range of sight, the child expects the parent to return—immediately! Why? Because the child does not yet understand the concept of time. The baby knows the parent is gone but doesn't know when or if the beloved parent will return. No wonder they feel anxious![76]

This week the disciples find themselves in a similar situation. During their last evening with Jesus, He talked about leaving them to go to the Father. As His "little children" they were experiencing separation anxiety. They didn't know when they would see Him again. To help them overcome their anxieties, He went into great detail to explain His coming and going.

Day 1: John 16:5–11	CONVICTION OF SIN
Day 2: John 16:12–15	INSTRUCTION OF TRUTH
Day 3: John 16:16–19	INTERRUPTION OF THOUGHT
Day 4: John 16:20–21	TRANSITION OF FEELINGS
Day 5: John 16:22–24	SUPPLICATION OF SPIRIT

DAY 1

Conviction of Sin

LIFT UP ...

Lord, thank You for the sacrifice of Your Son, and thank You for the work of the Holy Spirit in this world. We are never alone because You are always with us. Amen.

LOOK AT ...

Last week we saw Jesus warn the disciples of some of the calamities that lay ahead for believers at the hands of those in the world. But He balanced His words by offering the promise of the Holy Spirit. Today He continues this theme by elaborating on the need for the Holy Spirit. Although difficult to believe, it was to the disciple's advantage for Jesus to leave so that the Holy Spirit might come. Among His many functions, Jesus described how the Holy Spirit has the critical job of convicting the world of sin through faith in Christ, of righteousness through His atoning death, and of the judgment of Satan accomplished by the power of the cross.

Though the disciples were faced with losing Jesus in person, He comforted them with the knowledge that they would gain the person of the Holy Spirit in their hearts. When you feel lost and afraid, to whom do you turn? The Holy Spirit is living inside you to offer you the hope and help you need for any situation.

READ JOHN 16:5–11.

"But now I go away to Him who sent Me, and none of you asks Me, 'Where are You going?' But because I have said these things to you, sorrow has filled your heart. Nevertheless I tell you the truth. It is to your advantage that I go away; for if I do not go away, the Helper will not come to you; but if I depart, I will send Him to you. And when He has come, He will convict the world of sin, and of righteousness, and of judgment: of sin, because they do not

believe in Me; of righteousness, because I go to My Father and you see Me no more; of judgment, because the ruler of this world is judged." John 16:5–11

1. Where was Jesus going and when?

2. What had the disciples failed to ask? Why do you think Jesus noticed the failure to question Him about His destination?

3. Describe how the disciples felt about Jesus' departure.

4. Jesus explained that it was to their advantage that He went away. Explain why this was so.

5. The Helper will convict the world of sin, righteousness, and judgment. Explain in your own words why the world needs the Helper to convict the world in these three areas:

   Of sin because:

   Of righteousness because:

   Of judgment because:

LIVE OUT...

6. a. Christ's coming and going is one of the key themes of this discourse. Review John 13:31—14:31 and record how often Jesus talked about going and coming.

   b. Reflect on the lessons you have learned. What things do you still have questions about?

LEARN ABOUT ...

2 Coming and Going

The theme of Jesus' coming and going is central in the Upper Room Discourse. Jesus repeatedly shared that He was going to the cross but would be coming back from the dead. The other layer of meaning was that He would be going to the Father in heaven but would be coming again a second time.

3 Deep Sorrow

Sometimes sorrow leaves us speechless. Earlier, in John 13:36, Peter had asked, "Where are you going?" Now the disciples seemed not to have the heart to question Jesus further. The word *sorrow* here means heaviness or grief.

5 Conviction

Conviction is a legal term that means to be found guilty. In common language it means to be persuaded or convinced. Conviction is the work of the Holy Spirit, who exposes the wickedness of sin, the righteousness found only in Christ, and the judgment of Satan at the cross.[77]

LEARN ABOUT …

6 Christ's Coming

The disciples probably expected Christ to come back soon after His ascension. Yet it has been over two thousand years. Skeptics say Christ isn't coming. But Peter said, "The Lord is not slack concerning His promise, as some count slackness, but is longsuffering toward us, not willing that any should perish but that all should come to repentance" (2 Peter 3:9).

---

7 Hope

Hope is a confident expectation. It means to anticipate good, especially in the future. The object of our hope as believers is fixed on "the Lord Jesus Christ, our hope" (I Tim. 1:1). In Paul's letters, hope is often tied to the resurrection from the dead and Christ's second coming.[78]

7. The disciples were deeply sorrowful at Christ's words. But Paul wrote that believers have a sorrow that is blended with hope when our loved ones die. Read 1 Thessalonians 4:13–18.

   a. When Christ comes again, what will happen to the "dead in Christ"?

   b. What will happen to those who are alive at His coming?

   c. Does this comfort you? Why or why not?

8. We know one reason the Holy Spirit came to the world is to convict of sin. Describe how the Holy Spirit speaks to you. How do you respond when He talks to you about the ways you fall short of God's highest?

° ° • ° °

Jesus explained that it was for the disciples' good that He leave and take His place beside the Father. If He did not, the Holy Spirit would not come to work in and through the disciples to spread the gospel message. Jesus predicted that the Holy Spirit would bring the world to faith by imparting three key truths:

1. *Humans are sinful.* Romans 3:23 tells us that "*all* have sinned and fall short of the glory of God." We've heard people say, "I'm a good person." "I haven't murdered anyone." "I pay my taxes." But even the best person is sinful. The Holy Spirit helps us to recognize and acknowledge our sinfulness.

2. *Only faith in Jesus brings righteousness.* Though we may try to act right, only one person is truly righteous—Jesus Christ. The

Holy Spirit convinces us of this fact and beckons us to accept the righteousness that comes through faith in Christ. Romans 5:18 tells us, "Through one Man's righteous act the free gift came to all men."

3. *Jesus' death and resurrection brought judgment to Satan.* The Holy Spirit reminds us that Satan is a defeated Enemy who Jesus will return to judge just as He will judge those who fail to believe in Him. Have you experienced the convicting power of the Holy Spirit? We *are* sinful. Faith in Jesus brings righteousness. Jesus judged Satan on the cross and will one day return to judge the world. Won't you allow the Holy Spirit to draw you to faith in Jesus Christ?

LISTEN TO ...

Beware of being in bondage to yourself or to other people. Oppression and depression never come from the Spirit of God. He never oppresses, he convicts and comforts.

—*Oswald Chambers*

DAY 2

Instruction of Truth

When Nicodemus came to Jesus, Jesus said to him, "'Most assuredly, I say to you, unless one is born again, he cannot see the kingdom of God.' Nicodemus said to him, 'How can a man be born when he is old? Can he enter a second time into his mother's womb and be born?' Jesus answered, 'Most assuredly, I say to you, unless one is born of water and the Spirit, he cannot enter the kingdom of God. That which is born of the flesh is flesh, and that which is born of the Spirit is spirit" (John 3:3–6).

One day after Sunday school, a schoolgirl named Ellen came home and said, "Daddy, I'm a Christian!"

He said, "Tell me all about it."

She said, "Pastor Dave said that if we received Him, God would come in and live in our hearts."

The father said, "What else happened?"

Frustrated, the little girl said, "I prayed and the Holy Spirit came into my heart." The father persisted, "How do you know that?"

Ellen replied, "Because He said He would!" Whether we're young or old, the Holy Spirit promises to reside in the hearts of those who believe.

The Holy Spirit's name describes His character. Holy comes from the word *hagios,* meaning "set apart, sacred, or pure." Spirit is *pnuema,* which also means "a breath, a breeze, or a strong wind." The Holy Spirit is the unseen God who promises to help you. He is the One who is able to put power into your life. He's the One who comforts and instructs you in the truth. Let Him breathe new life into your soul.

LIFT UP ...

Lord, You are the perfect teacher. You give us just what we can handle, when we can handle it. Thank You for the Holy Spirit, who guides us in every aspect of our lives. Help me to listen when You instruct me. Amen.

LOOK AT ...

Yesterday Jesus spoke of the Holy Spirit's power to convict the world. Now Jesus reveals to the disciples the Holy Spirit's wisdom to instruct believers. Jesus knew the Eleven had reached their limit on receiving spiritual truth. They were sorrowful over His departure. They were probably disturbed that a traitor had left them. Jesus had prophesied Peter would betray Him. But they needed to know more. The only possible way for them to learn was through the ministry of the coming Holy Spirit. Thus, Jesus explained another function of the Holy Spirit: He would instruct believers in truth. Peter wrote, "Holy men of God spoke as they were moved by the Holy Spirit" (2 Peter 1:21). The Holy Spirit is still active today. If you need instruction, ask the Spirit to guide you into truth.

LEARN ABOUT ...

3 Instruction

Rather than hearing Jesus' audible voice, believers can rely on the Word of God and the Spirit of truth to guide and illuminate us. The Spirit brings understanding about what is true. When the visible departed, the invisible Spirit embarked on a new relationship with believers to indwell our hearts and instruct us in truth.

READ JOHN 16:12–15.

"I still have many things to say to you, but you cannot bear them now. However, when He, the Spirit of truth, has come, He will guide you into all truth; for He will not speak on His own authority, but whatever He hears He will speak; and He will tell you things to come. He will glorify Me, for He will take of what is Mine and declare it to you. All things that the Father has are Mine. Therefore I said that He will take of Mine and declare it to you." John 16:12–15

1. How much more did Jesus want to share with His followers?

2. Explain why Jesus didn't reveal more at this point.

3. What did Jesus call the Holy Spirit? What did He promise concerning this attribute?

LEARN ABOUT ...

5 Declaration

To declare means to announce, report, or bring back tidings from another person or place.[79] The Holy Spirit supernaturally imparted the truth of God's Word from the Father and Son to the disciples. He helped fulfill the promise that what the disciples only partially understood about Jesus as Messiah would be completely understood later.

---

6 Revelation

Most scholars agree that this passage speaks of the authorship of the New Testament through the power of the Holy Spirit. James Montgomery Boice said, "The Holy Spirit would lead the disciples into a supplementary but definitive new revelation that thereafter would be the church's authoritative standard of doctrine."[80]

---

7 Witness

The word *witness* comes from the Greek word *martur*, from which we get our word *martyr*. It carries the idea of a person proclaiming belief in the gospel despite personal suffering. By using this word, Jesus was predicting that His followers would be persecuted for proclaiming the gospel message.

4. What does the Holy Spirit speak and tell about? Why?

5. How does the Holy Spirit treat Jesus and the things of Jesus?

6. Who possesses the Father's things? What will the Spirit do with these things?

LIVE OUT...

7. a. Jesus promised that the Holy Spirit would guide His followers. Read Acts 1:8. Explain where the Holy Spirit would guide them, how He would help them, and why.

   b. Who have you told about Jesus Christ? Name someone in another town, state, and country who needs to hear about Him, and talk about how you can be a witness to Him through the power of the Holy Spirit.

8. a. According to Acts 2:38, how does a person receive the gift of the Holy Spirit?

   b. Talk about when you personally accepted this gift. If you have not, offer a prayer of repentance and ask God to send His Spirit into your heart.

9. a. The Holy Spirit declared things about the Father and Son so the New Testament might be written. Read 2 Timothy 3:16 and explain the supernatural process God engaged in between men and Himself to compose the Scriptures.

   b. What does the Word accomplish in the life of humans? How has it done this in your life?

It is amazing that God would use imperfect humanity to compose the most perfect book ever written. And yet that is just what He did. Through the inspiration of the Holy Spirit, God has given us the Bible. The word *inspired* literally means "divinely breathed in." This fits with what we have learned about the Holy Spirit. It is the Holy Spirit's character to breathe the inspiration for God's Word to those men who were chosen to put the Old and New Testament Scriptures into written form.

The Bible is comprised of sixty-six books written by different authors with different writing styles. Though they lived in different time periods, they wrote a cohesive book with one central theme: the redemption of humanity from sin by the Messiah. The Old Testament has four sections: *Law, History, Poetry, Prophets.* The New Testament is divided into two sections: *History and Letters.* It's been said that the Old Testament contains Christ concealed; the New Testament shows Christ revealed.

The Holy Spirit flows throughout the Bible, making the Scriptures come alive to those who read it. We know that the Bible is not just any book. It holds the very power of life. The writer of Hebrews said, "The word of God is living and powerful, and sharper than any two-edged sword, piercing even to the division of soul and spirit, and of joints and marrow, and is a discerner of the thoughts and intents of the heart" (Heb. 4:12).

LEARN ABOUT ...

8 Repentance

To repent is to change one's mind or purpose; to turn and go in a different direction. Dwight L. Moody said, "Man is born with his face turned away from God. When he truly repents, he is turned right round toward God; he leaves his old life." When this occurs, God's Holy Spirit indwells the believer.

LISTEN TO ...

Christ departed so that the Holy Spirit could be imparted.

—Anonymous

DAY 3

Interruption of Thought

The toughest questions young children ask can be about death. They ask questions like, "If you die, who will I live with?" "Is Spot going to die too?" "Can we go to heaven to see Grandma?" When death occurs, they know something has changed and grow concerned about their own security.

My (Penny) daughter Ryan was in elementary school when Grandmother moved to Albuquerque so my side of the family could help take care of her. We went to visit the day before she died. Then we received the call that Grandmother had died suddenly. We made arrangements and took her home to Texas for her funeral. Little Ryan couldn't process the events verbally. So she drew a picture book with crayon drawings. One was of Grandmother's arrival as we wheeled her to the car from the plane. One was sitting and eating cookies with her. One crayon drawing showed Ryan's face flowing with bright blue tears. Another showed a picture of "heaven" with a yellow sun, white clouds, angels, and my grandmother smiling happily. Interestingly, my grandmother didn't have her wheelchair in heaven. Ryan was trying to work things out in her drawings.

The disciples found themselves in a similar situation. Jesus explained He was leaving. Then He explained they would see Him again. But the disciples seemed unable to process the information. Unfortunately, they turned to one another in confusion. But they couldn't work it out.

LIFT UP ...

Dear Jesus, my heart's desire is to see You. I long for the day when You come in the clouds. Until then, please show me Yourself through the power of Your Holy Spirit and through Your holy Scriptures. Amen.

LOOK AT ...

Yesterday we saw Jesus speak compassionately of the Holy Spirit's role in the world and to the believers following His departure. Today we find the disciples again perplexed about what Jesus was saying. Rather than simply asking Him, they interrupted His train of thought and began to discuss what He was saying as if they could figure it out for themselves.

But we'll see that Jesus was speaking about complex matters. He again brought up the idea of the disciples seeing Him for a while and then not seeing Him. This had to have been confusing and frightening for them. Without the Holy Spirit's aid, they could not understand the implications of what Jesus said. Nor can we. Jesus was unfolding a plan that has still not come to complete fruition. He was speaking of three events that many still do not understand: The disciples would literally see Jesus after the resurrection; they (and all believers) may "spiritually" see Him through the ministry of the Holy Spirit; and one day all believers will literally see Him when He comes again. When you have questions, don't hesitate to ask the Lord. He will give you eyes to see.

LEARN ABOUT ...

I Ticking Time

Jesus often spoke of time intervals. He said, "The kingdom of heaven is at hand" (Matt. 4:17) and, "My hour has not yet come," (John 2:4). He spoke of the "time of your visitation" (Luke 19:44). One interpretation of "a little while, and you will not see Me" is that He is speaking about His imminent crucifixion and burial.

READ JOHN 16:16–19.

"A little while, and you will not see Me; and again a little while, and you will see Me, because I go to the Father."

Then some of His disciples said among themselves, "What is this that He says to us, 'A little while, and you will not see Me; and again a little while, and you will see Me'; and, 'because I go to the Father'?" They said therefore, "What is this that He says, 'A little while'? We do not know what He is saying."

Now Jesus knew that they desired to ask Him, and He said to them, "Are you inquiring among yourselves about what I said, 'A little while, and you will not see Me; and again a little while, and you will see Me'?" John 16:16–19

1. Explain what would happen after "a little while"?

2. Jesus explained that in "again a little while" they would see Him. What reason did He give for this?

LEARN ABOUT ...

3 Tomb Time

The most obvious interpretation of seeing Jesus again was at His postresurrection appearances. Even before this, Jesus had spoken of His death and resurrection with His disciples. He had predicted "as Jonah was three days and three nights in the belly of the great fish, so will the Son of Man be three days and three nights in the heart of the earth" (Matt. 12:40).

5 Squandered Time

If we only knew then what we know now. The disciples had no idea that this was their last evening with their Master. If they had, what would they have changed? Perhaps they would have asked more questions. Perhaps they would have poured out their love. Perhaps they would have sat and gazed at Him in worship rather than talking among themselves.

7 Time Up?

The Pharisees and Sadducees had hardened their hearts, opposing Jesus and refusing to recognize Him as the true Messiah. Matthew Henry said, "Those who rejected the true Messiah when he did come were justly abandoned to a miserable and endless expectation of one that should never come."[81] Yet at this point Jesus' time was not up.

3. What do you think Jesus was referring to when He said they would not see Him and then see Him?

4. Recount the disciples' discussion among themselves.

5. What conclusion did they reach?

6. How did Jesus respond to their conversation? What does this show you about Him?

LIVE OUT ...

7. a. Jesus told the disciples that He would be going to the Father "in a little while." Read John 7:32–36. Recount the conversation Jesus had with the Pharisees and Sadducees at the Feast of Tabernacles.

   b. Jesus told the Pharisees and Sadducees they could not come where He was going. But earlier He told Peter he could not follow Him *now* (see John 13:36). Explain why some can go where Jesus goes and others cannot. Please provide Scriptures to back up your answers.

8. Jesus has gone to sit at the Father's right hand. We will not "see" Him as those privileged to "see" Him during His incarnation saw Him. What do you most wish you could have seen during His lifetime on earth?

9. Sometimes we get so caught up looking at our present difficult circumstances that we forget to look ahead to the far-reaching things God has promised. In the columns, list some ways you might be shortsighted, and list some of God's far-reaching promises.

SHORTSIGHTED   FAR-REACHING

° ° • ° °

8 Lifetime

Charles Spurgeon said, "Now, what has taken place as to the physical sight of Christ by the sons of men, will take place with all of you as to your mental sight of Christ unless you receive from the gospel an inner and spiritual sight of him. All of you have, in a certain sense, seen Jesus Christ."[82]

I (Penny) always had good eyesight. Therefore it came as quite a shock when my vision began to blur. I started to become nearsighted in my twenties. I went to the eye doctor and got contact lenses to address the issue. The problem was that when I wore my contacts I couldn't read up close. But when I took my contacts out, I couldn't see distances. So my ophthalmologist suggested mono-vision.

With mono-vision, one eye is used for distance and the other for proximity. However, my doctor told me my brain would have to adjust to this type of vision. Unfortunately my vision isn't perfect. I don't see with the eyes of my youth. Now I take my glasses off when I want to see up close. And when I want to see at distances, I wear my glasses.

As believers we face the same conundrum—it's hard to see clearly. The disciples literally saw Jesus in the past, and the promises about literally seeing Jesus again are in the future. We won't see Him face-to-face until He comes again. Yet there is a way we can "see" Him through the ministry of the Holy Spirit, the truth of His Word, and the people who are being conformed into His image. We "do not look at the things which are seen, but at the things which are not seen. For the things which are seen are temporary, but the things which are not seen are eternal" (2 Cor. 4:18).

LISTEN TO ...

In the beginning was the Word, and the Word was with God, and the Word was God.

—John

DAY 4

Transition of Feelings

Women who have gone through natural childbirth know that transition is the most intense part of labor. The contractions are very strong and indicate that your baby is coming very soon. Though often transition lasts for only a short period of time, it can be very emotional and painful. One of the greatest markers for this stage of labor is giving up. Many women have said, "I can't do this anymore!" Another physical sign is an inability to get comfortable. The laboring woman may continually want to shift around. During this time the mother is emotionally needy. She feels unsure and needs reassurance that things will be okay. Most women respond well to encouragement. Following transition comes the time to push the baby out of its warm womb environment. This, too, can be a painful and intense experience. But when the baby is finally born, women often feel a wide range of emotions: joy, elation, awe, pride, exhilaration, and intense relief that it's all over. Though they may be exhausted from their labors, most new mothers find that the joy of giving birth leaves them wide awake and longing to hold their baby, the pain quickly forgotten.

In His classic teaching style, Jesus used the metaphor of childbirth to teach His followers about the things to come. While this text probably spoke of the time between Christ's death and resurrection, it could also refer to the transition between Christ's ascension and the coming of the Holy Spirit. A third interpretation is that it refers to the time while the world awaits the second coming of Jesus Christ.

LIFT UP ...

Lord, thank You for the Bible. In it I can find Your words and Your works to build up my faith. Teach me to trust You as I study the Scriptures. Amen.

LOOK AT ...

The disciples had been puzzling over Jesus' words regarding His departure and return. Now in His masterful way, He drew a word picture taken from everyday life to help them understand the suffering they were destined to experience. He promised that the end of their suffering would be transformed into great joy.

Jesus wanted the disciples to understand that they needed a transition of feelings. They could not mature spiritually without enduring affliction. But the pain would be well worth the gain. God would use them to birth a great work that would literally change the world. Often God does not choose to spare us from trouble but empowers us through the trouble. He uses us to share what we've learned to tell others about His grace and the hope of joy to come. Why don't you share that hope with someone who is downcast and brokenhearted?

READ JOHN 16:20–21.

"Most assuredly, I say to you that you will weep and lament, but the world will rejoice; and you will be sorrowful, but your sorrow will be turned into joy. A woman, when she is in labor, has sorrow because her hour has come; but as soon as she has given birth to the child, she no longer remembers the anguish, for joy that a human being has been born into the world." John 16:20–21

1. Look back to yesterday's lesson and recount what Jesus and the disciples were discussing.

2. Because of this, what negative emotions would the disciples surely experience?

3. How would the world respond?

4. How would their feelings change? What analogy did Jesus use to illustrate His point?

5. a. Why does a woman in labor first feel sorrow?

LEARN ABOUT …

3 Rejoicing World

The ruler of this world (Satan) did not know that Jesus would be resurrected, thus he and others rejoiced at his crucifixion. But Jesus had predicted, "Now is the judgment of this world; now the ruler of this world will be cast out. And I, if I am lifted up from the earth, will draw all peoples to Myself" (John 12:31–32).

5 Fear of the Future

Anxiety over the future is a very human condition. At this point, Jesus was probably beginning to feel this anxiety as He faced the shadow of the cross and could relate it to the sorrow His beloved disciples would feel when they finally realized what would transpire in the next few hours.

b. Have you ever felt this (in pregnancy or a similar situation such as "giving birth" to a new venture)? If so, what was it like?

6. How did Jesus describe the progression of emotions when a woman gives birth?

LIVE OUT...

7. a. Jesus, like the woman in labor, felt great anxiety that His hour had come. Read Mark 14:32–36. What did He ask concerning His hour (see v. 35)?

  b. What did Jesus know about His Father (see v. 36)?

  c. What did Jesus ultimately conclude (see v. 36)?

  d. Are you able to pray in this way to the Father? Why or why not?

8. Jesus knew that the disciples' sorrow would turn to joy when they saw Him after His resurrection. Read John 20:19–20 and describe the disciples' encounter with the risen Lord.

9. The psalmist perhaps wrote it best: "Weeping may endure for a night, But joy comes in the morning" (Ps. 30:5). If you or someone you know is full of sorrow, rewrite this psalm into a personal prayer asking God to transform grief into joy.

○ ○ ● ○ ○

Louisa May Alcott wrote a beautiful poem called "Clover-Blossom" about a little worm that crept into a pleasant meadow and sought shelter among the flowers. He promised that when he awoke he would be a beautiful new creature: "Ah! pity and love me," sighed the worm, "I am lonely, poor, and weak; A little spot for a resting-place, Dear flowers, is all I seek." But none of the flowers would agree to let the worm live with them. The wild rose was too proud and showed her thorns. The violet turned away. The blue-eyed grass looked down on the worm. Finally the Clover called out, "Poor thing, thou art welcome here; Close at my side, in the soft green moss, Thou wilt find a quiet bed." The next spring all the flowers bloomed again, but the worm lay still and unmoving. The flowers mocked the Clover saying, "We pity thee, foolish little flower, To trust what the false worm said; He will not come in a fairer dress, For he lies in the green moss dead." The flowers tried to convince Clover to give up on the worm. But Clover remained faithful and she was not disappointed: "At last the small cell opened wide, And a glittering butterfly, From out the moss, on golden wings, Soared up to the sunny sky."[83]

It is a mystery that a lowly worm can be transformed into a butterfly. But with God all things are possible. The dead can live. Sorrow can be transformed into joy through the power of the Holy Spirit.

LISTEN TO ...

The most perfect being who has ever trod the soil of this planet was called the Man of Sorrows.

—*James Anthony Froude*

DAY 5

Supplication of Spirit

Lillian Lester-Redcross believes that etiquette should begin at an early age and become a way of life. Her school, the "Renaissance Academy of Social Graces," a Christ-centered finishing school, offers classes for children and teens. She has some interesting things to say about why etiquette is so important. She notes, "Etiquette isn't just about table manners; it is more than that. The emphasis is mostly on people getting along and respecting each other.... Etiquette is about consideration, respect and honesty."

When asked which manners young children should exhibit, she replied, "The words 'please' and 'thank you' should be an early part of a child's vocabulary. Children will imitate what they hear, so it is important to use polite words at a young age. They should be able to say 'please' and 'thank you' when things are done for them. Those are the very basics of manners." When queried about children of elementary school age she said, "Respecting elders and speaking respectfully to adults and their parents."[84]

For believers it is important to know how to approach our Father in prayer. It's not that He wants us to come to Him with a prepared speech or prayers that other people have uttered. In fact, He told us, "When you pray, do not use vain repetitions" (Matt. 6:7). But, as Lillian Lester-Redcross noted, speaking respectfully is the key. Our Father is worthy of all honor when we approach Him in prayer. The least we can do is give Him the respect He is due.

LIFT UP ...

Father, thank You for letting me approach You with my needs. I am amazed that You listen to my requests; I'm so grateful for Your faithfulness toward me. Amen.

LOOK AT ...

Things were about to change. Soon the disciples would not be able to go to Jesus with questions or requests. The events to come would result in a new kind of relationship. They would need a new way to communicate with Him. They would need to learn to pray. Prior to this, the priest had interceded on the people's behalf. But now Jesus was instructing the disciples that they had direct access to the Father through the Son. Just as Jesus loved to communicate with His disciples in an intimate manner, God loves to hear the prayers of His people. Prayer is simply talking to God as one would talk to a friend. Have you dialed into God the way you pick up the phone to dial into your friends? He's eagerly waiting to hear from you. What are you waiting for?

READ JOHN 16:22–24.

"Therefore you now have sorrow; but I will see you again and your heart will rejoice, and your joy no one will take from you. And in that day you will ask Me nothing. Most assuredly, I say to you, whatever you ask the Father in My name He will give you. Until now you have asked nothing in My name. Ask, and you will receive, that your joy may be full." John 16:22–24

1. Describe the current emotional state of the disciples and why they were feeling that way.

2. What would change their feelings?

3. a. What is remarkable about this joy?

   b. Are you filled with this type of joy? What helps or hinders joy in you?

4. a. What did Jesus predict the disciples would ask "in that day"?

   b. What day do you think He was speaking of?

LEARN ABOUT …

1 Everlasting Joy

Jesus confers upon His followers not only peace but joy. This joy is permanent compared to the sorrow of the world, which is fleeting. In the dark days of disappointment that followed the crucifixion, the disciples' joy waned. But at the resurrection and on the day of Pentecost, it reemerged and remained a characteristic of the early church.[85]

5 In His Name

We pray in Christ's name for three reasons: 1) We are personally identified with Christ through faith in Him. 2) We pray based on Christ's merit rather than any merit of our own. 3) We pray in Christ's name so we can ask for the things He would want, in line with His character.[86]

LEARN ABOUT ...

7 Ask and Receive

Believers are told to ask and keep on asking. The promise is that they will receive what they ask for in Jesus' name. The one who prays does not utter Jesus' name as a magic incantation to achieve her will. Praying in Jesus' name has the goal of achieving God's will on earth and fullness of joy for the believer.

---

8 Intercession

James Montgomery Boice wrote, "There are times when we do not know the will of God, and when that is the case we must pray cautiously allowing the Holy Spirit to interpret our prayers aright. But when we know God's will ... then we may pray confidently in the name of the Lord Jesus Christ."[87]

---

9 Confession

One element to prayer is confession—acknowledging that we are sinful and God is holy. When we confess, we regain right standing with Him. Then we can make our requests not only about our needs, but about the needs of others: "In everything by prayer and supplication, with thanksgiving, let your requests be made known to God" (Phil. 4:6).

5. What is the key to receiving from the Father?

6. Up to that point, what had the disciples *not* done?

7. What was the outcome of asking in Jesus' name and receiving of the Father?

LIVE OUT...

8. Jesus encouraged the disciples to pray in His name. Read Romans 8:26–27 and explain how God helps us to pray when we don't know what to pray for.

9. a. Read James 4:2–3. Why do people fail to have the things they want?

   b. Based on what you've learned today, what would be the right way to ask?

   c. Describe something you don't have that you have asked for in the wrong way or failed to ask for. (You don't have to share this with your small group.)

10. Jesus promised fullness of joy to those who prayed in His name. As a memory tool, you can use the word JOY as an acrostic to pray in His name: For example, Dear Jesus, I **O**ffer **Y**ou this prayer. Using this template, write a prayer from the heart in Jesus' name.

° ° • ° °

This may astound or amuse you, but there is actually a Web site that teaches people *The Top Ten Secrets to Unhappiness.* You could probably figure them out, but here they are:

1. Start by complaining a lot. Part of being unhappy is that everyone should know it.

2. Adopt the attitude that you are "deserving." This is America, and we are supposed to be taken care of by others.

3. Become defensive and closed minded, thinking only of yourself.

4. Impatience is vital. Subscribe to the idea that you should get what you want now!

5. Don't be responsible. That would require leadership and accountability. Then how could you possibly blame things on someone else?

6. Avoid decision-making situations. If you're confused about this, see #5.

7. Lack self-confidence. Self-confidence leads to secretion of endorphins that makes you feel good. All of a sudden you find yourself violating #4, 5, 1, 3. It could feasibly blow this whole thing apart.

8. Eliminate all trust and faith from your life. It's easy to justify not believing in something you can't see.

9. Be sure to be self-centered and selfish. Look out for number one, baby!

10. Go watch something on TV that promotes meaninglessness.[88]

We all know that happiness is different from joy. Happiness can be temporary and flee the moment circumstances change. Unhappiness can come upon us without our even cultivating it. Thankfully, Jesus offers us His true joy that will last into eternity. Are you filled with the joy of Christ?

Listen to ...

Joy is the serious business of Heaven.

—*C. S. Lewis*

LESSON EIGHT

We Shall Overcome

John 16:25–17:5

"We Shall Overcome" echoed from the choir lofts of black churches to the integrated meetings of black and white coal miners during the 1900s. Striking tobacco workers in the South joined the refrain in 1946. Eventually, the civil rights movement adopted the song as its unofficial anthem. Its verses have comforted underprivileged migrant workers and convicted overzealous politicians. Finally, this compelling song permeated the White House walls, where leaders were challenged to provide voting rights for *all* Americans. On March 15, 1965, President Lyndon B. Johnson concluded his speech to Congress with the promise that "We Shall Overcome."

According to the Library of Congress, "It was the most powerful song of the 20th century. It started out in church pews and picket lines, inspired one of the greatest freedom movements in U.S. history, and went on to topple governments and bring about reform all over the world. Word for word, the short, simple lyrics of 'We Shall Overcome' might be some of the most influential words in the English language."[89]

With the Emancipation Proclamation, Abraham Lincoln granted slaves their liberty. Reverend Martin Luther King Jr. had a dream to end segregation, and largely he did. However, Jesus stands as the greatest liberator of them all. He came to set us free from a greater enemy than prejudice. He came to release humanity from sin in all its ignominious forms. He was perhaps the first leader to inspire His followers with the promise of overcoming. "Be of good cheer, I have overcome the world" (John 16:33).

Day 1: John 16:25–27   **SAY A LITTLE PRAYER**

Day 2: John 16:28–30   **BLOWIN' IN THE WIND**

Day 3: John 16:31–33   **GIVE PEACE A CHANCE**

Day 4: John 17:1–2   **THIS LITTLE LIGHT OF MINE**

Day 5: John 17:3–5   **HE'S GOT THE WHOLE WORLD IN HIS HANDS**

DAY I

Say a Little Prayer

LIFT UP ...

Lord, thank You for speaking to my heart in the true language of love—salvation. I am humbled to know that because of Your sacrifice I can come to the Father. When I ask anything in Your name, He will hear my voice. Amen.

LOOK AT ...

Last week Jesus left the disciples with a bold promise—that whatever they asked the Father in the name of Christ they would receive. Today Jesus continues to prepare the disciples for His imminent departure. Throughout the Upper Room Discourse, Jesus has used examples to impart important lessons. He has washed their feet and shared their bread. He has spoken of houses, vines, and children. But now we see Him become more literal in His speech. Likely, because He knows He will soon be leaving.

Jesus wanted the disciples not just to know about His Father, but also to grow into a deeper relationship with Him. His lessons were meant to lead to love. Bible study is not merely reading the Word; it must include relating to the Father as well. If it doesn't, you are missing the point. Paul said, "Knowledge puffs up, but love edifies. And if anyone thinks that he knows anything, he knows nothing yet as he ought to know. But if anyone loves God, this one is known by Him" (1 Cor. 8:1–3). In God's book, it's better to have a big heart than a big head!

READ JOHN 16:25–27.

"These things I have spoken to you in figurative language; but the time is coming when I will no longer speak to you in figurative language, but I will tell you plainly about the Father. In that day you will ask in My name, and I do not say to you that I shall pray the

Father for you; for the Father Himself loves you, because you have loved Me, and have believed that I came forth from God. John 16:25–27

Learn about …

2 Figuratively

Jesus used illustrations to drive home a point. *Figurative* literally means parable or proverb. It describes an enigmatic or fictitious illustration.[90] A parable lays one thing alongside another to describe it. Jesus said: "To what shall we liken the kingdom of God? Or with what parable shall we picture it?" (Mark 4:30).

5 Factually

Previously Jesus had spoken in parables: "Without a parable He did not speak to them." (Mark 4:34). He introduced a time when He'd speak "plainly," which means outspokenness. It implies frankness or bluntness.[91] This marked a change in tone.

7 Fatherly

Jesus says that we don't need intermediaries, such as the Old Testament priests, to reach the Father. We can go directly to the Father in the name of the Son. We don't pray to saints or Mary, either. "For there is one God and one Mediator between God and men, the Man Christ Jesus" (I Tim. 2:5).

1. Jesus began with a familiar phrase: "these things." Look back through previous verses to catch up on what "things" Jesus referred to.

2. How had Jesus spoken to the disciples so far?

3. Jesus again referenced the time. What do you think His concern was about the time He had left?

4. Jesus used the term "figurative language," referring to the stories and parables He told to drive His point home to the disciples. Recall an example of Jesus' use of figurative language and describe what it was meant to portray. Be sure to include the Scripture reference for your example.

5. How would Jesus now begin to speak to them? Who would He speak about?

6. a. In whose name would the disciples be able to make their requests?

   b. How would they be able to draw near to the Father because of this?

7. What two reasons did Jesus give for the Father loving the disciples?

Live out…

8. Jesus described Himself using many figurative terms, from the Lion of the tribe of Judah to the Lamb that had been slain.

Recount one of your favorite metaphors used to describe God and explain why this is dear to you. Be sure to include the Scripture reference.

LEARN ABOUT …

9. Today's lesson is in the context of prayer. Jesus told His disciples that after He was glorified they could pray directly to God. They must simply do so in His name. Fill in the following chart to discover what else can be done in His name.

9 In His Name

Jesus repeats "in My name" three times in three verses for impact. This implies three things: 1) We pray because we're identified with Christ as Christians. 2) We ask on the basis of His works, not our own. 3) We pray in keeping with His character, which is revealed through His many names.

SCRIPTURE	IN HIS NAME
Acts 3:1–6	
Acts 5:41	
Acts 10:42–43	
Acts 15:14	

10 In His Love

Are you afraid of God, too fearful to approach Him personally? Don't be timid. Be assured that the Father loves *you!* "How great is the love the Father has lavished on us, that we should be called children of God! And that is what we are!" (1 John 3:1 NIV).

10. a. Jesus says that the Father Himself loves us. Write about an experience you had with your earthly father that taught you something about love, whether it was delightful or disappointing.

b. How did this circumstance make you feel about your heavenly Father? Compare and contrast these two relationships.

c. Rewrite the following Scripture into a personal prayer to Father God:

God has sent the Spirit of his Son into our hearts, prompting us to call out, "Abba, Father." Now you are no longer a slave but God's own child. And since you are his child, God has made you His heir. (Gal. 4:6–7 NLT)

○ ○ ● ○ ○

Jesus included a little word with a large meaning in His teaching on prayer—ask. In fact, it encapsulates the concept of prayer. We must simply ask the Father in the name of the Son. So often we view prayer as something complicated. Or we relegate it to "professional" Christians. Instead we must view it more simply, like children carrying on a conversation with their father.

When my (Lenya) son Nathan was just starting to read, I bought him his first Bible, with colorful pictures to spark his imagination. Each night, as I tucked him into bed, I would read a portion of God's Word and say a prayer. One evening Nathan read something that prompted him to pray, "Lord, help me to obey You more. Teach me how to be a better Christian. In Jesus' name, Amen." I kissed my little towhead goodnight, pulled the flannel covers up around his ears, and then turned out the lights. The next day was full of normal activities, from brushing teeth to building a fort in Legoland. I did the laundry as Nathan did his homework. Around three o'clock, we made our daily trip to the mailbox. Inside we discovered a package decorated with bright and colorful stickers addressed to Nathan.

As Nathan tore into the package, he discovered a Beanie Baby and a book that was the perfect answer to his prayer the night before. Amazingly a dear friend, Patty Davis, had mailed Nathan a copy of *God's Little Instruction Book for Children*. Nathan blurted out, "Hey, look, Mommy! God sent me a book to show me how to be a better Christian." That night we both said our prayers a little more enthusiastically!

LISTEN TO ...

More things are wrought by prayer than this world dreams of.

—Alfred, Lord Tennyson

DAY 2

Blowin' in the Wind

Bob Dylan says the inspiration for "Blowin' in the Wind," a poetic song with deep political insight, came when he "was walking through Washington Square Park and heard a kid singing,

> How much wood could a woodchuck chuck
> If a woodchuck could chuck wood?
> The answer, my friend, is blowin' in the wind.[92]

The lyrics of Dylan's song possess a litany of metaphorical questions that continue to challenge listeners to this day. Mary Travers of the singing trio Peter, Paul, and Mary said, "To sing the line, 'How many years can some people exist before they're allowed to be free?' in front of some crummy little building that refuses to admit Jews in 1983, the song elicits the same response now as it did then. It addresses the same questions. 'How many deaths will it take till they know that too many people have died?' Sing that line in a prison yard where political prisoners from El Salvador are being kept. Or sing it with Bishop Tutu. Same response. Same questions."[93]

Our Lord's comments in the upper room have greater longevity than the lyrics of modern troubadours. The disciples believed they understood what was being said in current terms. Yet Christ's words possessed both an immediate and longer-term meaning. The disciples thought they finally understood what Jesus was saying. But they didn't. Warren Wiersbe wrote, "They claimed to understand what He had been teaching them, although this claim was probably presumptuous, as their subsequent actions proved."[94] More insight would continue to unfold after the Lord's departure and with the coming of the Holy Spirit. Gloriously, His words are eternal, reaching all generations and unfolding His wisdom to those who diligently seek it.

LEARN ABOUT ...

I Coming

Jesus came into the world through His incarnation, which is "the gracious voluntary act of the Son of God in assuming a human body and human nature. Jesus is one person with two natures indissolubly united, the one nature being that of the eternal Son of God, the other that of man, in all respects human, 'yet without sin.'"[95]

LIFT UP ...

Lord, forgive me for the times I do not acknowledge Your great sacrifice of leaving heaven because I needed a Savior. I know You know all things. Please teach me what I need to know. Amen.

LOOK AT ...

It must have been encouraging to hear how much the disciples were loved by the Father since they loved Jesus and believed He came from God. Now Jesus tells them again that He came from the Father and will be leaving this world to go back to Him. Because of this direct speech from Jesus, the disciples make a bold statement. They claim to truly know who Jesus is and sincerely believe that He came from God.

Whether or not the disciples understood all that He had spoken to them, we don't know—but they wanted to believe they did. It is hard to determine if they really understood the implications of what was to come—the cross, the tomb, and the subsequent resurrection. Many times in our daily walk we want to believe we know exactly what God is telling us, only to find that we had partial understanding. God's Word is so deep and rich, we could ponder it for a lifetime and still discover more.

READ JOHN 16:28–30.

"I came forth from the Father and have come into the world. Again, I leave the world and go to the Father." His disciples said to Him, "See, now You are speaking plainly, and using no figure of speech! Now we are sure that You know all things, and have no need that anyone should question You. By this we believe that You came forth from God." John 16:28–30

1. Where did Jesus say He came from? What does this tell us about His nature?

2. Jesus made it clear that He "came forth" from the Father rather than being sent against His will. Describe how you feel knowing He voluntarily came to die for your sins.

3. Jesus disclosed that He would leave the world and go to the Father. Why was He leaving and going to the Father? Give Scriptures to back up your answers.

4. Jesus made the disciples aware that He willingly came to the world and was willingly going back to the Father. What does this tell you about His crucifixion?

5. Once Jesus died for the sins of the world, He would go to the Father. What does this tell you about the finality of this act? Would there be a need for any other acts to procure salvation for the world?

6. a. What did the disciples believe Jesus knew?

   b. What was there no longer a need for? Why?

7. The disciples boldly proclaimed that they understood what Jesus was saying and that they believed Jesus knew all things. Do you think they truly understood? Why or why not?

Live out...

8. Today we learned that the incarnation made it possible for the Lord to come to earth. He was fully God yet fully man. In the appropriate columns fill in details you know about Him that illustrate His dual nature.

Learn about ...

3 Going

After the resurrection, Jesus returned to His Father in heaven. He is presently seated on a throne high above all principalities and powers. He is our advocate, interceding on our behalf. "[Jesus] is even at the right hand of God, who also makes intercession for us" (Rom. 8:34).

---

6 Knowing

Although the disciples may not have had a complete understanding of all that Jesus said, they made a strong statement of faith. They admitted that they were "sure" and that they "believed." Our faith, like a muscle, ever grows, being strengthened as we trust and obey. "Lord, I believe; help my unbelief!" (Mark 9:24).

---

8 Claiming

"Came forth from God" speaks of Christ's origin. The common belief among the Jews was that the Messiah was coming into the world. However, the phrase also means that Jesus is God: "He who came down from heaven, that is, the Son of Man who is in heaven" (John 3:13).

LEARN ABOUT ...

9 Calling

Jesus uses the term "to the Father" six times in the upper room. It's a privilege to call the omnipotent God your Father. Nothing is too big for Him! "You are of God, little children, and have overcome them, because He who is in you is greater than he who is in the world" (I John 4:4).

THE DEITY OF CHRIST   **THE HUMANITY OF CHRIST**

9. Jesus told the disciples that He would "go to the Father." Although we cannot go to the Father until our death or the return of Christ, we can run to Him in prayer. Read the Lord's Prayer in Matthew 6:9–13.

a. The prayer begins by worshipping God. What do you learn about God's nature from verses 9–10?

b. The prayer continues with personal requests. What three main topics are included in verses 11–13?

c. The prayer ends as it began with the focus on the Father. How does it make you feel to have access to a Father described in this manner? Do you take advantage of His resources in prayer?

10. The disciples made a bold statement of faith by using the words *sure* and *believe*. Using the word SURE as an acrostic, write your own statements of faith.

S (for example, I'm Sure that Jesus died for my sins.)

U

R

E

○ ○ ● ○ ○

In today's lesson the apostles made a bold statement of faith. They believed that Jesus was sent from God. A statement of faith is simply a declaration of beliefs. Eventually they become known as *creeds* derived form the Latin word *credo,* meaning "I believe."

The Apostles' Creed is the earliest declaration we have on record and the basis for most of the others that followed. Although not written by the original apostles it sprang from their teachings. It served as a litmus test of orthodoxy. Laypeople who did not have access to written documents could memorize it easily. The Apostles' Creed was intended to unite the early church against the rise of false apostles and teaching. It stated:

> I believe in God, the Father Almighty,
> the Creator of heaven and earth,
> and in Jesus Christ, His only Son, our Lord:
> Who was conceived of the Holy Spirit,
> born of the Virgin Mary,
> suffered under Pontius Pilate,
> was crucified, died, and was buried.
> He descended into hell.
> The third day He arose again from the dead.
> He ascended into heaven
> and sits at the right hand of God the Father Almighty,
> whence He shall come to judge the living and the dead.
> I believe in the Holy Spirit, the holy [universal] church,
> the communion of saints,
> the forgiveness of sins,
> the resurrection of the body,
> and life everlasting.
> Amen.

The Bible teaches "we walk by faith, not by sight" (2 Cor. 5:7). But how many of us actually stop to ponder what we believe? What is our faith? If you've never adopted your own statement of faith, perhaps it's time you did.

LISTEN TO ...

His life is the highest and the holiest entering in at the lowliest door.

—Oswald Chambers

DAY 3

Give Peace a Chance

The son of a blacksmith Quaker, Herbert Hoover was raised with a strict sense of morality. His beliefs shaped him into a man who was passionate about peace and determined to devote his life to public service. During his lifetime he served as food administrator, secretary of commerce, and eventually the thirty-first president of the United States. However, because of the stock market crash of 1929, he became the scapegoat for the Great Depression. He went from the heights of popularity to the depths of plummeting approval ratings.

A reporter asked President Hoover, "How do you handle criticism? Do you ever get agitated or tense?"

As if surprised by the question he responded, "No, of course not."

The reporter reminded him of the season when it seemed that everyone was against him and asked, "Didn't any of this meanness and criticism ever get under your skin?"

Hoover explained that those who enter politics expect opposition. When it comes, they're insulated against it. Then the Quaker president looked the reporter directly into the eyes and added, "Besides, I have 'peace at the center,' you know."[96]

"Peace at the center" is a Quaker term used to describe serenity at the heart, in the soul of a person. This concept springs from the pages of Scripture emanating from the Prince of Peace. Those who look for a source of peace from this planet will be sorely disappointed. The world seems incapable of producing peace despite its treaties and détentes. If it cannot procure outer peace, how in the world can it ever produce inner peace? Today Jesus gets to the heart of peace.

LIFT UP ...

Lord, I am thankful to know that You have overcome the world. Help me to be of good cheer knowing that I stand protected in Your kingdom. Please give me peace in the center. Amen.

LEARN ABOUT ...

3 Scattered

Scatter means to put to flight or disperse. In Mark's gospel Jesus quoted Zechariah, "It is written: 'I will strike the Shepherd, And the sheep will be scattered" (Mark 14:27). The disciples should have been a source of comfort during our Lord's trial, but instead they were embarrassed by His chains.

LOOK AT ...

Yesterday the disciples affirmed that they plainly understood the Lord. This knowledge resulted in a bold statement of faith: Jesus had indeed come from God. In past weeks we watched the disciples ask many questions and Jesus patiently supply the answers. Now we see Jesus question the disciples. He wondered if they truly understood all that He was trying to teach them. After spending years by His side, the disciples still did not completely understand Him. Yet we can sympathize with them. At one time or another, haven't we all been wrong in our assumptions about the Lord? Or haven't we had our eyes opened to a truth about the Savior we've previously missed? Because He was God, Jesus knew the disciples didn't truly understand and that soon their faith would be challenged. So Jesus gave them hope, assuring them that, while persecution would come, they could find peace in Him.

READ JOHN 16:31–33.

Jesus answered them, "Do you now believe? Indeed the hour is coming, yes, has now come, that you will be scattered, each to his own, and will leave Me alone. And yet I am not alone, because the Father is with Me. These things I have spoken to you, that in Me you may have peace. In the world you will have tribulation; but be of good cheer, I have overcome the world."
John 16:31–33

1. Jesus posed a question to the disciples. Look back to yesterday's text and record what prompted Jesus' question.

2. What time reference did Jesus employ? As you reflect on previous lessons, what do you think this refers to?

3. a. What startling prediction did Jesus make about His disciples?

b. How do you think this made them feel? Why?

4. Contrast the faithfulness of Jesus' friends with the faithfulness of His Father. How does this comfort you during those times you feel alone?

5. a. Describe the impact Jesus' words would have upon His disciples both at that time and in the future.

   b. How do you think this is accomplished?

6. What two lessons did Jesus give the disciples regarding the world? How should these lessons affect them emotionally?

LIVE OUT...

7. It was predicted that Jesus, the Shepherd, would be struck and that His sheep, the disciples, would scatter. Turn to Isaiah 53.

   a. Look for the personal pronoun "He" in verses 2–9. Describe the plight of the Savior.

   b. Look for the personal pronouns "we," "our," and "us" in verses 2–3. Describe how the world perceived Him.

   c. Look for the personal pronouns "He" and "Him" in verses 10–12. Describe the position of the Father.

   d. How do you relate to the sheep in verse 6? Spend time thanking Jesus for His beautiful sacrifice of willingly taking your iniquity upon Himself.

LEARN ABOUT ...

4 Secure

Even though the disciples would scatter, Jesus was secure in His Father's presence. He would not leave Jesus alone. Likewise, as Christians, we need never feel lonely because Jesus promises never to leave us alone: "He Himself has said, 'I will never leave you nor forsake you'" (Heb. 13:5). God doesn't abandon His own.

5 Serene

The peace that Jesus offers is not the absence of strife but the presence of the Savior. It is internal and based on eternal promises. Therefore external circumstances cannot rob us of serenity: "The peace of God, which surpasses all understanding, will guard your hearts and minds through Christ Jesus" (Phil. 4:7).

7 Suffering

The Jews missed the Messiah at His first coming because of a misunderstanding about His role and His reasons for coming. Many expected that His arrival would be displayed with power to topple political oppression. However, they missed many Old Testament prophecies declaring that the Messiah must be a suffering servant to do so.

LEARN ABOUT ...

8 Sorrow

Tribulation means great adversity and anguish; intense oppression or perse-cution. Tribulation is linked to God's process for making the world right again. Jesus underwent great suffering, just as His people undergo a great deal of tribulation in the world. This tribulation has its source in the conflict between God and the Devil.[97]

8. Jesus offers a stark contrast between what we can expect from the world and what He provides. One offers peace, the other problems. In the appropriate column list your life experiences that confirm this premise.

WORLDLY PROBLEMS	HEAVENLY PEACE

∘ ∘ • ∘ ∘

After having two beautiful girls, Don and Debbie were overjoyed when the doctor said, "It's a boy!" But their excitement turned to concern when they saw the worried look on the nurse's face. They knew something must be wrong. Sadly, Bobby's abdomen had not completely closed, leaving many of his internal organs exposed. Over several years and multiple surgeries, this beautiful boy would have his kidney, bladder, and intestines reinserted. Through it all, Bobby was a blessing. Despite the suffering, the little boy was always cheerful.

During one hospital visit, Don and Debbie felt nervous having their toddler rolled away on a gurney. So they prayed and then promised, "Mommy and Daddy will be right here waiting for you. Don't be afraid."

Bobby replied, "I'm not scared. That nice man always holds my hand."

"Who holds your hand?" they asked. "One of the nice doctors?"

"No," he explained. "He's the man from the book we read at night."

Stories like this continue to amaze us. We hear about angels who visit us unawares. People talk about feeling the presence of Jesus, who sticks closer than a brother. Nothing, from sickness to surgeries, from accidents to attacks, can separate believers from their Lord. Paul wrote, "I am persuaded that neither death nor life, nor angels nor principalities nor powers, nor things present nor things to come, nor height nor depth, nor any other created thing, shall be able to separate us from the love of God which is in Christ Jesus our Lord" (Rom. 8:38–39).

LISTEN TO ...

God takes life's pieces and gives us unbroken peace.

—W. D. Gough

DAY 4

This Little Light of Mine

"This Little Light of Mine" is a song known as a Negro spiritual because it was originally written by rural slaves to stress the importance of unity in the face of great adversity. It inspired listeners to remember the light they possessed and to gather it alongside others in order to break the darkness. The song illuminated those trapped in the shadow of bigotry and hatred. It, too, was adopted as an anthem by the civil rights movement.

Eventually, the church at large adopted this song into the beloved hymn sung by children and adults alike. Christians realize that Jesus is the Light of the World and that coming to Him is the true source of illumination. Once we're saved, we are to ignite others by sharing the gospel and performing good works. When we do this, we bring glory to the Lord. Jesus said, "Let your light so shine before men, that they may see your good works and glorify your Father in heaven" (Matt. 5:16). Light and glory are synonymous terms in Scripture.

Biblically, God's glory speaks of the visible manifestation of His moral beauty and perfection. Oftentimes, this presence was displayed by fire or radiant light, like the pillar of fire that lead the Israelites through the wilderness. Jesus embodied God's light. On the Mount of Transfiguration, His disciples saw the brightness of His glory. In the future, the heavenly Jerusalem will have "no need of the sun or of the moon to shine in it, for the glory of God illuminated it. The Lamb is its light" (Rev. 21:23). Obviously, there is nothing little about His light! Today Jesus prays that the Father and Son will glorify each other.

LIFT UP ...

Father, I lift my eyes to You, asking that You be glorified in my life. Help me to spread the gospel that others many know eternal life. Amen.

LOOK AT ...

Yesterday Jesus promised tribulation in the world. However, He also offered his disciples a glorious assurance—that He had overcome that same world.

Today we have the unimaginable privilege of watching as Jesus turns His attention from the disciples to His heavenly Father. We are privy to an intimate conversation as Jesus lifts His eyes toward the heavens in a remarkable example of prayer. From the very start of His earthly ministry, the goal for Jesus' coming was to save mankind, thereby glorifying the Father. We see today that He asks God to pour His glory down so that Jesus can extend the Father's glory. There is such beauty in the reciprocal relationship between the Father and the Son—each seeking to exalt the other. We can learn much from their example. As we exalt Jesus, He will in turn lift us up.

LEARN ABOUT ...

I Gazing

Prayer was generally done standing up. To express deeper devotion, the worshipper sometimes knelt or bowed the head. Hands were usually uplifted toward heaven or in the direction of the Holy of Holies. During penitential prayer, it was usual to strike the breast with the hand and to bend the head toward the bosom.[98]

3 Glory

Glory in Hebrew literally means weight. It carries the idea of adding value or respect to something. It can also portray beauty, honor, and power. Paul wrote to the Corinthians, "For our light affliction, which is but for a moment, is working for us a far more exceeding and eternal weight of glory" (2 Cor. 4:17).

READ JOHN 17:1–2.

Jesus spoke these words, lifted up His eyes to heaven, and said: "Father, the hour has come. Glorify Your Son, that Your Son also may glorify You, as You have given Him authority over all flesh, that He should give eternal life to as many as You have given Him." John 17:1–2

1. Describe the posture Jesus took in prayer.

2. Jesus once again talked about time. Think back to the other references Jesus made to time. How was this different?

3. a. What did Jesus first pray for? How would you put this into your own words?

   b. How do you think this was going be accomplished?

LEARN ABOUT ...

4 Given

The word *give* in its various forms is used seventeen times throughout this prayer. Seven times it refers to believers as a gift from the Father to the Son. We often think of Jesus as the gift God gave to the world (see John 3:16). But in this text we are God's love gift!

---

8 Glorify

"This request for glorification included sustaining Jesus in suffering, accepting His sacrifice, resurrecting Him, and restoring Him to His pristine glory. The purpose of the request was that the Father would be glorified by the Son, that God's wisdom, power, and love might be known through Jesus. Believers too are to glorify God."[99]

---

9 The Gift

A gift is something given to someone else out of one's own possessions. God gave Jesus to save a sinful world. To those who receive Jesus' gift of salvation He gives eternal life. But a gift must not only be offered, it must be accepted: "The gift of God is eternal life in Christ Jesus our Lord" (Rom. 6:23).

4. What had the Father given Jesus authority over?

5. Who would receive eternal life?

6. Jesus made His claim on mankind by revealing that He had come for *all*. Describe what it means to you to know that, as a believer, you are a gift to Jesus.

LIVE OUT...

7. a. During His prayer Jesus lifted His eyes to the Father. Check the positions you have taken in your prayer time.

   ☐ Standing   ☐ Walking   ☐ Prostrate
   ☐ Kneeling   ☐ Bowing   ☐ Sitting
   ☐ Lifting Hands ☐ Lifting Head ☐ Other ___

   b. Choose one of the positions you've rarely or never used in prayer. In that position spend time praying to your heavenly Father. Ask Him to be glorified in your life.

8. So far in today's lesson we've discovered several meanings for the word *glory*, including "to add weight," "to portray beauty," and "to manifest God's holiness." With this in mind, share some ways that you will glorify the Lord.

9. Jesus gives eternal life to those who are given to Him by the Father. According to 1 Timothy 2:3–4, who does God desire to come to the Son?

∘ ∘ • ∘ ∘

Have you ever met someone who is not practicing what they preach? Perhaps you're at a ball game and the drunk guy next to you sees your cross necklace and says, "Hey, I'm a Christian too!" At times like this we're tempted to say, "Please, don't tell anyone else that you're a Christian."

Recently Reuters News Agency reported:

> "A Mexican priest briefly ended up behind bars after punching a policeman who caught him driving drunkenly through the streets of the northern city of Monterrey. Priest Manuel Raul Ortega, who was not wearing clerical dress but was clutching a prayer book when captured, launched himself at the traffic cop who pulled him over earlier this week. 'The individual became very violent because they were going to tow away his car. He attacked a policeman and was taken away,' said transit department spokesman Hector Lozano on Thursday. Ortega's papers identified him as a priest. He was released a few hours after his arrest after paying the fines for his offenses."[100]

The prophet Nathan was jealous for God's glory. The Lord revealed to Nathan that King David had committed adultery with Bathsheba and then murdered her husband. Nathan accused David of despising the Lord's commands. The king's actions diminished God's glory. Nathan said, "By this deed you have given great occasion to the enemies of the LORD to blaspheme" (2 Sam. 12:14). Let's be careful to give God all glory. And let's especially be careful not to take any glory away from the Lord, who we love so much.

LISTEN TO ...

Rejoice, that the immortal God is born, so that mortal man may live in eternity.

—*John Huss*

DAY 5

He's Got the Whole World in His Hands

Composer Hamilton Forrest is remembered for his arrangement of American folksongs, especially "He's Got the Whole World in His Hands." He published this work in 1951 and dedicated it to the famous contralto Marian Anderson. Ms. Anderson once commented that Forrest "provided a piano part that fits the words like a glove." Her powerful rendition of this spiritual often compelled her audience to sing along. Beautiful music is made when accomplished composers and performers merge their talents into a harmonious refrain.

When you ponder the fact that God *has* got the whole world in His hands, it's both inspiring and comforting. Amazingly, though God rules the universe, in John 17 we see Him pray. Witnessing this prayer between Jesus and the Father must have been incredible. Thankfully, the disciples recorded this personal prayer for our benefit. Warren Wiersbe writes that this prayer "is certainly the 'holy of holies' of the Gospel record, and we must approach this chapter in a spirit of humility and worship."[101]

You can't help but ask yourself, "What did the Lord pray for and for whom?" Surprisingly, He started by praying for Himself. He prayed that God would be glorified in His finished work. Then He interceded on behalf of His disciples by asking that God would keep them safe and set them apart. He concluded His prayer by praying for you and me. He asked that one day we would be with Him and share His glory. Since Jesus, who is God, needed to pray, how much more do we? As you study this prayer, why not join in and make it your own? Remember, He's got the whole world in His hands. Hands that were locked together in prayer.

LIFT UP ...

Father, thank You for sending Your Son so I would know You, the one true God. Help me to finish the work You have for me to do on this earth. Amen.

LOOK AT ...

Yesterday we saw the beautiful heart of the Godhead as they unselfishly desired to bring glory, one to another. Jesus sought to exalt the Father, and in return the Father would lift up His Son. Jesus continued in what we could call the *real* Lord's Prayer. After all, it is the Lord who is praying. We've shared that this prayer is threefold: 1) for Himself; 2) for the disciples; 3) for those who would come to Christ because of their witness. It is interesting to note that the smallest portion of this request is Christ praying for Himself. Most of the prayer focuses on others. This is a wonderful example to follow. Too often we obsess about ourselves rather than concentrating on others. Yet Jesus, on the eve of His greatest trial and temptation, kept His sight on those He loved. And amazingly, while focusing on others, He was able to say, "I have finished the work you have given me to do."

Are you focusing on the work God wants to do in your life? It may not be all about you! Imagine the glory returned to you when you stand before the throne and say, "I have completed Your work."

LEARN ABOUT ...

2 Eternal Life

Eternal life is an intimate, personal relationship that is continuous and dynamic. The word *know* is often used in the Greek to describe the intimacy of a sexual relationship. Thus a person who knows God has an intimate personal relationship with Him. And that relationship is eternal, not temporal.[102]

READ JOHN 17:3–5.

"And this is eternal life, that they may know You, the only true God, and Jesus Christ whom You have sent. I have glorified You on the earth. I have finished the work which You have given Me to do. And now, O Father, glorify Me together with Yourself, with the glory which I had with You before the world was." John 17:3–5

1. This portion of Scripture begins with the word *and*. Look back at yesterday's lesson to connect what Jesus is talking about.

2. How did Jesus define eternal life? How does this differ from your previously held beliefs?

LEARN ABOUT ...

4 Finished Work

Although Christ's works included His entire earthly ministry, the work He refers to is our salvation in the finished work of the cross. Even though the cross was yet in the future, it was in Christ's mind and was a certainty—a done deal. "He said, 'It is finished!' And bowing His head, He gave up His spirit" (John 19:30).

6 Previous Glory

Glory is repeated eight times in this prayer. This verse refers to His preincarnate glory that He shared with the Father before He was born to die. "When the Son of Man comes in His glory, and all the holy angels with Him, then He will sit on the throne of His glory" (Matt. 25:31).

7 Life Eternal

Eternal life is not just quantity of years but quality of life. It is not merely endless existence, for this is something all humans will possess. All humans will live eternally, but where they will live eternally is the question. Jesus promised that eternal life starts in the present: "I have come that they may have life, and that they may have it more abundantly" (John 10:10).

3. Jesus said He had glorified God on earth. Based on what you've learned so far, explain how He had done this.

4. What did Jesus report about the work He had been given to do?

5. Based on Jesus' requests, how would you describe the relationship between the Father and Son? What did they seek to do?

6. Jesus speaks of a glory before the world was formed. Read Isaiah 6:1–5 and describe His glory in your own words.

LIVE OUT...

7. We've learned that eternal life is a free gift in which we enter into an intimate relationship with God. Fill in the following chart to discover more about eternal life.

SCRIPTURE	ETERNAL LIFE
John 3:15–16	
John 10:27–28	
1 Timothy 6:12	
1 John 5:11–13	

8. Jesus could say at the end of His life, "It is finished." Paul, too, could say "I have finished the race, I have kept the faith" (2 Tim. 4:7). Journal about the work God has given you to do. What can you do to be about the Father's business in your daily routine?

9. Jesus referred to the many facets of glory—from His works that added value to the Father's name, to the glory of God's holiness. Today He spoke of His preincarnate glory.

   a. Jesus was the cocreator (see Col. 1:16). What prerogatives of glory do you think He laid aside at His incarnation?

   b. Jesus is the exact image of God, expressing the brightness of God's glory (see Heb. 1:1–3). Explain how approaching God in the Old Testament differed from approaching Jesus in the New Testament. What do you think made this possible?

LEARN ABOUT …

8 Finish the Work

Jesus said that He finished His Father's work. Yet there were still broken people to be healed, sinners to be saved, and disciples to be called. How is His work completed? Through His body, the church. One day we'll hear the Father say: "Well done, good and faithful servant" (Matt. 25:21).

∘ ∘ • ∘ ∘

Everybody has someone on their Christmas list for whom buying a gift is harder than winning the lottery. Some make the task impossible because they already have everything. Often this includes our parents, who have begun offloading their belongings to future generations. Others are tricky because they are so picky. You know the type. Inevitably you'll pick out the wrong color, the off-brand, or something that just doesn't fit. Then there are those who claim, "I don't need anything, just give me a card. Your phone call is all I need." Sure … right. On Christmas morning they watch everyone else open presents—that just doesn't seem right, does it? Don't they understand that giving is a joy?

Gifts are an expression of love. Gifts likely started in the heart of God, who has been a gift giver from the beginning: "For God so loved the world that He *gave*" (John 3:16, emphasis added). When God desired to give His Son the perfect gift, what did He choose? Companionship. It came in the form of a people to call His very own—the church. This includes you and me! This is the gift that kept on giving, for our gift was wrapped up in Him—because He loved, we are loved. And since Jesus is the eternal God, He imparts to His bride eternal life. And unlike unwanted or ill-fitting Christmas gifts, we'll never need to exchange it for something else. It's a perfect fit!

LISTEN TO ...

God, I pray Thee, light these idle sticks of my life, that I may burn for Thee. Consume my life, my God, for it is Thine. I seek not a long life, but a full one, like You, Lord Jesus.

—Jim Elliot

Band of Brothers
John 17:6-19

One of the themes flowing through the Bible is warfare. Some of the earliest Scripture accounts describe war between the worldly and the godly. Cain slew Abel in a fit of jealousy over God's accepting Abel's sacrifice. When God asked Cain where his brother was, Cain replied, "I do not know. Am I my brother's keeper?" (Gen. 4:9). King Chedolemaer invaded Canaan with his allies and kidnapped Lot. Abraham came to his nephew's rescue, waging war against five kings. Abraham took it personally when outsiders interfered with his family. The Bible is rife with war and peace; alliances and broken promises; love and hate. The history of humanity has been called a time of war during which nations sometimes stop to reload their weapons. As believers, our hope is that one day the Prince of Peace will come to put an end to all wars.

Perhaps nothing draws men closer together than uniting together to face great danger. In William Shakespeare's *Henry V*, the English troops prepare for battle against the French at Agincourt. King Henry rallies the troops by urging them on to victory. One line from this speech has struck a chord in the hearts of warriors for generations:

> From this day to the ending of the world,
> But we in it shall be remembered—
> We few, we happy few, we band of brothers.

Jesus would soon leave His beloved disciples to face battles alone in the world. They would become a band of brothers united in a common goal to fight a common enemy. So Jesus prayed fervently for this group of men in the short time He had left. His prayer has been remembered as one of the most poignant and perfect prayers ever offered.

Day 1 John 17:6–7   **THE LEADER**

Day 2 John 17:8–10   **THE LORD**

Day 3 John 17:11–13   **THE LEAVING**

Day 4 John 17:14–16   **LEFT BEHIND**

Day 5 John 17:17–19   **LAUNCHED OUT**

DAY 1
The Leader

LIFT UP ...

Lord, thank You for sending Your Son to the world. Help me to keep Your Word and to continually grow in the grace and knowledge of the truth. Amen.

LOOK AT ...

Last week we saw Jesus as He began praying to the Father. The first part of this prayer, also known as the High Priestly Prayer, was personal. How refreshing to know that God *does* want to hear what is on our hearts and longs to hear our requests. Jesus, the Sovereign Leader, prayed to the Father for the things His disciples would need. He acknowledged that all the things they received had been given from the Father through the Son. He prayed they would stick together and fight any dissension that could deter them from spreading the gospel message. Then He prayed that God would supernaturally empower them to face what would happen in the future. He also prayed that they would be secure. Prior to this, most spiritual attacks had been directed at Jesus. Now the Enemy would turn his attention to the disciples. Last He prayed for their spiritual purity. Though Jesus prayed for the Eleven, His words apply to all believers. As you study this week, ask God to remind you that everything you have comes from Him. Ask for His power to fortify you from within, to unify your relationships with those in the church, and to make you holy. When you do, you'll find strength you never knew you had.

READ JOHN 17:6–7.

"I have manifested Your name to the men whom You have given Me out of the world. They were Yours, You gave them to Me, and they have kept Your word. Now they have known that all things which You have given Me are from You." John 17:6–7

1. On Day 5 of Lesson Eight, Jesus began this prayer. Let's look back in order to move

LEARN ABOUT ...

3 Manifested

In ancient times a name represented the nature of a person. To manifest means to plainly show, to make visible, or to shine. On earth Jesus revealed the Father's character to the disciples. Through His life, words, and works, Jesus shone forth the very essence of the Father. Jesus said, "He who has seen Me has seen the Father" (John 14:9).

4 Obeyed

The disciples were separated from the world through the electing work of the Father. They responded in faith to God's message of salvation through Christ. This is the only place where people are said to have kept God's word in contrast to being commanded to keep His commands.

5 Things Given

The word *things* can refer to words, business, or the whole of everything. It seems that Jesus was saying that His entire ministry, everything He had been doing, was of divine origin; springing from the Father. Leon Morris wrote, "What is central is that all we see in Him is of God."[103]

forward. Review verse 5 and describe what Jesus prayed.

2. a. Now let's turn to Jesus' prayer for His disciples in verses 6–7. How many times did Jesus use the pronoun "You" (or a variation) in referring to the Father?

b. How many times did He speak of "the men," "they," or "them"?

c. As you see Jesus link the Father and the disciples in this prayer, what do you learn about the disciples' connection with the Father?

3. What do you think it means that Jesus manifested the Father's name to the disciples?

4. Jesus said that God gave the men to Jesus. From where had they come and what had they kept?

5. Explain what the disciples now knew.

6. Based on your knowledge of Scripture, talk about some of the things the Father had given the Son.

LIVE OUT...

7. In this prayer, Jesus reminded His Father that He had manifested the Father's name to the men God had given Him.

a. According to 1 John 3:5–8, what two things did Jesus accomplish by being manifest?

b. According 1 John 4:9, how did God manifest His love toward us?

c. How do you know you have embraced this manifestation of God's love?

8. a. Jesus prayed about how the disciples had been given to Him from "out of the world." On the left side of the globe below, describe what you've learned about "the world" from our study in the upper room.

b. On the right side of the globe, describe some of the worldly things you'd like to be taken "out of."

c. Below the globe, journal a prayer asking the Father to supernaturally empower you to be "in the world" but not "of the world."

9. Among the "things" given by the Father to the Son were the disciples. Talk about some of the people God has given to you and how you are encouraging them to keep God's Word.

° ° • ° °

What are some of the best gifts you've ever received? As a child you probably received dolls, stuffed animals, and other toys for birthdays and Christmas. As you grew up, maybe you began to receive more "grown-up" presents like clothing, TVs, and music equipment. Some of us may have received elaborate gifts like jewelry and cars.

LEARN ABOUT ...

7 Love Given

Through perfect love and absolute obedience, Jesus was made manifest in order to manifest God's love for the world. He willingly offered Himself as the perfect sacrifice in order to pay the price for the sins of the world: "He has appeared to put away sin by the sacrifice of Himself" (Heb. 9:26).

---

9 People Given

It's been said that we cannot take possessions with us to heaven, only people. As followers of Christ, it is our responsibility to follow in the footsteps of the disciples who carried the good news of the gospel to the world. "Preach the word! Be ready in season and out of season" (2 Tim. 4:2).

But no one is a greater gift giver than our heavenly Father. He is not consigned to giving us temporal gifts. His gifts are eternal: life unending, joy unfolding, peace unsurpassed, and love unfathomable. James wrote, "Every good gift and every perfect gift is from above, and comes down from the Father of lights, with whom there is no variation or shadow of turning" (James 1:17). Did you catch that? *Every* good gift comes from above. The amazing truth is that everything we have comes from the Father.

We saw today that our Father gave to Jesus the gift of people. What a precious gift—it should not be overlooked. He also modeled another gift—the gift of prayer. Jesus' death on the cross accomplished a divine purpose. Paul tells us in Ephesians 2:14 that "He … has broken down the middle wall of separation" that once stood between sinful people and holy God. Now we have access to the Father. We can go to Him in prayer without an intermediary. Thank God for His marvelous gifts!

LISTEN TO …

God is so good that he only awaits our desire to overwhelm us with the gift of himself.

—*François Fénelon*

DAY 2

The Lord

In 1798 Rear Admiral Sir Horatio Nelson formed his own band of brothers as he pursued the French expeditionary force led by Napoleon Bonaparte to Egypt. The mission was long and difficult. It often seemed doomed for failure, but Nelson was an inspiration to the fleet.

The decisive battle occurred on the Nile when the fleet found the French anchored in Abu Qir Bay. Recognizing an opportunity, Nelson ordered an attack. Without forming a battle line, the fleet worked with amazing teamwork, flair, and military skill throughout the unfolding situation. By the end of the battle eleven of thirteen French battleships had been taken, sunk, or burned. Nelson became a national hero. In a conversation with Admiral Lord Howe, who questioned the actions of some of the participants in the battle, Nelson said, "I had the happiness to command a Band of Brothers." On August 3 the surviving captains commissioned a sword and a portrait of Nelson as "proof of their esteem" for his "prompt decision and intrepid conduct." Nelson responded by stressing that "the conduct of every officer was equal."[104]

Jesus, our Lord and Savior, willingly deprived Himself of the glories of heaven as He "did not consider it robbery to be equal with God" (Phil. 2:6). However, in this portion of the prayer, Jesus reveals that He is, indeed, equal with the Father—He is the Lord who deserves glory and honor.

LIFT UP ...

It's amazing to me, Lord, that You would pray for Your people. I praise You that You have given me an Advocate to stand beside the Father and intercede on my behalf. Help me to pray for those who need it as well. Amen.

LOOK AT ...

The disciples must have been fascinated to listen in as Jesus prayed to the Father on their behalf. We've heard how God gave the disciples to Jesus and how the disciples understood

LEARN ABOUT …

2 Caught

To receive means to seize, to catch, or to obtain. Jesus heard truth from the Father. In turn, the Son passed truth to the disciples. They would then pass the truth to anyone willing to grab hold of it. Some say that ministry is caught not taught. Have you caught it? Will you pass it on?

---

4 Called

At this time Jesus was not praying for the world. Rather, He was praying for those He was sending into the world. This does not mean that it is inappropriate to pray for the world: "God so loved the world that He gave His only begotten Son, that whoever believes in Him should not perish but have everlasting life" (John 3:16).

that all things came from the Father. This prayer must have given them greater insight into the Father and Son's relationship. Now we'll see Jesus remark on the steps the disciples had already taken toward faith: revelation and response.

These two steps are key to every believer's experience, not just at salvation but as we grow in the faith. When we hear God's Word, we must make a decision to *do* something with what we know. Jesus knew that the disciples had responded in faith. But this is not a once-and-for-all experience. God's Word continues to speak to us throughout our lives, helping us to grow and change. Today and every day let God's Word reveal new insights to your heart and make a conscious choice to respond.

READ JOHN 17:8–10.

"For I have given to them the words which You have given Me; and they have received them, and have known surely that I came forth from You; and they have believed that You sent Me. I pray for them. I do not pray for the world but for those whom You have given Me, for they are Yours. And all Mine are Yours, and Yours are Mine, and I am glorified in them." John 17:8–10

1. Describe what Jesus had given to the disciples. What does this tell you about His relationship with the Father?

2. Jesus said the disciples "have received" God's words—it was something they'd already done at the time of the prayer. Describe the process the disciples underwent upon receiving God's words.

3. How have you followed this process in your journey of faith?

4. a. Who did Jesus pray for, and who did He not pray for? Why?

b. Do you think this means He never prayed for the world? Please explain.

5. In this passage Jesus talked about "Yours" and "Mine." Explain how this dynamic seems to work between the Father and Son.

6. How is Jesus glorified?

LIVE OUT...

7. Today we saw that believing in God and growing in the faith involves a process of revelation and response. Describe how you are following this path in order to grow in the faith. If you have fallen behind, write about how you will move forward in your faith.

I hear God's words when ...

I have received God's Word about ...(name a specific instance God is speaking to you about. You don't have to share this with your small group if you don't feel comfortable.)

I know that God wants me to ...

8. Today Jesus prayed not for the world but for those disciples He was sending into the world. Journal a prayer for the people God has sent to disciple you in the faith. When you see them, say an encouraging word for the work they do for God's kingdom.

9. a. Jesus remarked that He would be glorified through the disciples. Fill in the following chart to discover how we can glorify Him.

LEARN ABOUT ...

5 Connected

The Father and Son are intimately connected as one in essence. Though they are two distinct persons, they are uniquely unified and exhibit an inexhaustible oneness. God the Father and God the Son are coequal in power and glory. Each willingly defers to the other. Jesus said it very simply, "I and My Father are one" (John 10:30).

7 Receive and Respond

God speaks to us through His Word, His Holy Spirit, godly people, and circumstances. When you spend time in His Word, you can trust that you will hear His "still small voice" guiding you (1 Kings 19:12). Make sure you are receiving God's truth and responding accordingly. Scripture confirms Scripture, so look for cross-references for confirmation.

8 Pray and Say

A disciple is a student, learner, or pupil. In the Bible the word is used most often to refer to a follower of Jesus. It is sometimes used in a more specific way to indicate Jesus' twelve apostles.[105] Jesus said, "It is enough for a disciple that he be like his teacher" (Matt. 10:25).

SCRIPTURE	HOW TO GLORIFY GOD
Romans 15:9	
1 Corinthians 6:18–20	
2 Corinthians 9:12–13	
1 Peter 2:11–12	
1 Peter 4:16	

b. In what ways would you like to glorify God more?

○ ○ ● ○ ○

One of the earmarks of a disciple is being like Jesus. Throughout His public ministry, Jesus exhibited two key characteristics: He prayed and He interacted with people. We can follow His lead. Jesus maintained consistent communication with His Father. He set aside time to pray and also spontaneously prayed during the course of the day. For instance, Jesus rose "a long while before daylight … went out and departed to a solitary place; and there He prayed" (Mark 1:35). Though He was equal with God, He burst into thanksgiving when Lazarus was raised from the dead, saying, "Father, I thank You that You have heard Me" (John 11:41). From the cross, Jesus offered a heartfelt prayer for those who persecuted Him: "Father, forgive them, for they do not know what they do" (Luke 23:34). What a wonderful example He left us to follow.

Jesus was also a people person. He walked among them telling stories and breaking down barriers. Jesus told the disciples to go into the world and make disciples just as He had done. You don't have to be a preacher or an evangelist to talk about Jesus. You simply need to be able to tell a good story. There are three types of stories you can tell: 1) God's stories. Tell others the stories you have learned from the Bible. These are the greatest stories ever told. 2) Your stories. Talking about your experiences before and after meeting Christ can have a powerful effect on the people you meet. 3) Others' stories. Relate how television, movies, and current events correlate (or not) with scriptural truth.[106] When you pray and move among people with the message of God's love, you'll have an amazing impact for the kingdom of God.

LISTEN TO ...

Salvation is free, but discipleship costs everything we have.

—Billy Graham

DAY 3

The Leaving

"United We Stand" unfurled across the United States in 1942 as a campaign adopted by magazines nationwide who agreed to feature the American flag on their covers. Nearly five hundred publications waved the Stars and Stripes to display the nation's solidarity in the shadow of World War II. Their goal, inspired by the National Publishers Association and the U.S. Treasury Department, was to promote national unity, rally support for the troops through war bonds, and celebrate Independence Day. The magazines brought home a message of patriotism and ideals worth fighting for. "United We Stand" originated from a verse of a 1768 patriotic ballad—"The Liberty Song" by John Dickinson: "Then join hand in hand, brave America all, by uniting we stand, by dividing we fall."[107]

During His prayer in the upper room, Jesus prayed that His disciples would be one as He and the Father were one. Because Jesus would be leaving the world, His disciples would be His ambassadors. The persecution that He faced would now be turned upon them. Therefore, it would be important for them to stand strong and united. The unity they were to promote would be patterned after that of the Father and the Son. It would be evidenced in their will and purpose to glorify the Son. Unity finds its root in a common good beyond that of the individual. Division springs from selfish ambition. Have you made your pledge of allegiance to God's kingdom and glory, or do you selfishly stand aside? When you seek first God's kingdom, you are an ambassador of hope.

LIFT UP ...

You give us joy unspeakable, Holy Father. You fulfill your Word, just as You promised. You are the giver of all good gifts. You bless us and keep us. We cannot praise You enough for all that You do for us. Amen.

LOOK AT ...

Yesterday, Jesus affirmed in His prayer that the disciples had received His words, which sprang from the Father's heart. They accepted these words wholeheartedly by believing that Jesus was the Christ. These words inspire people to accept Jesus as their personal Lord and Savior and to go make disciples of other people.

Now we see Jesus turn His prayer toward unity and protection. The safety of the disciples was a major concern to the Savior. It's important to note that the manner of protection was divine rather than human. Because the disciples were a gift from the Father to the Son, they had been handed over from one set of heavenly hands to another. Jesus affirmed that He had kept them throughout His tenure on earth. In His absence He would pass their safekeeping back to God through the power of His name. Solomon wrote that "The name of the LORD is a strong tower; The righteous run to it and are safe" (Prov. 18:10). Do you ever feel vulnerable or insecure? Where do you turn for security? Take comfort in knowing that you are His special treasure tucked away for safekeeping. His name provides a strong fortress.

READ JOHN 17:11–13.

"Now I am no longer in the world, but these are in the world, and I come to You. Holy Father, keep through Your name those whom You have given Me, that they may be one as We are. While I was with them in the world, I kept them in Your name. Those whom You gave Me I have kept; and none of them is lost except the son of perdition, that the Scripture might be fulfilled. But now I come to You, and these things I speak in the world, that they may have My joy fulfilled in themselves." John 17:11–13

1. Though Jesus was physically on earth, how did He view Himself now? Why do you think this was so?

2. We see Jesus revisit one of the major themes in the Upper Room Discourse: "the world." Circle each use of this phrase in the text. Based on what you've learned, what are the various meanings for "the world"?

3. a. Look for two other repeated words in Jesus' prayer. Underline them and record your finding here.

LEARN ABOUT ...

3 Keep Safely

Keep means to preserve, defend, sustain in trials, and save from apostasy.[108] God can keep you from fights on the outside as well as flaws on the inside. "Now to Him who is able to keep you from stumbling, And to present you faultless Before the presence of His glory with exceeding joy" (Jude 24).

4 Holy Father

When Jesus referred to God as "Holy Father," He made a distinction between sinful creatures and the spotless Creator. Believers are also called to holiness, implying separation from the world. They find protection from the sin and enmity of the world through the power of His name.

5 Son of Perdition

This term refers to Judas Iscariot. John Walvoord wrote, "Judas did what he wanted (he sold Jesus). Yet he was an unwitting tool of Satan. Even people's volitionally free acts fit into God's sovereign plan. Thus Judas' betrayal of Jesus fulfilled the words in Psalm 41:9 about David's betrayal by his friend."[109]

b. In your own words describe what He prayed for the disciples.

4. Describe the type of intimacy Jesus enjoyed with the Father and prayed that His church would enjoy too. What earthly relationship does this resemble?

5. Explain why the son of perdition was lost.

6. As Jesus prayed about coming to the Father, where did He speak and why?

7. When Jesus prayed about "these things," what do you think He was talking about?

LIVE OUT...

8. a. Jesus described His Father as holy. The word *holy* means separate from others or venerated (exalted) in worship. Write about the ways you can separate (differentiate) your relationship with God from all others.

b. Now spend time exalting the Lord in worship. Lift up His holy name!

9. a. Jesus promised to safeguard His disciples in His name. Place a check in the boxes that describe some of the things that have made you feel secure.

☐ Legal System   ☐ Shelter   ☐ Numbers of people

☐ Finances   ☐ Armed Forces   ☐ Drugs

☐ Relationships   ☐ Weapons   ☐ Other _____

b. Rewrite the following verses into a personal prayer for safety. "Some trust in chariots, and some in horses; But we will remember the name of the LORD our God. They have bowed down and fallen; But we have risen and stand upright" (Ps. 20:7–8).

10. a. Jesus prayed that the disciples would be one, united with God and one another. Read Ephesians 4:1–6. Describe the walk that is worthy of the Lord according to verses 1–2.

b. How can believers maintain unity (see v. 3)?

c. Note the repeated word *one* in this text. List all of the things Christians have in common.

d. Do you experience the unity Paul spoke of? What will you do to foster more unity among your fellow believers?

° ° • ° °

Some missionaries in the Philippines set up a croquet game in their front yard. Several of their Agta Negrito neighbors became interested and wanted to join the fun. The missionaries started the game, each with a mallet and ball. As the game progressed, the opportunity came for one of the players to take advantage of the other by knocking the opponent's ball out of the court. A missionary explained the procedure, but his advice only puzzled the Negrito friend. "Why would I want to knock his ball out of the court?" he asked. "So you will be the one to win!" a missionary said. The short-statured man, clad only in a loincloth, shook his head in bewilderment. Competition is generally ruled out in a hunting and gathering society, where people survive not by competing but by sharing equally in every activity.

LEARN ABOUT …

8 Perfect Holiness

God calls His followers to "be holy, for I am holy" (1 Peter 1:16). *Holy* and *perfect* are synonymous terms. With holiness "character is in view, perfect in the case of the Lord, growing toward perfection for the Christian. Love is the means God uses to develop the likeness of Christ in His children (see 1 Thes. 3:12–13)."[110]

10 Unity

Unity literally means one. This number is indivisible. It describes the harmony of the Trinity as our example. For the church it portrays oneness of belief, affection, and behavior. "Unity of the Spirit" portrays Jesus and the saints in whom the same Spirit dwells. They have the same disposition and aims.[111]

The game continued, but no one followed the advice to knock their opponent's ball out. When a player successfully got through all the wickets, the game was not over for him. He went back and helped his friends. As the final player moved toward the last wicket, the play was very much a team effort. When the last shot was made, the Agta Negrito "team" shouted happily, "We won! We won!" Isn't that how the church, the body of Christ, should be? We're a team—we all win together.[112]

LISTEN TO ...

There can be no unity, no delight of love, no harmony, no good in being, where there is but one. Two at least are needed for oneness.

—*George MacDonald*

DAY 4

Left Behind

On December 26, 2004, an earthquake in the Indian Ocean triggered a series of tsunamis that devastated the coastlands across Southeast Asia. Almost 230,000 people were lost in this natural disaster. Amazingly, an American woman survived the powerful tsunami. Here's what CNN reported:

> Faye Wachs, 34, was diving with her husband, Eugene Kim, Sunday morning off Ko Phi Phi Island in Thailand when they noticed the water visibility worsened and felt as though they were being sucked downward, Helen Wachs said. Their dive master signaled to them to surface, "but we still didn't know what happened," Faye wrote in an e-mail to her mother Tuesday. The enormity of what was happening while they were scuba diving was not immediately apparent after they surfaced, Helen Wachs said her daughter told her. "She said she saw a lot of trash in the water. The dive master said it was really rude for people to throw trash. Then they saw large bits of debris and thought there might have been a boat crash," Helen Wachs said. She said her daughter didn't know what had happened until the dive master got a text message from his wife telling him about the catastrophe.[13]

The tsunami wave released more than twice the total explosive energy used during all of World War II (including the two atomic bombs).[14] Yet Faye Wachs was completely unaware of the destructive power unleashed above her. She was kept safe from the storm.

In a figurative sense, Jesus prayed that as believers we be like Faye Wachs. Wouldn't it be lovely to so submerge ourselves in Christ, that when the tsunamis of life hit hard we are not swayed? That's what it could mean to be *in* the world but not *of* the world.

LIFT UP ...

Father, we know that the world hated You before it hated us. Help us to stay strong despite the way others may feel about us. In Your Son's name I pray. Amen.

LEARN ABOUT ...

1 The Word's Power

One reason the world hates believers is because the Word exposes how dark and dangerous the world and the prince of the world really are. The Word offers enlightenment about a better way to go: "Your word is a lamp to my feet And a light to my path" (Ps. 119:105).

3 Not of this World

Jesus was not of this world, because He was of divine origin—He was conceived by the Holy Spirit (see Matt. 1:20). The disciples were also not of the world, because they had been born again into the kingdom of God. In this state, they could consider that their "citizenship is in heaven" (Phil. 3:20).

LOOK AT ...

Yesterday we saw that unity among the disciples was dear to Christ's heart. He prayed that this unity would bring them great joy. Today we see that they would need to be unified, because following Christ would bring hatred from the world. It's important to remember that Jesus was not referring to the physical world: the grass, flowers, trees, oceans, rivers, and plains. After all, God created the world for us to inhabit. The psalmist said, "The earth is the LORD's, and all its fullness, The world and those who dwell therein" (Ps. 24:1).

Clearly, God is also not talking about the people who inhabit the earth either. The world referred to by Christ is the "morals, standards, ideas, and principles that are opposed to God.... The *world* in this sense is the system of ideas, activities, and people ruled by the ethics of Satan, who is called the 'god of this evil world' (2 Cor. 4:4)."[115] Jesus prayed that the disciples who would be left behind in the world be protected from the Evil One. You need not fear the Evil One either. Jesus "is even at the right hand of God, who also makes intercession for us" (Rom. 8:34).

READ JOHN 17:14–16.

"I have given them Your word; and the world has hated them because they are not of the world, just as I am not of the world. I do not pray that You should take them out of the world, but that You should keep them from the evil one. They are not of the world, just as I am not of the world." John 17:14–16

1. What had Jesus given the disciples?

2. How did the world feel about the disciples and why?

3. How did Jesus relate this to Himself?

4. Because of this, what did He not pray for them?

5. a. What did He pray for them?

   b. How do you think they might have felt upon hearing this prayer?

6. a. What point about the disciples and the world did Jesus reiterate?

   b. Why do you think He made a point to say this again?

LIVE OUT...

7. a. We've seen that the world hates believers because the Word exposes the world's darkness. Read Romans 12:1–2 and describe how believers can live differently from the world.

   b. What will you accomplish when you live this way?

8. Believers are considered to be "in" this world but not "of" this world. This is an important concept in the Upper Room Discourse (and throughout Scripture).

   a. What city, state, and country are you a citizen of now?

   b. Have you ever changed residences? How did you feel when you moved? Did you feel like you were "in" one place but not "of" that place?

   c. Now relate those feelings to your experience with Jesus Christ. How did it feel when you became a Christian? Did it feel

LEARN ABOUT ...

5 The World's Leader

The phrase "the evil one" depicts Satan's fundamental nature. He opposes God's plans and seeks to exalt himself above God. He is the source of all evil and wickedness. He is also known as *the adversary, the accuser, Beelzebub,* and *the Devil.* He is a real, created being but is in no way God's equal.

7 Transformation

Transform comes from the Greek word *metamorphoo,* which means "to change or transfigure." As followers of Christ, we should not be conformed, either inwardly or outwardly, to the philosophies, principles, and practices of a fallen world. Believers can renew their minds through prayer and the study of God's Word in the power of the Holy Spirit.[116]

8 Citizenship

Citizenship contains certain rights and privileges. It also carries the idea of certain duties. As citizens of heaven, we have the right to approach our heavenly Father in prayer. We will one day live with Him in a heavenly home. We have been saved by grace. But our Lord expects us to keep His commands and keep away from the world.

foreign to you, or were you raised in the church? Does your citizenship in heaven seem like a distant country or a near reality? Please elaborate.

9. a. We saw that "the Evil One" opposes the kingdom of God and that Jesus prayed to protect believers from him. Have you ever given the Evil One more credit than he is due? If so, please give an example.

    b. Have you ever overlooked his influence in the world? If so, what happened when you did?

○ ○ ● ○ ○

Christians have a powerful Enemy but an even more powerful God. God has given us great weapons to use against this Enemy—the Word of God and prayer. Paul explained that "the sword of the Spirit ... is the word of God" (Eph. 6:17). Following His baptism, Jesus went to the wilderness and was tempted by the Evil One. Satan tempted Jesus to take the easy way—the worldly way—so that Jesus would lose the battle against the adversary. Satan even twisted Scripture to entice Jesus to take the throne of the world without going the way of the cross. In essence, Satan tempted Jesus to forsake His role as Messiah. But Jesus knew the power of God's Word. Each time Satan tempted Him, Jesus defended Himself with Scripture. When Satan enticed Jesus to turn the stones into bread, Jesus said, "It is written, 'Man shall not live by bread alone, but by every word that proceeds from the mouth of God.'" (Matt. 4:4). When the Evil One tried to get Jesus to prove He had power over angels by throwing Himself off the temple, Jesus said, "It is also written: 'Do not put the Lord your God to the test.'" (Matt. 4:7 NIV). When the Devil offered Jesus the kingdoms of the world if Jesus would bow down to him, Jesus replied, "Away with you, Satan! For it is written, 'You shall worship the LORD your God, and Him only you shall serve.'" (Matt. 4:10). Are you feeling under attack? Let God's Word come to your defense!

LISTEN TO ...

I believe Satan to exist for two reasons: first, the Bible says so; and second, I've done business with him.

—*Dwight Lyman Moody*

DAY 5

ℓaunched Out

Since NASA was founded in 1958, space flight has become a commonplace occurrence. Men have walked on the moon, more than six hundred people have ventured into space, and space shuttles take off and land on a regular basis, docking with the International Space Station. Thousands are employed around the world in pursuit of a mission: to pioneer the future in space exploration, scientific discovery, and aeronautics research. How did it begin?

Robert Goddard loved rockets. On March 16, 1926, on his aunt Effie's farm, Goddard and an assistant launched the world's first successful rocket. It rose forty-one feet in the air then plummeted into a frozen cabbage patch 184 feet from the launchpad. Goddard continued to build bigger and bigger rockets, known as Nells. Goddard's rockets led to the design of the Saturn moon rockets and indirectly to every other rocket flown by the United States. From such small beginnings an entire industry was launched.[117]

Anyone watching Jesus the last evening before His death might not have thought He was a success story. He had only a ragtag group of male followers and a small group of women who remained loyal. Following His crucifixion, the men ran and a few women went to the tomb to dress His body. But through this small group of men and women, Jesus launched a mission to change the world one heart at a time.

LIFT UP ...

You are a holy God, perfect and set apart in every way. Help us to be a holy people, set apart for Your service. Sanctify us with Your Word as we seek to serve You with our lives. Amen.

LOOK AT ...

Jesus prayed for the disciples to be protected by God's Word as they lived in the world and endured the enmity of the Evil One. Now we'll see Him pray that they be purified by the

Word as they were launched out into the world. In other words, they were being sent out to do what they had been taught. Jesus did not want the disciples to hole up in a monastery or keep to themselves. He wanted them to go out among the people to live lives different from the world. This was both a challenge and a privilege. They were called by Christ to live as Christ lived. They had been given a template to follow: the Word of God. Just as no two snowflakes are exactly the same, God does not expect Christians to be exactly the same. But He does call us to seek the same goal: "To be conformed to the image of His Son" (Rom. 8:29). Are you growing more like Christ every day?

READ JOHN 17:17–19.

"Sanctify them by Your truth. Your word is truth. As You sent Me into the world, I also have sent them into the world. And for their sakes I sanctify Myself, that they also may be sanctified by the truth." John 17:17–19

1. What did Jesus ask God to do for the disciples and how?

2. According to this passage, what is truth?

3. Who sent Jesus into the world?

4. a. Now who was Jesus sending into the world?

   b. How do you think this cycle can be carried on continuously?

5. Explain why Jesus sanctified Himself.

6. How would the disciples be sanctified?

LEARN ABOUT …

1 Sanctified

To be sanctified is to be made holy, separated from the secular world for a sacred purpose. The believer is separated from sin and becomes dedicated to God's righteousness. Sanctification is accomplished by the Word of God (see John 17:17) and the Holy Spirit (see Rom. 8:3–4). Sanctification results in holiness and purification from the guilt and power of sin.[118]

4 Sent

In this prayer, Jesus was looking forward to the time when He would send the disciples out into the world in the power of the Holy Spirit. According to the Great Commission, Jesus instructed the disciples to "be witnesses to Me in Jerusalem, and in all Judea and Samaria, and to the end of the earth" (Acts 1:8).

5 Set Apart

Jesus was sanctified in that He had a special work to do on earth. He was the pure and perfect "Lamb of God who takes away the sin of the world!" (John 1:29). He did not need to *become* holy, for He embodied holiness. Nevertheless, He set Himself apart to do the Father's will and die on the cross.

LEARN ABOUT ...

7 Holiness

Growing into God's likeness and being set apart for His use is prominent throughout the Bible. Like Jesus, the apostles taught that sanctification (true holiness) expresses itself in growing love and service. Warren Wiersbe said, "As you grow in the faith ... you love sin less and you love God more."[119]

---

9 True Sanctification

We need the Son of God, the Word of God, and the Spirit of God, for true sanctification is personified in Jesus Christ as the ideal for humanity; He is the Word made flesh who expresses truth; the Holy Spirit is the Spirit of truth whose function is to guide all into truth.[120]

LIVE OUT...

7. a. Believers bear personal responsibility in the process of sanctification. Fill in the following chart to learn what you can do to become set apart from the world.

SCRIPTURE	HOW WE ARE SANCTIFIED
Acts 26:18	
1 Thessalonians 4:3	
1 Peter 1:15	

   b. In what ways do you sense that God is sanctifying you?

8. The disciples were sanctified and sent to Jerusalem, Judea, Samaria, and the ends of the earth. Journal a prayer asking God to empower you to witness for Him wherever you go, whether it's your neighborhood, out of town, or to a foreign location.

9. Today we learned that the Word is truth. According to the following verses, what else is truth?

   John 14:6

   1 John 5:6

   ° ° • ° °

After hearing his father preach on "justification," "sanctification," and all the other "-ations," a pastor's son was ready to answer when his Sunday school teacher asked, "Does anyone know what procrastination means?"

The pastor's son raised his hand and said, "I don't know what it means, but I know we believe in it!"

You may feel the same when you hear a term like sanctification. But you can remember it simply as the ongoing process of becoming a saint. John Wesley taught his congregation this little poem to encourage them on their journey throughout life:

> Do all the good you can,
> To all the people you can,
> At all the times you can,
> In all the ways you can,
> By all the means you can,
> As long as ever you can.

As you continue on your spiritual journey, remember that sanctification is not a destination to reach so much as it is a lifelong journey to take with God's truth as your guide.

LISTEN TO ...

Sanctification is not a heavy yoke, but a joyful liberation.

—*Corrie ten Boom*

One and the Same

John 17:20—18:2

Americans love acting as individuals. Yet they also understand the power of a coalition. They have learned the lesson that strength is in numbers. The Associated Press printed an amusing article about how a group of post office customers got results by acting together. Twenty-six clients found themselves crammed into two long and winding lines. According to those who were there, the lines "were moving slower than paint dries." One man said, "It was like watching grass grow." They could hear employees conversing in the back and realized they were being ignored. So a seventy-three-year-old man organized the group by encouraging them to chant, "We want service!" Within minutes an additional clerk appeared and without cracking a smile said, "Next." Overjoyed by the results of their uncommon show of unity, they repeated their cheer, "We want service!" Before they knew it, another clerk arrived. An amused customer summed it up: "I got through that line in four minutes. I've never seen anything like it."

Throughout His prayer, Jesus asked the Father to help His disciples find security and sanctity. Now He asked the Father to provide them with solidarity. Sadly, throughout history Christians have failed to show the world this sacred unity. Although churches have developed different organizational styles and methods of worship, we still have the same Lord. Our commonalities far outweigh our individualities! Paul shared how we can be different yet the same: "There are diversities of gifts, but the same Spirit. There are differences of ministries, but the same Lord. And there are diversities of activities, but it is the same God who works all in all" (1 Cor. 12:4–6). Let's remember that we are one and the same when we love the same God and are loved by God.

Day 1: John 17:20–21   **ARE YOU ONE?**

Day 2: John 17:22–23   **ONE + ONE = ONE**

Day 3: John 17:24   **ONE WAY**

Day 4: John 17:25–26   **THE HOLY ONE**

Day 5: John 18:1–2   **ONE WALKS AWAY**

DAY 1
Are You One?

LIFT UP ...

Lord, I'm astounded that You included me in Your prayer two thousand years ago. You prayed that I would become part of a community with You and others. Help me to join hands with God and bring unity to others who believe in You. Amen.

LOOK AT ...

The Upper Room Discourse began with Jesus answering His disciples' many questions. He patiently explained to Peter why He must be allowed to wash the disciples' feet. He revealed to John the identity of His betrayer. Because Thomas didn't know the way to heaven, Jesus explained that, "I am the way." After He answered these inquiries, Jesus made requests of His heavenly Father in the form of an intercessory prayer.

So far we've seen that this prayer included petitions for Himself as well as His disciples. Here in John 17:20 Jesus directed His prayer toward the future—reaching forward to believers today! It's amazing that Jesus hasn't stopped praying for *you:* "He always lives to make intercession for [us]" (Heb. 7:25). Do your troubles seem insurmountable? Take heart, dear friend, you can pray *to* God and *with* God. In prayer, you are never alone. He will even send His Spirit to articulate the prayers you don't know how to pray: "For we do not know what we should pray for as we ought, but the Spirit Himself makes intercession for us" (Rom. 8:26).

READ JOHN 17:20–21.

"I do not pray for these alone, but also for those who will believe in Me through their word; that they all may be one, as You, Father, are in Me, and I in You; that they also may be one in Us, that the world may believe that You sent Me." John 17:20–21

LEARN ABOUT ...

2 Their Word

In the New Testament the apostles recounted the words and works of Jesus. The Scripture records their testimony. The author of Hebrews writes, "In the past God spoke to our forefathers through the prophets at many times and in various ways, but in these last days he has spoken to us by his Son" (Heb. 1:1–2 NIV).

---

4 Their Example

Don't confuse unity with uniformity. John Walvoord writes, "Jesus was not praying for the unity of a single, worldwide, ecumenical church in which doctrinal heresy would be maintained along with orthodoxy. Instead He was praying for a unity of love, a unity of obedience to God and His word, and a united commitment to His will."[121]

---

6 Their Witness

Jesus repeated the word *believe* twice. First, we believe the word of the disciples. Second, the world believes our witness expressed in unity. To believe means to commit one's trust or to put one's faith in something: "He who believes and is baptized will be saved; but he who does not believe will be condemned" (Mark 16:16).

1. What two groups did Jesus include in this prayer?

2. Explain how the second group became part of this prayer.

3. What time frame do you think this prayer includes? Please explain.

4. What did Jesus ask that the Father do for these people, and what example did He give?

5. Do you think there is unity among believers today? Explain why or why not.

6. What would be the outcome when this prayer was answered?

LIVE OUT...

7. Jesus prayed for those who would come to faith in the future. Moses also prayed for future generations: "I make this covenant and this oath, not with you alone, but with him who stands here with us today before the LORD our God, as well as with him who is not here with us today" (Deut. 29:14–15).

   Journal a prayer asking God to save those who will one day hear the word of your testimony.

8. a. Read 1 Corinthians 12:12–25. What metaphor does Paul employ to describe the diversity and unity of the church?

   b. Who are included in this entity and how are they joined to it?

c. Draw a stick man and label different parts with members of Christ's body who you've encountered. Which part best describes you?

d. Who decides what function each member will possess? What results should this encourage?

9. Faith in Jesus Christ has been shared from the disciples in the early church to the saints of today. Take a moment to describe how you heard the Word of the gospel. Who shared it with you? Thank God for their faithful witness.

° ° ● ° °

"It was November 17, 1991, and Detroit Lions guard Mike Utley was doing what he always did which was protecting his quarterback and blocking his heart out to help his team win.

Late in the fourth quarter of that game against the Los Angeles Rams, Utley attempted to throw a block in pass protection when he went down with an injury that would change the course of the rest of his life. He had fractured the 6th and 7th cervical vertebrae in his spine and was paralyzed."[123]

It's a strange phenomenon, but sometimes when a key player gets hurt, the team actually performs better. That's exactly what happened with the Detroit Lions. Mike's injury inspired the team to greater unity than they'd ever known. The next game the team wore T-shirts in Utley's honor under their jerseys. They utterly defeated their opponent. After the game, the players credited their victory to a spirit of unity with their injured teammate.

Jesus would leave His disciples shortly after He finished this prayer. His absence could have demoralized His followers, but it didn't. Much like Mike Utley's teammates, they bonded together. Although Jesus was

LEARN ABOUT ...

7 Our Witness

This prayer reaches to those who would come to faith through the apostles' witness. Directly or indirectly, that is how we've all been saved. Their mission has become our Great Commission. "He said to them, 'Go into all the world and preach the gospel to every creature'" (Mark 16:15).

9 Our Mark

"Joy is the mark of the Christian relationship to [Jesus]. Holiness is the mark in relationship to God. Truth is the mark in his relationship to the Bible. Mission is the mark in his relationship to the world. In this mark, unity and the last, love ... summarize them all."[122]

no longer with them in body, they became His body and continued the work He had begun. His work continues today as each new believer joins the body of Christ. When we act as one, we are all winners!

LISTEN TO ...

We do not find in the gospel, that Christ has provided for the uniformity of churches, but only for their unity.

—Roger Williams

DAY 2

One + One = One

Growing up with an older, intellectually smarter sister, I (Lenya) always felt as if I didn't quite measure up. She had the verbal sparring skills of a great debater. Whenever I attempted to spar with her, I'd get tongue-tied and end up saying something utterly lame. One day we were engaged in a silly argument. I braced myself and tried to arouse all of my mental acumen. "You're so stupid," Suzanne said.

I insisted, "I am not, I know everything you know." We both knew that wasn't true, but I wasn't about to back down.

"Oh, really," she challenged, "I bet you don't even know what two plus two equals."

"Uh, huh," I quickly responded, "it equals two." I looked stunned then burst into laughter. I was so intimidated I couldn't even add in the heat of the moment.

God's math defies convention. Somehow He can multiply through subtraction. After Jesus departed, the church grew exponentially. God imparted the Holy Spirit, and the disciples began to testify about the resurrection of Christ. Another anomaly in God's math is the unusual equation: One + One = One. The Trinity displays this concept. How can three separate entities equal one God? Yet the Bible teaches that it's true. During His prayer in the upper room, Jesus built on this equation and added the disciples. He knew that they could be part of the one. But He didn't stop there. He continued with those who would be joined to the church as a result of their witness. Therefore, we being many are one.

Lift up ...

Lord, thank You for sharing the glory of the Father with me. Help me to be unified with You in my thoughts and actions. Help me to add others to Your kingdom that they may be one with You. Amen.

Look at ...

Yesterday we saw Jesus sound a call for unity among the church. Why is this call so

important? Jesus knew that the world would be watching. He also knew that the world wants any excuse to discount the message of the gospel based on the actions of the church. We've all seen disunity displayed because of organizational and philosophical differences. But true Christian unity is not based on programs, preaching styles, or numbers of people in attendance. Christian unity begins internally. Today we'll see that Jesus used the word *in* to describe where Christian unity must begin. It begins in our hearts and spreads outward. This unity is a product of our God dwelling in us. It exists when we become part of God's spiritual family. God has given us a role to display unity not only among churches, but also through our lives. When we do this, we show the world that believers are different from the world and our Savior had a cause worth dying for.

READ JOHN 17:22–23.

"And the glory which You gave Me I have given them, that they may be one just as We are one: I in them, and You in Me; that they may be made perfect in one, and that the world may know that You have sent Me, and have loved them as You have loved Me." John 17:22–23

1. What did Jesus give to the disciples?

2. a. Why did He give the disciples His glory?

   b. Based on the first question and the corresponding sidebar, what do you think this glory might entail?

3. Jesus used the preposition *in* to describe the unity He imparted to believers. Explain who would be "in" whom and why.

4. What would the world know about Jesus?

5. What would the world know about God's love?

LIVE OUT...

6. a. Jesus found glory by going the way of the cross. Fill in the following table to describe the path to glory for Christ's followers.

SCRIPTURE	PATH TO GLORY
Romans 5:1–3	
Ephesians 3:13	
1 Peter 5:10	

   b. What hardships have you faced along the path to glory? How have God and other believers helped you on this journey?

7. a. Jesus prayed that His disciples would be made perfect. Read Matthew 5:48. What did Jesus command?

   b. Have you ever met anyone who was perfect? What do you think Jesus means by this command?

8. Jesus prayed that through the unity of believers, the world would know that God had sent Him. In what ways have you seen believers work together to show God's love to an unbelieving world?

☐ Missions   ☐ Outreach Teams
☐ Disaster Relief   ☐ Music or evangelistic crusades
☐ Medical Aid   ☐ Other_____

LEARN ABOUT ...

5 Made Loveable

This Scripture tells us that God loves the world as much as He loved His Son. It's not surprising that we love God—He's completely loveable. But God's love is incomprehensible: "In this is love, not that we loved God, but that He loved us and sent His Son to be the propitiation for our sins" (I John 4:10).

6 Given Glory

God's glory was revealed in Christ, who shares His divine glory with His followers. Believers will be fully glorified at the end of time in God's heavenly presence. There the glory of God will radiate everywhere: "The city had no need of the sun or of the moon to shine in it, for the glory of God illuminated it" (Rev. 21:23).

7 Grown Perfect

Can believers be "perfect" on earth? In one sense the answer is yes. We are positionally perfect when we are *in* Christ. God sees us as He sees Christ—without the stain of sin. Yet experientially we will not attain perfection until we reach heaven. We can only hope to grow more perfect as we become more like Christ.

○ ○ • ○ ○

Looking around at the different types of birds in the air or fish in the sea helps us realize that God loves variety. When we think about Jesus' prayer for unity, we can infer that He wasn't praying for uniformity among believers. If He had wanted clones, He would have created cookie-cutter followers from the start.

Jesus said, "The very hairs of your head are all numbered" (Matt. 10:30). He created blondes, brunettes, and redheads. Some are tall, while others are short or in between. The point is that God loves variety. He also allows for a variety of personalities, gifts, and styles of worship within the church. Pastor Skip Heitzig wrote, "Variety is thrilling! Why can't there be unity and diversity at the same time? The vast nature of God demands it. No single Christian movement, denomination, or assembly could ever embody all of God's personality."[125]

On the other hand, some essential truths are nonnegotiable. These include: humanity's sin nature; salvation by grace through faith; Christ's nature as God and man; the virgin birth; vicarious atonement; and Christ's bodily resurrection and imminent return. On these essentials there must be unity. Christians disagree about other issues, such as baptism, Communion, the Sabbath, and other important subjects. When these are broached, we've found that the best approach is to agree to disagree agreeably in a spirit of Christian love. Let's not let unity disintegrate by placing more emphasis on doctrinal interpretation or organizational structure than we place on loving submission to Jesus as our Savior and Lord.

LISTEN TO ...

God loves each of us as if there were only one of us.

—Augustine of Hippo

DAY 3
One Way

One day I (Penny) went to my grandfather's home for breakfast and found him reading the obituaries in the newspaper. I said, "Granddaddy, that seems kind of depressing. Wouldn't you rather read the sports page?"

He chuckled and said, "Honey, when you get to be my age, you know more people in heaven than you do on earth. I'm just lookin' to see if any of my friends have been called home."

At the time, I thought it was very strange and kind of macabre. I didn't know very many people in heaven. But now that I'm older and hopefully wiser, I understand where he was coming from. Some of my favorite people live in heaven. Jesus is there preparing a place for us. And like my granddaddy, I find myself thinking about heaven more and more. What will it be like? Will there be animals? How will we get around? Will my grandmother bake my favorite cinnamon rolls? Some of my thoughts turn sentimental about the people I'll see. Some turn silly about the things I'll want to do. But in reality, I know that in heaven I'll only want to worship my Lord Jesus. Make no mistake, heaven is a real place. The Bible speaks of heaven as God the Father's home. I believe that God is interested in reassuring us with thoughts of heaven. He wants to make sure that we know how to get there. Thankfully, He makes it easy. There's only one way to reach heaven: You must come through faith in Christ.

LIFT UP ...

Lord, I am humbled to know that it is Your desire to be with me in heaven and to shower Your glory upon me. Help me to make the desire of my heart to serve You in all my ways. Amen.

LOOK AT ...

For the past two days we've studied Jesus' heartfelt prayer for unity in the church. His omniscience in this matter gives us insight into His divine nature, knowing that He caught a

LEARN ABOUT ...

2 His Desire

Christ's desire was not simply a request. The word used implies that it was a choice, an intention, and even a delight that His desire be fulfilled.[126] Knowing that His Father delights in answering prayers, Jesus was certain that His desire would be fulfilled: "Ask what you desire, and it shall be done for you" (John 15:7).

3 His Home

Jesus was headed home to heaven and desired that all who believed in Him might come live with Him forever. Though Jesus didn't give a name to this place, we know where He was going: "In My Father's house are many mansions; if it were not so, I would have told you. I go to prepare a place for you" (John 14:2).

5 His Glory

The glory spoken of here is different from Christ's glory on earth. Here He is speaking of the unveiled glory that can be seen only in heaven. As Moses learned on Mount Sinai, no human can see God and live (see Ex. 33:18–20). Only resurrected, transfigured bodies can see the visible splendor, beauty, and magnificence of God's true glory.

glimpse into the future of the world and even the divisions and discord that would come to the church following His departure. Nevertheless, as true believers we must follow His example and continue the quest for unity among the brethren. Today we see Him turn His gaze toward His heavenly home. Jesus beseeched the Father that His followers may be with Him there. By doing this, they would behold the true glory of God. This prayer has implications for life and death. Believers throughout the ages have prayed to see God's glory. They long for Christ to return so that they might not see death. Or they are comforted knowing that when they or their loved ones die, they will go to heaven. If this life's fears are holding you hostage, take comfort. Jesus has a place for you that is filled with His glory.

READ JOHN 17:24.

"Father, I desire that they also whom You gave Me may be with Me where I am, that they may behold My glory which You have given Me; for You loved Me before the foundation of the world." John 17:24

1. Look back to yesterday's lesson and explain who you think "they" are Jesus is referring to in this passage.

2. Explain what Jesus desires for them.

3. Jesus prayed that His followers would be where He is. Where is this place, and what do you know about it?

4. What will Christ's followers behold there?

5. Where did this glory originate?

6. Explain why God gave Jesus this heavenly glory. How does this confirm Jesus' deity?

LIVE OUT...

7. a. Today we discovered that Jesus desires His followers to be where He is. According to Matthew 9:13, what else does Jesus desire?

   b. How was Jesus merciful in offering Himself as a sacrifice?

   c. In what ways can you be merciful to others in your life?

8. a. Jesus talked about His followers going home to be with Him in heaven. Fill in the following table to catch a glimpse of heaven.

SCRIPTURE	A GLIMPSE OF HEAVEN
Acts 7:55–56	
2 Corinthians 5:1–2	
Revelation 4:2–3	
Revelation 21:3–4	

   b. Which of these snapshots into heaven offers you the greatest comfort? Which makes you most motivated to let others know about heaven as a reality?

LEARN ABOUT ...

7 His Mercy

Christ's mercy became evident in one great act of sacrificial love on the cross. With that act, no more ritualistic sacrifices would be required as payment for sin. This was love in action: "But this Man, after He had offered one sacrifice for sins forever, sat down at the right hand of God" (Heb. 10:12).

8 His Resurrection Power

Since heaven is a place unlike any other, it is impossible for human beings to live in heaven with earthly bodies. At death or at Christ's return, believers will receive resurrected bodies. The idea of resurrection is expressed in Scripture through such images as a transformed or transfigured body, a new dwelling place, or a new set of clothing.

○ ○ ● ○ ○

Although he was known as "The Man in Black," country music legend Johnny Cash was a man of faith. The son of a cotton farmer, Johnny idolized his older brother Jack. In Johnny's eyes, his brother was everything he was not: full of promise and full of faith. Jack was the apple of their father's eye. One day a horrible tragedy occurred. Jack was working with a table saw when he was cut open from chest to groin. His injuries were grave. Nevertheless he survived for a number of days. As he lay dying, Jack asked his mother if she could see the river. His mother told him she couldn't see what he was seeing. He told his mother he could see heaven and the angels and said it was beautiful. This experience shaped Johnny Cash's faith. He struck out for Nashville to record a gospel album. Johnny Cash had a long career filled with ups and downs. He was highly successful, yet developed a drug addiction and faced other public problems. When he reached bottom, Johnny repented and returned to Christ. At his death, Johnny was assured that he would have a place in heaven along with his beloved brother Jack.[127]

The question for every human being is not what you have done but where you are going. The thief on the cross recognized Jesus as the sinless One and asked Jesus to remember him when he died. Jesus promised, "Today you will be with Me in Paradise" (Luke 23:43). If you died today, would you have the assurance of heaven?

LISTEN TO ...

Heaven would hardly be heaven if we could define it.

—William Edward Biederwolf

DAY 4

The Holy One

My (Penny's) great-grandfather was the pastor of a small church in rural Oklahoma. He was also the head of a large family with eleven children. Resources were often slim. The congregation would sometimes pay him by holding a "pounding." They'd bring a pound of butter, a pound of chicken, a pound of sugar, etc. The children had chores to do around the house. Bob, the youngest, was responsible for shining his daddy's shoes on Saturday night in preparation for Sunday-morning services. Bob recalls that there was a "scarcity of light bulbs" in the house, so he would fumble around in the dark to find his father's good shoes. But he was familiar with the closet, because he shared it with his father.

One Saturday night, Bob decided he was tired of groping around in the dark. So he lit matches to help him find the shoes. Once he grabbed the shoes, Bob went to the living room, which had the only light bulb in the house, to polish them. Soon, the family smelled smoke. The clothes closet had caught on fire! His father had been at the store, so he followed the fire truck—only to see it turn into his driveway. Thankfully, the house didn't burn down, but Bob's beloved hand-me-down white suit was burned along with his father's Sunday suits. But his father didn't punish him. He said, "Son, the fact that your clothes smell like smoke is punishment enough. Hopefully, this is the nearest you'll ever get to the fires of hell."

Today we'll see that God, our heavenly Father, is a righteous God who knows how to deal lovingly with His children as well.

LIFT UP ...

Father, thank You for Your righteous nature. Please give me a heart to declare Your name in everything I do. Amen.

LOOK AT ...

Jesus ended this prayer with a moment of retrospection. Before He moved forward to the cross, He looked back to what He had done in the lives of His disciples. Throughout His

LEARN ABOUT ...

1 Righteousness

Jesus knows His Father is fair and just. The word *righteous* only occurs two other times in John's gospel. In both cases, Jesus linked righteousness with judgment (see 5:30; 7:24). The significance seems to be that His Father is in the right and will one day set things right: "For the LORD is righteous, He loves righteousness" (Ps. 11:7).

---

3 Knowledge

The disciples' knowledge was different from Christ's knowledge. As a member of the triune Godhead, He had complete and perfect understanding of God the Father. On the other hand, the disciples' knowledge was connected to Christ and His incarnation. "It is not said that they knew God, but that they knew God sent Jesus."[128]

ministry Christ had declared the Holy One's name to the disciples. In the first chapter of John we read, "No one has seen God at any time. The only begotten Son, who is in the bosom of the Father, He has declared Him" (John 1:18). Jesus had accomplished His task of revealing God's name to those who were willing to hear it and would soon finish His work on the cross. From that point forward, the job of spreading God's name and God's love would be left to the small group of disciples. So Jesus ended this prayer for His followers by reinforcing the topics of His prayer: the world's indifference, the disciples' reliance, and our Savior's confidence that His message of love would spread. In a world that is hostile to the gospel message, are you increasingly reliant on the Lord Jesus? Do you place your confidence in the name of the Father and share the love of Christ with people around you?

READ JOHN 17:25–26.

"O righteous Father! The world has not known You, but I have known You; and these have known that You sent Me. And I have declared to them Your name, and will declare it, that the love with which You loved Me may be in them, and I in them." John 17:25–26

1. What did Jesus call His Father? How have you found this to be true?

2. Jesus stated that the world has not known God. Based on what we've learned in the Upper Room Discourse, why is this so?

3. Jesus made two "I have" statements about God in this portion of His prayer. Each of these statements reflects a cause and effect. Because Jesus did something, something else occurred. How did Jesus' knowledge of the Father affect His disciples?

4. a. Why did Jesus declare the Father's name to His disciples?

b. What do you think declaring the Father's name involved? Was this simply uttering the word *Father* aloud, or was there more to it than that?

5. What do you think it means that He "will declare" the Father's name?

LIVE OUT...

6. Jesus was able to call His Father righteous despite the fact that for the next three days things would seem to go terribly wrong. Describe a situation in your life where wrong seemed to prevail for a period of time. How did God set it right? If He has not, do you still trust that He will?

7. Jesus proclaimed that the disciples knew that God had sent Him. How has this study increased your knowledge that God sent Christ as Messiah?

8. Jesus taught the disciples God's name. Which of God's names means the most to you and why (see partial list below)?

- Jehovah—I Am

- Jehovah Jireh—the Lord will provide

- Jehovah Nissi—the Lord is my banner

- Jehovah Shalom—the Lord is peace

- Jehovah Tsebaoth—the Lord of hosts

LEARN ABOUT ...

5 Declaration

When Jesus promised to declare the Father's name, He could have meant several things: 1) declaring God's name through the written word; 2) declaring the Father's name through the work of the Holy Spirit; 3) declaring God's name at the cross: "Father, forgive them, for they do not know what they do" (Luke 23:34).

---

6 Righting Wrongs

Asaph was almost undone when he saw how the wicked prospered. He wrote: "My steps had nearly slipped.... When I saw the prosperity of the wicked" (Ps. 73:2–3). Then he went to the sanctuary of God and "understood their end" (Ps. 73:17). It's good to get a perspective check to remind us of God's mercy and judgment working together.

---

8 Naming Names

Perhaps the loveliest name Jesus taught His disciples is "Father." Prior to Christ's coming, God was not referred to as God the Father. When Jesus taught the disciples to pray, He taught them to say, "Our Father." In the garden of Gethsemane He prayed, "Abba, Father." In this way, Jesus taught us that we can call our heavenly Father, "Daddy."

- Elohim—God of gods

- El Roi—the God who sees

o o · o o

Born in 356 BC, Alexander the Great made quite a name for himself. He was taught by Aristotle, overthrew the mighty Persian Empire, and laid the foundations for the Hellenistic world. Though he didn't know it, he was instrumental in preparing the way for the Messiah. Through Alexander's conquests, the Greek language was established as the common language of the Roman Empire, allowing the gospel to be spread far and wide.

The story is told how on one of his military campaigns, Alexander heard that one of his troops acted with cowardice on the battlefield. Alexander was stunned to learn that the soldier's name was also Alexander. So he sent for the soldier to answer to him. The young soldier arrived at his commander's tent and stood before the great man. The commander asked, "What is your name, soldier?"

The young man replied timidly, "Alexander, sir."

The commander asked again with more force, "Soldier, I said what is your name?"

The young man shrank back and said even more timidly, "Al-Al-Alexander, sir."

By now the commander was filled with disappointment. The soldier had not lived up to his namesake. He said, "Soldier, I suggest you either change your attitude or change your name."

This story has a lesson for each of us. When we call ourselves Christians, we are identified with the name of Christ. Let's ask ourselves if we are living as Jesus prayed we would do. Let's pray we have the courage to represent Christ as He represented the Father.

LISTEN TO ...

I am with you is good indeed. I am in you is better still.

—F. F. Bruce

DAY 5
One Walks Away

God loves gardens. The Bible tells us that He came to meet with Adam and Eve in the "garden in the cool of the day" (Gen. 3:8). In this paradise, God had an intimate relationship with His human friends.

Sadly, sin entered the world in the garden after Satan tempted Eve to take a bite of forbidden fruit (see Gen. 3:5). When Adam and Eve ate it, fellowship with God was broken, and God banished the couple from the garden. In order to resume a relationship with the wayward couple, God conducted the first animal sacrifice to cover their sin: "For Adam and his wife the LORD God made tunics of skin, and clothed them" (Gen. 3:21).

Jesus also cultivated relationships in a garden. In the garden of Gethsemane He "often met ... with His disciples" (John 18:2). Sadly, in this garden Jesus was betrayed by one who had walked away. From there, Judas turned Him over for trial and crucifixion.

Victoriously, God displayed His power over death in a garden. Jesus was buried in the garden tomb and laid there for three days. But on the third day He arose, ultimately to ascend to the Father's right hand.

One day Jesus will return to earth and take us to live with Him in paradise. The Greek word for paradise literally means "an Eden." We will live with God in a perfect place where we can "eat from the tree of life, which is in the midst of the Paradise of God" (Rev. 2:7). How beautiful that much of salvation's story finds its setting in gardens.

LIFT UP ...

Lord, thank You for traveling across the dusky and gloomy waters to bring me salvation. Thank You for promising me paradise. I long to live in the place You dwell. Amen.

LOOK AT ...

Yesterday Jesus prayed that the disciples would experience the indwelling love of the Father and Son. Today we see Jesus and the disciples begin their journey toward Gethsemane. From

LEARN ABOUT ...

3 Going to the Garden

Matthew and Mark give this garden the name Gethsemane. It was situated on the Mount of Olives just east of Jerusalem, across the Kidron Valley, opposite the temple. Since Gethsemane means "olive press," scholars believe it was situated in an olive grove that contained a press.[130]

---

4 Resisting Temptation

Temptation means to prove or try one's faith; to test the character. In the garden Jesus urged the disciples to pray lest they be tempted. Here He was warning them to avoid temptation from carelessness or disobedience. "God is faithful, who will not allow you to be tempted beyond what you are able" (I Cor. 10:13).

there Jesus would head to the cross. To reach Gethsemane they would cross the Brook Kidron, which, according to Warren Wiersbe, "means 'dusky, gloomy,' referring to the dark waters that were often stained by blood from the temple sacrifices. Our Lord and His disciples were about to go through 'dark waters' and Jesus would experience the 'waves and billows' of God's wrath."[129] Throughout Christ's ministry, He would leave the multitudes to retreat to the garden of Gethsemane for peace and rest. However, this time would end much differently—not in rest, but in betrayal and crucifixion. However, John portrays this as an appointment with destiny. Jesus was not shirking His divine duty. Rather, He was meeting it head-on. Judas, the one who had walked away, walked back into Jesus' life.

As we end this study in the Upper Room Discourse, spend time thanking Jesus for the sacrifice He gladly made on your behalf. Purpose in your heart never to walk away from His love.

READ JOHN 18:1–2.

When Jesus had spoken these words, He went out with His disciples over the Brook Kidron, where there was a garden, which He and His disciples entered. And Judas, who betrayed Him, also knew the place; for Jesus often met there with His disciples. John 18:1–2

1. Our text today reminds us that "Jesus had spoken these words." Look back to yesterday's lesson and explain what words He had spoken.

2. Where did Jesus go with His disciples?

3. Who entered the garden with Him?

4. Read Luke 22:39–46 for a further account of what occurred in the garden.

a. Explain what Jesus told the disciples to do and why. Why is this still good advice today?

b. What did Jesus pray?

c. How did God send comfort to His Son during His darkest hour?

5. Explain how Judas knew Jesus would be in this place.

LIVE OUT...

6. a. Jesus, the King of Kings, passed by the Brook Kidron on the way to cleanse the world of sin. Fill in the following table to discover what some other kings of Judah destroyed at the Brook Kidron.

SCRIPTURE	THE KING AND WHAT HE DESTROYED
2 Kings 23:4, 6	
2 Chronicles 15:16	
2 Chronicles 30:14	

b. Journal about how knowing Jesus has helped you tear down some of the idols in your life.

7. Jesus went to the garden where there was an olive press. There He pressed into God in prayer and was pressed out to the point where "His sweat became like great drops of blood" (Luke 22:44). As we conclude this study, rewrite Paul's prayer into a personal prayer to press on in your journey of faith: "I press toward the goal for the prize of the upward call of God in Christ Jesus" (Phil. 3:14).

LEARN ABOUT ...

5 Meeting There

Jesus didn't avoid the place where He and His disciples had previously rendezvoused. Having prepared Himself in prayer and knowing that His hour had come, He went forward to meet His betrayer. It could perhaps be said that Jesus knew where Judas would be and did not avoid meeting Judas there.

6 Destroying Idols

Today, not many people worship carved images. But we do spend time and energy on things that are *in* this world and *of* this world. Jesus died to help us overcome what we can't overcome on our own. Paul said, "Put to death your members which are on the earth: fornication, uncleanness, passion, evil desire, and covetousness, which is idolatry" (Col. 3:5).

LEARN ABOUT ...

8 Meet Him There

Jesus is willing to meet you anywhere. When you meet with a group of believers, He is there. He said, "Where two or three are gathered together in My name, I am there in the midst of them" (Matt. 18:20). He's also available anytime. He said, "I am with you always, even to the end of the age" (Matt. 28:20).

8. a. Jesus often met with His disciples in the garden of Gethsemane, spending time in friendship and fellowship. Where do you meet with Jesus and how often?

   b. How has meeting Jesus in the upper room made an impact on your life?

° ° ● ° °

What lessons will we take away from this time spent with Jesus in the upper room? There are so many that to consign them to a few paragraphs is impossible. Please allow us to leave you with some final thoughts. Jesus began this special evening by modeling servant leadership as He washed His disciples' feet. Don't leave the upper room without letting the Savior wash the sins of the world from your heart. And be willing to kneel down in order to lift others up just as Jesus did.

Jesus also taught a new commandment based on old truths: "Love one another; as I have loved you, that you also love one another" (John 13:34). He reiterated the idea of love as the distinguishing mark of believers throughout His discourse. As you leave the upper room, ask yourself if the world recognizes who you are by those you love.

Jesus knew He was going home to the Father. So He gave the disciples an amazing promise that we can all cling to: "I go to prepare a place for you. And if I go and prepare a place for you, I will come again and receive you to Myself; that where I am, there you may be also" (John 14:2–3). These words offer hope and help to believers struggling with issues of life and death.

He also promised to send the Holy Spirit to come to dwell with and in the hearts of believers. Do you have the abiding presence of the indwelling Holy Spirit? If the answer is yes, then you can trust that He will give you peace for every circumstance. He said, "Peace I give to you;

not as the world gives do I give to you" (John 14:27). May you continually walk in His love and peace as you abide in the true Vine—Jesus Christ.

LISTEN TO ...

That which was lost in the Garden of Eden will be reclaimed in the Garden of Paradise—all because of the Garden of Gethsemane.

—Jon Courson

Notes

1 Herbert Lockyer, *Nelson's Illustrated Bible Dictionary* (Nashville: Thomas Nelson, 1986), adapted.

2 *McClintock and Strong Encyclopedia*, Electronic Database (Biblesoft, 2000).

3 "Harvard's Howard Gardner: Changing Minds is Difficult," *CIO* April 1, 2004, www.cio.com (accessed Jul 16, 2007).

4 Dr. Thomas Stuttaford, "Out, damned spot: why the Macbeth instinct is still with us," *New York Times*, September 15, 2006, www.thetimesonline.co.uk (accessed on July 17, 2007).

5 Allison Klein, "A Gate-Crasher's Change of Heart," *Washington Post*, July 13, 2007, www.Washingtonpost.com (accessed July 17, 2007)

6 Warren Wiersbe, *Be Transformed* (Colorado Springs: Cook Communications, 2005), 18–19.

7 "Face to Face," Bible Illustrator for Windows, version 3.0F (Parsons Technology, 1998).

8 *Biblesoft's New Exhaustive Strong's Numbers and Concordance with Expanded Greek-Hebrew Dictionary* (Biblesoft and International Bible Translators, Inc., 1994).

9 John E. Barbuto, Jr., and Dan W. Wheeler, "Becoming a Servant Leader: Do You Have What It Takes?" October 2002, www.ianrpubs.unl.edu (accessed July 22, 2007).

10 Herbert Lockyer, *Nelson's Illustrated Bible Dictionary* (Nashville: Thomas Nelson, 1986), adapted.

11 Matthew J. Slick, "Prophecy, the Bible, and Jesus," 1995–2007, www.carm.org/bible/prophecy.htm (accessed July 26, 2007).

12 Hugh Sidey, "Washington's Hottest Spot for 100 Years," *Time,* November 2002, www.TIME.com (accessed July 26, 2007).

13 Roseline Wiseman, "Girls Cliques, What Role Does Your Daughter Play?", 2002, parenting.ivillage.com (accessed July 26, 2007).

14 Dolores Flaherty, "Hanssen, the spy with two faces," *Chicago Sun-Times,* November 23, 2003 (accessed, July 30, 2007).

15 Matthew Henry, *Matthew Henry's Commentary on the Whole Bible: New Modern Edition,*

Electronic Database (Hendrickson Publishers, Inc., 1991), adapted.

16 Herbert Lockyer, *Nelson's Illustrated Bible Dictionary* (Nashville: Thomas Nelson, 1986), adapted.

17 "The Blaspheme Challenge," http://www.blasphemychallenge.com/ (accessed July 30, 2007).

18 Illustrated "Adelphon Kruptos": The Secret Work of the Knights of Labor, quoted in Peter J. Rachleff, *Black Labor in the South: Richmond, Virginia, 1865–1890* (Philadelphia: Temple University Press, 1984), 135.

19 Merrill F. Unger, *The New Unger's Bible Dictionary*, in PC Study Bible, version 4.2b (Seattle: Biblesoft, 2004).

20 Ibid.

21 *Crucible of War: A Journey Back to the Balkans*, Crucible of War Productions, 2006, www.crucibleofwar.com (accessed June 30, 2007).

22 Adapted from www.museum.tv.com (accessed on August 8, 2007).

23 W. E. Vine, *Vine's Expository Dictionary of Biblical Words* (Nashville: Thomas Nelson, 1985), adapted.

24 Ibid.

25 *Biblesoft's New Exhaustive Strong's Numbers and Concordance with Expanded Greek-Hebrew Dictionary* (Biblesoft and International Bible Translators, Inc., 1994).

26 Herbert Lockyer, *Nelson's Illustrated Bible Dictionary* (Nashville: Thomas Nelson, 1986), adapted.

27 Josh McDowell, *Evidence That Demands a Verdict*, (Nashville: Thomas Nelson, 1972), 103.

28 Ethen Kim Leiser, *Like Father, Like Son*, March 1, 2007, www.twicethericeword press.com (accessed August 10, 2007).

29 Warren Wiersbe, *Be Transformed* (Colorado Springs: Cook Communications, 2005), 29.

30 "Family Business," wikipedia.org (accessed August 11, 2007), adapted.

31 Matthew Henry, *Matthew Henry's Commentary on the Whole Bible: New Modern Edition*, Electronic Database (Hendrickson Publishers, Inc., 1991), adapted.

32 Warren Wiersbe, *Be Transformed* (Colorado Springs: Cook Communications, 2005), 30.

33 Herbert Lockyer, *Nelson's Illustrated Bible Dictionary* (Nashville: Thomas Nelson, 1986), adapted.

34 "Gallup Poll," Index *#432, Bible Illustrator for Windows,* version 3.0F, (Parson Technology, 1998), adapted.

35 Matthew J. Slick, "The Trinity," www.carm.org Christian Apologetics and Research Ministry, 2006 (accessed August 15, 2007).

36 Luis Palau, "Five Ways God Answers Prayer," *Today's Christian*, February 2002 (accessed August 13, 2007), adapted.

37 Herbert Lockyer, *Nelson's Illustrated Bible Dictionary* (Nashville: Thomas Nelson, 1986), adapted.

38 "Earnestness in Prayer," Index #1071-1072, *Bible Illustrator for Windows,* Version 3.0F, (Parson Technology, 1998), adapted.

39 *Strong's Greek/Hebrew Dictionary,* in PC Study Bible, version 4.2b (Seattle: Biblesoft, 2004), adapted.

40 Justin Mullens, "Invisibility Cloaks: Now you see them …" newscientist.com, February 16, 2007 (accessed August 16, 2007).

41 Herbert Lockyer, *Nelson's Illustrated Bible Dictionary* (Nashville: Thomas Nelson, 1986), adapted.

42 James Montgomery Boice, *The Gospel of John*, Vol. 4 (Grand Rapids, MI: Baker Books, 1999), 1145.

43 Harriet Hanngan, "The Sense of Sight," www.whalonlab.msu.edu (accessed August 20, 2007).

44 Arthur Pink, "The Eye of Faith," www.pbministries.org (accessed August 20, 2007).

45 James Montgomery Boice, *The Gospel of John*, Vol. 4 (Grand Rapids, MI: Baker Books, 1999), 1146.

46 "Lead and Follow," wikipedia.com (accessed August 17, 2007).

47 "Trinity," Index #3694, *Bible Illustrator for Windows*, version 3.0 F, (Parson Technology, 1998), adapted.

48 Herbert Lockyer, *Nelson's Illustrated Bible Dictionary* (Nashville: Thomas Nelson, 1986), adapted.

49 Matthew Henry, *Matthew Henry's Commentary on the Whole Bible: New Modern Edition*, Electronic Database, (Hendrickson Publishers, Inc., 1991), adapted.

50 A.W. Tozer, "Omniscience," *Bible Illustrator For Windows* version 3.0 F, (Parsons Technology, 1998), adapted.

51 James Montgomery Boice, *The Gospel of John*, Volume 4 (Grand Rapids, MI: Baker Books, 1999), 1160.

52 Carl Jacobsen, "Pruning Grapevines," January 2003, http:ucce.ucdavis.edu/files/filelibrary/616/5855.htm (accessed August 26, 2007).

53 John MacArthur, "Abiding in Christ," 1986, http://www.biblebb.com/files/MAC/1553.htm (accessed August 26, 2007).

54 Warren Wiersbe, *Be Transformed* (Colorado Springs: Cook Communications, 2005), 41

55 Herbert Lockyer, *Nelson's Bible Dictionary*, in *PC Study Bible*, version 4.2b (Seattle: Biblesoft, 2004).

56 Esteban Herrera and Darrell Sullivan, "Why Fruit Trees Fail to Bear," Nov. 20, 1995, http://cahe.nmsu.edu/pubs/_h/h-308.html (accessed August 27, 2007).

57 Herbert Lockyer, *Nelson's Illustrated Bible Dictionary* (Nashville: Thomas Nelson, 1986), adapted.

58 Billy Graham, *How to Be Born Again* (Waco, TX : Word Books Publisher, 1977), 37.

59 Lenya Heitzig, *Holy Moments,* (Ventura, CA, Regal/Gospel Light, 2006), 26.

60 *International Standard Bible Encyclopedia, PC Study Bible*, version 4.2b (Seattle: Biblesoft, 2004), adapted.

61 *Adam Clark Commentary, PC Study Bible*, version 4.2b (Seattle: Biblesoft, 2004), adapted.

62 Adapted, "Tips to Keep Friendship Going," July 24, 2007, Aero Smith, www.associatedcontent.com (accessed September 11, 2007).

63 James Montgomery Boice, *The Gospel of John Volume 4,* 1999, Grand Rapids, MI: Baker Books, 1185.

64 *The New Unger's Bible Dictionary.* (Chicago: Moody Press, 1988).

65 *McClintock and Strong Encyclopedia*, Electronic Database (Seattle: Biblesoft, 2000).

66 www.perecution.org (accessed Septemeber 17, 2007).

67 "Christians Beaten, Church Burnt by Militants," The Voice of the Martyrs, www.persecution.net (accessed September 17, 2007).

68 James Montgomery Boice, *The Gospel of John*, Volume 4 (Grand Rapids, MI: Baker Books, 1999), 1191

69 Brigitte Gabariel, *Because They Hate* (New York: St. Martin Press, 2006), 18–19.

70 Ibid

71 *An Anonymous Brief for Christianity Presented to Diognetus: The Mystery of the New People* (Christian Classics Ethereal Library), ccel.org (accessed November 23, 2007).

72 James Montgomery Boice, *The Gospel of John*, Volume 4 (Grand Rapids: Baker Books, 1999), 1197–1198

73 Sherri Jackson, "To Snitch or Not to Snitch," CBS 42 News, www.wiat.com (accessed September 26, 2007).

74 Dave Kiffer, "Beware: Dangerous Curves Ahead!" *Stories in the News*, June 26, 2007, www.sitnews.us (accessed September 28, 2007).

75 *Biblesoft's New Exhaustive Strong's Numbers and Concordance with Expanded Greek-Hebrew Dictionary* (Biblesoft and International Bible Translators, Inc., 1994).

76 Michael J. Harkness, M.D., "Separation Anxiety," *Kid's Health*, July 2005, www.kid-shealth.org (accessed October 3, 2007).

77 Merrill F. Unger, *The New Unger's Bible Dictionary*, in PC Study Bible, version 4.2b (Seattle: Biblesoft, 2004).

78 *Vine's New Testament Bible Dictionary,* in PC Study Bible, version 4.2b (Seattle: Biblesoft, 2004).

79 *Vine's New Testament Bible Dictionary,* in PC Study Bible, version 4.2b (Seattle: Biblesoft, 2004).

80 James Montgomery Boice, *The Gospel of John*, Vol. 4 (Grand Rapids, MI: Baker Books, 1999), 1217.

81 *Matthew Henry's Commentary,* in PC Study Bible, version 4.2b (Seattle: Biblesoft, 2004).

82 Spurgeon's Sermons, Electronic Database. (Seattle: Biblesoft, 1997).

83 Louisa May Alcott, *Clover Blossom,* www.repeatafterus.com (accessed October 8, 2007).

84 Kelsey Good, "Please Mind Your Manners, Thank You," http://blog.al.com/enjoy/2007/09/ (accessed October 8, 2007).

85 *International Standard Bible Encyclopedia,* in PC Study Bible, version 4.2b (Seattle: Biblesoft, 2004).

86 James Montgomery Boice, *The Gospel of John*, Volume 4 (Grand Rapids, MI: Baker Books, 1999), 1231

87 Ibid.

88 John F. Edwards, "10 Best Secrets to Unhappiness," http://www.edwardsmotivational.com/5-secrets.htm (accessed October 8, 2007).

89 "We Shall Overcome: Historical Period: Postwar United States, 1945–1968," Library of Congress, www.loc.gov/teachers/lyrical/songs/overcome (accessed October 8, 2007).

90 *Biblesoft's New Exhaustive Strong's Numbers and Concordance with Expanded Greek-Hebrew Dictionary* (Biblesoft and International Bible Translators, Inc., 1994), adapted.

91 Ibid.

92 Tim De Lisle, ed., *Lives of the Great Songs* (New York: Penguin, 1995), 143–144, quoted by Jasper Rees.

93 Joe Smith, *Off the Record* (New York: Warner Books, 1988), 161–162.

94 Warren Wiersbe, *Be Transformed* (Colorado Springs: Cook Communications, 2005), 67

95 *The New Unger's Bible Dictionary.* (Chicago: Moody Press, 1988).

96 "Peace at the Center" Index #3013 *Bible Illustrator for Windows,* version 3.0F, (Parson Technology, 1998), adapted.

97 Herbert Lockyer, *Nelson's Illustrated Bible Dictionary* (Nashville: Thomas Nelson, 1986), adapted.

98 *The New Unger's Bible Dictionary.* (Chicago: Moody Press, 1988), adapted.

99 J. F. Walvoord, *The Bible Knowledge Commentary: An Exposition of the Scriptures* (Jn 17:1) (Wheaton, IL: Victor Books).

100 Reuters, "Drunken Priest Punches Cop, Jailed," October 12, 2007, www.reuters.com (accessed October 15, 2007).

101 Warren Wiersbe, *Be Transformed* (Colorado Springs: Cook Communications, 2005), 70

102 J. F. Walvoord, *The Bible Knowledge Commentary: An Exposition of the Scriptures* (Jn 17:1) (Wheaton, IL: Victor Books).

103 Leon Morris, *The Gospel According to John* (Grand Rapids, MI: Wm. B. Eerdmans Publishing, 1971), 724.

104 Andrew Lambert, *Oxford Dictionary of National Biography*, "Nelson's Band of Brothers," http://www.oxforddnb.com/public/themes/96/96379.html (accessed October 20, 2007).

105 Herbert Lockyer, *Nelson's Bible Dictionary*, in *PC Study Bible*, version 4.2b (Seattle: Biblesoft, 2004).

106 "Influencing the Body of Christ to Make Disciples of All Learners," International

Orality Network, http://www.oralbible.com/Booklet_chap_6_page_3.php (accessed October 22, 2007), adapted.

107 "July 1942: United We Stand," Smithsonian Museum of American History, www.americanhistory.si.edu/1942/campaign (accessed October 10, 2007, adapted.

108 Barnes' Notes, Electronic Database (Seattle: Biblesoft, 1997).

109 J. F. Walvoord, *The Bible Knowledge Commentary: An Exposition of the Scriptures* (Jn 17:1) (Wheaton, IL: Victor Books).

110 W. E. Vine, *Vine's Expository Dictionary of Biblical Words* (Nashville: Thomas Nelson, 1985), 108, 115, adapted.

111 *McClintock and Strong Encyclopedia*, Electronic Database (Seattle: Biblesoft, 2000), adapted.

112 James S. Hewett, *Illustrations Unlimited* (Wheaton IL: Tyndale House Publishers, 1988), 123–124.

113 Author unknown, "American Diver Underwater During Catastrophe," December 29, 2004, www.CNN.com (accessed October 22, 2007).

114 Tad Murty, "Facts about Indian Ocean Tsunami 2005," http://www.factsnfacts.com/disasters_facts/tsunamis/indian_ocean_2005 (accessed October 22, 2007).

115 Skip Heitzig, *When God Prays: Discovering the Heart of Jesus in Prayer* (Wheaton, IL: Tyndale House Publishers, 2003), 84.

116 Herbert Lockyer, *Nelson's Bible Dictionary*, in *PC Study Bible*, version 4.2b (Seattle: Biblesoft, 2004).

117 Jeffrey Kluger, "TIME 100: Scientists & Thinkers," *Time* (2003), http://www.time.com/time/time100/scientist/profile/goddard02.html (accessed October 23, 2007).

118 Merrill F. Unger, *The New Unger's Bible Dictionary*, in *PC Study Bible*, version 4.2b (Seattle: Biblesoft, 2004).

119 Warren Wiersbe, *Be Transformed* (Colorado Springs: Cook Communications, 2005), 78.

120 *International Standard Bible Encyclopedia*, PC Study Bible, version 4.2b (Seattle: Biblesoft, 2004), adapted.

121 J. F. Walvoord, *The Bible Knowledge Commentary: An Exposition of the Scriptures* (Jn

17:1) (Wheaton, IL: Victor Books).

122 James Montgomery Boice, *The Gospel of John*, Volume 4 (Grand Rapids, MI: Baker Books, 1999), 1328

123 Luke Sacks, "Mike Utley Still Giving a Thumbs Up," January 25, 2006, www.nflplayers.com (accessed October 26, 2007)

124 Leon Morris, *The Gospel According to John* (Grand Rapids, MI: Wm. B. Eerdmans Publishing), 734.

125 Skip Heitzig, *When God Prays: Discovering the Heart of Jesus in Prayer* (Wheaton, IL: Tyndale House Publishers, 2003) 131.

126 *Strong's Bible Dictionary*, in *PC Study Bible*, version 4.2b (Seattle: Biblesoft, 2004)

127 Adapted, Christopher Stratton, "Johnny Cash Walked the Line," 2005, www.explorefaith.org (accessed Oct. 27, 2007).

128 Leon Morris, *The Gospel According to John,* (Grand Rapids, MI: Wm. B. Eerdmans Publishing), 737

129 Warren Wiersbe, *Be Transformed* (Colorado Springs: Cook Communications, 2005), 84

130 Herbert Lockyer, *Nelson's Bible Dictionary*, in *PC Study Bible*, version 4.2b (Seattle: Biblesoft, 2004).

About the Authors

Lenya Heitzig is an award-winning author and sought-after speaker at conferences and retreats worldwide. Serving as the director of Women at Calvary, one of the core ministries at Calvary Albuquerque, she delights in seeing God's Word do His work in the lives of women. Her husband, Skip Heitzig, is the senior pastor of the fourteen-thousand-member congregation that has been ranked one of the fastest-growing churches in America. She received the Gold Medallion Award for coauthoring *Pathway to God's Treasure: Ephesians,* which also includes *Pathway to God's Plan: Esther* and *Pathway to Living Faith: James* in this same series. She also contributed a number of devotionals to *The New Women's Devotional Bible,* which was a finalist in the 2007 Christian Book Awards. Her most recent book, *Holy Moments,* published by Regal, enlightens the reader to see God's hand of providence move miraculously in daily life. Lenya loves jogging with her dog, Winston, as well as sampling pastries wherever she goes, fulfilling her motto, "Run so you can eat!" She lives in Albuquerque, New Mexico, with her husband, Skip, and their adult son, Nathan, who is a youth pastor.

Penny Rose is the Gold Medallion Award winning coauthor of *Pathway to God's Treasure: Ephesians,* as well as *Pathway to God's Plan: Esther,* and *Pathway to Living Faith: James* published by Tyndale House. She contributed to Zondervan's *True Identity: The Bible for Women* and was the general editor and a devotional writer for their *New Women's Devotional Bible,* a finalist for the 2007 Christian Book Awards. She wrote *A Garden of Friends* published by Regal as an ode to biblical friendship. A longtime member of the Women at Calvary Steering Committee, Penny thrives on teaching at conferences and retreats nationwide. Penny lives in Albuquerque, New Mexico, with her husband, Kerry, a pastor at Calvary Albuquerque. They have two daughters, Erin and Ryan, and one son, Kristian. She loves to spend time with family and friends, read, travel, and take naps.